GERRY
ARMSTRONG

THE GERRY ARMSTRONG AUTOBIOGRAPHY

MY STORY, MY JOURNEY

First published by Curtis Sport, 2021

Curtis Sport

Unit 24, Empire Industrial Park

Empire Close

Aldridge

West Midlands

WS9 8UQ

www.curtis-sport.com

info@curtis-sport.com

CONTENTS

FOREWORD

....

BY PAT JENNINGS

I first met Gerry when he came over to join Tottenham from Bangor back in 1975 and I've been lucky enough to have had him as a friend nearly 50 years now.

Gerry followed the same path as I had into the game, coming across from Northern Ireland as a youngster, though he was a bit older than I was when I came to England at 17. Players like myself would always give a special welcome to any of the boys that came over from Northern Ireland or the Republic, because you knew what they were going through, how hard it was fitting in, having moved away from home.

He was able to settle in pretty quickly because he was such a bubbly character, great company and always able to make friends quickly. Then on the football field, even if he'd been only playing the game seriously for two or three years by then, his attitude was fantastic. Whatever he might have been short of in terms of experience of the game at that time, he quickly made up for with the work he put in and the determination he had to succeed. Every time he went out on the field, he made sure he gave the opposition a hard time, whatever the result. Once Gerry had made his mind up to do something, nothing was going to stop him.

Spain certainly weren't going to stop him on that night in Valencia at the World Cup in 1982. His game was always to chase everything, to work hard, never give the defenders a moment's peace. But that night, he never stopped for a second. The poor Spanish left-back, he had a terrible time because Gerry kept coming and coming at him. Whenever I got the ball, I just knocked it down Gerry's side and let him get on with it.

When we arrived in Spain, all the posters around the cities had Arconada on them, the Spanish goalkeeper, the captain. I felt a bit sorry for him on that night because when Billy Hamilton's cross came in, there wasn't much else he could do but push it out, but typical of Gerry, he'd carried on running into the box and there he was to finish it off.

Gerry got all the glory after the game – it's always the goalscorer! But rightly so, that goal turned him into a star. Before then, I used to get more calls from journalists wanting interviews and stories, so Gerry would be answering the phone and making excuses for me if I didn't want to talk to them. After that goal, it was the other way round! The whole world wanted to talk to Gerry, so I was there taking the calls and fending them off for him.

After beating the host nation, winning a game nobody else expected us to win, everyone was buzzing. We stayed up all night and watched the sun come up the next day – but Gerry always had that kind of energy anyway, whatever the situation. When we used to play in Belfast during the Troubles, you couldn't go out into the city at night, so we would bring in Mike Kerry and Noel McMaster from the group Bakerloo Junction to where we were staying and have a sing-song after the game. That would go on for hours. When Gerry was at Watford, Graham Taylor would organise training for the day after the international matches, because maybe he thought that would get his players to bed early. Not Gerry. He'd stay up until first light and then get himself off to the airport, he never went to bed!

That was a very special group of players that we had with Northern Ireland. To qualify for two World Cups, to win two British Championships, to beat West Germany home and away, those were incredible days for the country and Gerry was at the heart of it, because he always seemed to be there with the important goals. That was a real gift he had. The one against Israel that took us into the World Cup in 1982, that was as important in its way as the one he scored in Spain.

He was always a real team man, he would work himself into the ground for the good of the team. When we were away in Romania late in qualifying for the 1986 World Cup, Gerry was on the bench for some reason. I think we got out of our half twice in the first 45 minutes and fortunately we scored and were 1-0 up, but we were under constant pressure. I never gave managers advice during my career, that wasn't my job, but that night I said to Billy Bingham, "Billy, I think we need Gerry on here." He came on and because he could make the ball stick, because he worked so hard, he gave us an out ball and we got a little breather every now and again.

All through the years ever since, Gerry has always been one of those people who you're delighted to see whenever your paths cross, because you know you're in for a great time. He's a great bloke who is fantastic company, as I'm sure you'll discover as you read the book.

INTRODUCTION

....

ONE GOAL IN VALENCIA

June 25th 1982, Estadio Luis Casanova, Valencia. Northern Ireland were at the World Cup finals for the first time since 1958 and we'd been drawn in the same group as the hosts, Spain. They were our final game and after drawing with Yugoslavia and Honduras, we knew what the job was – win and we would go through, lose and we were on the way home. A draw most likely wouldn't be enough.

At half-time, it was so far, so good. The game was goalless, we were doing well, frustrating them. The day before, Martin O'Neill, the captain, had talked us through the game, saying we would keep Spain at bay, quieten the crowd and then we'd get a chance and win the game 1-0. He was already halfway to be being right.

Out we went out for the second half. I was playing on the right side, just in front of Jimmy Nicholl, Billy Hamilton was up front with young Norman Whiteside, 17 years old. A couple of minutes into the half, I saw Gordillo coming forward, he had the socks round the ankles, about 20 yards inside our half. He came inside and I knew he was going pass the ball wide to Lopez Ufarte, who was a little winger and so I intercepted the pass and away I went.

I picked up speed and went past a couple of players - one of them was Periko Alonso, Xabi Alonso's father. He knew he wasn't going to catch me, so he tried to kick me as I reached the halfway line, but I kept going and going, on into the other half, about 20 yards into their territory. Billy had pulled out wide right, Norman had gone left, trying to stretch things.

I knocked the ball out to big Billy and Tendillo, the other centre-half, went with him. I thought, "Am I going to go forward here, or wait and see what Billy does?" I was surprised, but he knocked the ball past Tendillo and pushed him out of the way with his left arm. He went sprinting down the right hand side and put in a fantastic cross as I was arriving towards the box.

I had to make a decision, whether to go for the ball from the cross initially or not. Listen, with the heat and everything else, the pressure was unbelievable! But I decided not to go for the cross, it was that bit too far in front of me. I thought I'd wait and see what the outcome was.

Arconada, the goalkeeper, he decided to come for it and he made a bit of a hash of it. He pushed it out, it came straight in front of me, maybe 10 yards, 11 yards out. I remember thinking, "This is my chance", and it was the only real chance we had in the game.

My only thought was to keep the ball low, get my head over the top and my knee over the top of the ball and keep the ball low. I hammered it. I can still see the goalkeeper jumping to spread himself. But as he spread himself, his legs are open and the ball went below his outstretched leg. If you see the goal, you'll see it go under him.

Alexanko was behind him, his reaction was to get back on the line to try to cover. He had stretched and it went through his legs as well. Then Camacho was coming across, but he wasn't really in the line of fire, he couldn't do anything about it, and it went in the back of the net.

There was a silence for a split second that seemed a very long time, because obviously the home crowd was not going to celebrate a goal against them! I saw big Billy putting his arms up and Norman was running, celebrating, then Sammy McIlroy, all of them coming running towards me. We were ahead. Then the hard work really started!

We went down to ten men after an hour, there were 50,000 Spaniards baying for every decision, trying to will the ball into the net, everything was against us holding out for that win, as I'll explain later on. But when the final whistle went, we'd done it. We'd won the game 1-0, we topped the group, we were still in the World Cup. Crazy!

Looking back across nearly 40 years now, that goal was probably the defining moment of my career, the thing I'm best remembered for, a move that lasted 10, 15 seconds but changed so much. It opened a lot of doors for sure, including going and playing my football in Spain for a couple of years, learning the language, then commentating on their league for TV for many years and living out there again for a spell later on in my life.

More than that though, I think that period defined a lot more. The "spirit of '82" was a huge thing for all of us, in all our lives. The bond that we had as a group was very special and that's something that is so important, not just in football, but in life. That bunch of lads, as David McCreery always says, we were a band of brothers and we've been like that ever since, a family. That carried us to the World Cups of 1982 and 1986, to beating West Germany home and away in the qualifiers for the 1984 Euros and to two British Championships, in 1980 and 1984. That is something that I'm so proud of.

I love being part of a team, all working together towards achieving a common goal, the way we did over that period in the 1980s. I've done it in football, I've done it working in television, I've done it working on various projects and charities in Northern Ireland, as we'll see. But for a lot of my life, Northern Ireland was a divided country. It was them and us, no two ways about it. I think that the politicians over the years allowed that to happen, some encouraged it. That attitude is just so different to what we had, that spirit of '82. Forget about the football side of it, that World Cup team, we brought people together, we did a lot for our country at a really hard time. We had people who could not find common ground and we brought them together by the way we stuck together and achieved things through pure determination and hard work.

CHAPTER ONE

....

BELFAST BOY

I'm a child of Northern Ireland, through and through, and that's something I'm fiercely proud of. The Northern Irish people are the best in the world, very friendly, very homely and I'm very happy that after so many adventures all over the world, my journey has now brought me back home to settle again in Belfast.

There have been three very different Northern Irelands, three different Belfasts through my lifetime. I was born on May 23rd 1954 in the Mater Hospital on the Crumlin Road, and grew up in a city that was still recovering from the bombardment it had taken during the war. It was a tough, working class city, rough and ready. I don't suppose it was that different from a lot of other towns and cities around that time. There wasn't a lot of money to go around, and as kids we tended to live our lives out on the streets, playing games, getting into fights every day, learning how to look after yourself.

That Belfast changed very quickly in 1969 when the Troubles started. Suddenly, barricades were going up, the Army was on the streets, you'd see buses burning in the middle of the road every week. It's amazing how people adapt to things and just get on with it, but looking back, it was anything but normal. That became what Northern Ireland was known for all over the world – I found that out when I was at Tottenham Hotspur and we had a couple of new team-mates arrive from Argentina in the summer of 1978, Ossie Ardiles and Ricky Villa, both great lads. They'd been with us a week or two and Ricky came over to talk to me.

"Gerry, amigo", then he starts talking in Spanish to Ossie, who was translating for him.

"Ricky wants to know, is it true you are from Northern Ireland?"

"Yes, I come from Belfast."

Ricky said, "Belfast!!" and then he mimed pulling the pin out of a hand grenade and throwing it! That was the way everybody thought about Northern Ireland then, but I didn't think I'd have a lad from Argentina taking the mickey out of me about it!

Thankfully, all of that came to an end in the late 1990s, creating the Northern Ireland we have today. The Good Friday Agreement made a huge difference to life here. I watched it happening and I must admit that, like most people probably, I thought there was no way the two sides would ever come to an agreement because they were so far apart and had been so stubborn over the years. You know, when a bomb goes off, it doesn't pick out a Catholic or a Protestant, it kills whoever is closest to it. Bombs going off in the city centre, they killed indiscriminately. It was so wrong. The vast majority of the people who were killed over the years were innocent people but for all those years, that never made a difference to the groups on either side, they carried on with the violence. Yet in the end, they put this deal together and it worked. We've become a great advert for the rest of the world. All the trouble that went on and on, the bombs and the killing, but in the end, we've got peace from it.

Hopefully we've learned the lessons. Time will tell. Most of the people I know have had enough, they don't want all this nonsense anymore. They suffered it for 30 years, it's time it was left behind and that people looked to the future. We have to bring our kids up and give them an opportunity to live in a decent world. It's more important to me that they would think about global warming and what those dangers are going to be in future rather than go back to the sectarian nonsense from when I was growing up.

I suppose a lot of people had that same idea of Belfast as Ricky had, because when they hear that I grew up in Belfast, people go, "Oh, my God, that must have been horrendous!" But I loved my childhood, I had so much fun and I found quite a lot of trouble!

Initially, I lived on the Springfield Road - it's a Catholic area but it borders a Protestant area, but we were definitely apart from each other. I was a teenager before I ever met a Protestant. I owe so much to my parents and my family for the way they brought me up. We were a big family, just as my parents had come from big families too - I had an older sister and then a younger sister and every year, there was another member of the family came along. I ended up with five sisters and four brothers. It was a real clan.

My father is one of ten as well - he had six brothers and three sisters. His family came from Fintona in County Tyrone, which is about 70 miles west of Belfast, and he grew up on a farm there. He moved to Belfast when he was 17 to get a job and he worked in the shipyards, building a dock with a construction company for Harland & Wolff. He liked driving, he was a good driver, he loved machinery and engines, and he just got jobs wherever he could. Good opportunities to get on in life were few and far between at that time. Dad was a milkman, a bus driver, a taxi driver. He ended up becoming a driving instructor and then he went on and had his own driving school. After that he became a driving examiner.

He's still with us and he's got a great memory. He remembers growing up as a boy on the farm, he talks about how tough it was back then and how it was that that made him always have big ideas for the future, just to try and get on. He was always very well dressed, always in a shirt and tie. I can remember him shaving every morning in the kitchen. There was a little mirror on the wall, nine inches by ten, and he'd get the brush with the shaving soap, then get the blade out. He'd tuck his collar into this shirt then, once he was done, he'd take the collar out, put his tie on and off he'd go to work. He had a real discipline and a determination to him and that's why he did so well. I think I've inherited a bit of that from him.

I hope I've inherited a bit more too, because he's coming up to 91 now, but he's still fit and well. Six months ago, he bought himself a brand new car. It looks like a sports car, black, alloy wheels. He's into all the gadgets, he's brilliant with electrics, with mechanical stuff. He loves phones, he loves cameras. He's on the ball. I'll phone him and ask him what he's up to at the weekend. "Oh, I just thought I'd drive down to Bundoran and spend the weekend down here. I've checked into the hotel, just going to have a pint of

Guinness and listen to some music and look at the scenery." He just goes off and does it.

He was at my sister's recently and he saw Nicco's bike in the garden – that's his grandson, my nephew. He said, "I wondered if I could still ride a bike, so I took it for a wee pedal around the garden. It's true, you never forget how to ride a bike!" That's inspirational for me. The fact that he wants to enjoy his life and live it to the full. That's a shining light for me. If I can do half of that at his age, I'll be very, very pleased!

My mum had had to leave school early, at 13, because my grandmother had so many children that she had to leave to stay at home and help look after them. She had seven brothers and two sisters, so she had to help bring the others up. Both my parents were hard workers, they both had two or three jobs at a time. It was tough because we didn't get to see much of them, they were off working away at eight every morning and wouldn't get back until five o'clock. Then my mum was running to try and make dinner. My older sister Mary and I used to help, I'd peel potatoes and she would do some vegetables, just whatever we could do.

Because I had so many siblings, it was difficult for my mum looking after us all and working multiple jobs. I was a handful, I remember that. My mum used to call me a holy terror! I used to play in a place called the Blackie, by the river. I was attracted to anything dangerous, I was drawn to it like a magnet! I would just be mischievous. I'd be in the water every day as a boy. I used to love the river, love the water. I'd come back home soaking, walking in the house with my wet shoes on, and she'd go crazy and give me a hiding! It never deterred me.

When my mum had a few shillings put together, she'd manage to buy some nice cups and saucers and plates. We had the river at the back of the house, and yours truly used to throw the plates and the cups and saucers into the water because I liked to watch them float down the river. My mum had to run and paddle into the water and get them back out! I was very impressionable I suppose. On TV we had the westerns like "The Lone Ranger". I was very much into that. There wasn't much to watch on TV then, there was only one or two channels and anyway, I spent my time outside, they couldn't get me in!

At weekends, to give my parents a break from looking after me, I would go and stay with my grandmother, Hannah Gallagher, and eventually, I ended up living permanently there, along with some of my mum's brothers and sisters who hadn't left home yet, who were still in their late teens. It was only a street away from Springfield Road, 150 yards down the road in Logan Street, Beechmount, so I still saw my mum and dad and my brothers and sisters every day, but I grew up with my grandmother most of the time. It was very family orientated, everybody looked after each other. The oldest one looked after the youngest ones and that was the way it was.

The people in the street round there called me Gerard Gallagher, not Armstrong, I was just part of that clan there. I loved being down there with them and I lived there until I was 15 or 16, there for ten years. They were all big Gaelic football fans, so I used to go with them and watch the games every week. I loved the fact there were always lots of fights!

My grandmother was a very strict woman, she was the boss and I learnt an awful lot from her. She tried to keep me in check, she'd send me grocery shopping and then when I got back, I wasn't allowed to go out again until I'd done my jobs. That was good for me I think because I could never sit still - I still can't sit still. I'll have to be doing something keep busy. My grandmother always used to say to me, "Don't stop, because you may not be able to get up again afterwards!" She lived until she was 94!

Mary is my older sister, she's a year older than me, then Rosaleen is a year younger than I am. Kevin came along next, then Sean. After that was my brother Joseph. He only lived a few hours and then sadly died. There were two sisters after that, Joanne and then Sinead. My youngest brother is Eugene and my youngest sister is Gráinne, she's the last in line. Mary and I used to babysit for a lot of the young ones, and we'd babysit my cousins as well, we'd look after them for my Uncle Herbie and Auntie Margaret. When you're ten or eleven and you're babysitting, you think you're very grown up! But that's how the families were, you just relied on each other to help out. Money was scarce, everybody wanted to work and was working long hours when they did, so everybody mucked in. The neighbours were great as well. If you ran out of milk or sugar or whatever, you'd knock on each other's door to get a drop of milk for a cup of tea. The community was very close.

You'll have already noticed that I was a mischievous boy, getting into trouble all the time. I'd be getting into fights, smashing windows, I was like Dennis the Menace! I had loads and loads of energy, I'd run everywhere and so it was all about trying to keep me under control, to put a ball and chain on me. Whatever anyone did though, it didn't deter me, I had the determination to go out and do it again the next day. But the crazy thing with that is that I was asthmatic as a boy. When I was three or four, I used to get it really bad in October and November and the doctor warned my mum that I was going to have problems with it. "Make sure he gets a good education because he's not going to be doing anything that involves athleticism or anything physical." Boy did I prove him wrong!

I remember having to go to hospital a lot of times because of problems with my chest and with my breathing, but then around the time I turned 14 or 15, it just disappeared and it hasn't bothered me again. But as a boy I was always going to the Children's Hospital for appointments to do with asthma, and in the months when it was wet, I couldn't breathe properly. Yet I was always running everywhere. I never stopped running. I loved being outside playing games, hide and seek, chasing games, all different ball sports. Everybody played handball, we played football in the streets and used the lampposts as a goal. If you had a football, you were happy, because you could make your own fun. We used to play "kerby", which was a game where you would stand on one side of the pavement, throw the ball and try and hit the kerb so it would bounce back to you from there. If you did it, you got a goal. We made up all sorts of sports and games.

I just had so much enthusiasm for things, so much adrenaline. I couldn't walk down the street to go to the shops, I'd have to run to the shop, or run to the park to use up my energy, but it was fun. I set myself challenges like how quick I could get to the shop and back. I grew up competitive. I think my father and my uncles were always competitive anyway. How many goals did you score? How many points did you score?

That was another family trait. My father had been a sprinter, he'd won competitions, so those fast, twitch muscles that you need, I think we inherited then from him. My sisters were all quick too, they could all run. Gráinne, Sinead, Rosaleen, they were all runners. Mary was the dance champion of all Ireland from when she was seven until she was 11 or 12 and then she started getting into fashion. Unfortunately, Joanne had a bad accident when she was very young, when she was run over by a lorry. She had a fractured skull, an arm and leg too and she spent months in hospital. Thankfully, she recovered and was able to come back home.

My brothers were all good athletes, they all did really well in their sports. My brother Kevin played soccer for Cromac Albion and could have played at a higher level for a lot of Irish league clubs and both Kevin and Sean played Gaelic football for Antrim. Eugene, the youngest, he was so quick, very athletic, he could score breaks of 70 or 80 at snooker, he'd beat you at table tennis, at tennis, so we were all naturally gifted. Eugene actually went over to Blackpool on trial and Sam Ellis, the manager, wanted to sign him. But he didn't want to stay, he was only 18 at the time and he was homesick, which happens a lot with boys from Northern Ireland, they don't like leaving home to go to England.

We were lucky to have had the athletic inheritance from both my mum and dad's sides of the family. My mum's dad was Joe Gallagher. He died when I was around seven, and as I said, he had seven sons. He had been a fantastic hurler for Antrim and a Gaelic footballer as well. He was only a small man, but they called him Joe "Hack" Gallagher because if you put a hurling stick in his hand and put him on the pitch, he hacked anything that moved! He didn't take any prisoners! He was the groundsman for Casement Park, where all the big Antrim matches were played. He had the tractor and the trailer on the back and I remember driving in it with him, going back up the Falls Road when I was three or four. He'd do his work and I'd run around the pitch with a football, kicking it and throwing it about - the ball was probably bigger than me! I think putting me on a pitch like that, two or three times a week, psychologically it prepared me for the future. That was the lead in. It was great having the encouragement to go and play sport.

My grandfather was one of the founders of St. John's GAC at Corrigan Park, along with a lot of other famous names like Andy McCallion, Tommy Hall, the Morgan family, the Crawford family was another that were very heavily into it. A lot of families came together to form the club. As a kid, I just loved the chance to get out onto a big, green pitch. I played a lot of football there, I played a lot of football in the Falls Park. That was a great place for people to go because of the football pitches but also it had a place at the back called The Cooler, an outdoor swimming pool. As you can imagine, with the weather in Northern Ireland, even in June, July, August, it was freezing! But to us, it was paradise, it was a place to go and learn to swim and have fun.

At Corrigan Park, there were no showers. Basically, there was just a big hut there for changing in. In the winter, the pitches got really badly cut up, thick with mud. You'd come off after a game and there was a water tap on the side of the building, cold water only, and you'd go and clean as much mud off your legs and your face and your arms as you could! Those days were very basic, but I think it prepares you very well for what's to come in life. It's very different to how we bring up the kids these days and I do wonder sometimes if we mollycoddle them too much. We all do the best we can and most of us try to give our kids the things we didn't have, but sometimes in doing that, maybe we do them a disservice in making it too easy? I think we maybe overprotect them.

That sure didn't happen when I was a boy! In the summer, we'd go down to Fintona as a family and spend time there on the farm where my dad grew up. It was great to learn about life on the farm, how different it was. They were getting up at five and six in the morning to milk the cows and they had a hard life, but it was like a holiday for me. I looked upon everything as an adventure at that stage. I tell my daughter now that she misses out on so much because the kids sit inside watching TV, they've got 200, 300 channels to choose from, then they've got the internet. They've got it all to hand, but I still think they miss out on what we had.

At the farm, we'd go out working in the fields and help out. We helped to pick up bales of hay and throw them on the back of the trailer when they were picking it up and you just did your bit. That was an adventure, it was great. Being able to work and do stuff that you'd never done before was interesting. The other big job was bringing in turf in the summer. It was dried out and then you packed it into the bags and carried it from the bog and put it in a big shed to keep it dry through winter. We filled the shed right to the very top with turf. I was on the top of the shed, and as the bags were coming in, I was pouring the turf out and standing on top of it. It was going higher and higher until eventually we reached the top of the barn and I had to come down. The trailer was about 10 feet below me so, me being me, I took a running jump off the top of the turf, caught hold of one of the rafters, swung on it over the top of the trailer, and then let go to drop down onto the trailer, which I didn't think was a problem.

Unfortunately, one of the boards on the trailer was really rotten, so my leg went straight through the board. As I did that, the nut that held the plate on at the back, it just cut me open. I didn't feel too much at the time, I just remember seeing that I'd ripped my trousers and I thought that was a disaster, I'd have to tell my mum! But then when I looked inside, I had a four inch gash on my leg where I'd cut it wide open. So that was another visit to the hospital - I used to have a season ticket there! It seemed like every week I was back there. Even later on when I was playing professional football, I broke my nose seven times, just by jumping for the ball and clashing heads or catching an elbow. I broke my leg and ankle at Watford, I broke metatarsals, metacarpals, I broke my knuckles as well, though that was mostly from fighting people!

You had to learn to take care of yourself and I had to look after my brothers and sisters as well. At school, I used to get into fights all the time, that was part and parcel of growing up in an area like the Falls Road. You'd be in a fight on the way to school and a fight on the way back, but it was no big deal. It's just part of growing up, part of developing yourself as a person. I think that gives you confidence. I remember Martin O'Neill saying to me, "I wish I had your confidence Gerry!" It was rough and ready I suppose, but that's how the world was at that time.

We made our own adventures, but it was an innocent sort of a trouble, it all stemmed from us just being inquisitive. For instance, we had a brickyard at the top of the road and when they closed down for the night at five o'clock, there was only railings to keep you out, so we would climb over and just explore the place and see what they were doing in there. I went in and jumped on one of the wee dumper trucks. My mate said, "My dad drives one of these. Pull that lever and it empties everything out the back." Of course, I had to try it. Next thing, there's 1,000 bricks coming off the back of it and we're legging it because the watchman heard all the bricks falling off and chased after us!

There was a Walls' ice cream factory at the top of our road, just over some wasteland heading towards the Springfield Road, on an industrial estate. We could see this factory, we could see the vans coming in and out and the one day, the gates were left open, so I went in through them, found the vans were open and helped myself to some ice cream. I gave it my brothers and sisters and the rest of the kids in the street because none of us had any money to buy anything much.

From then, that became the norm. The kids were always asking me for ice cream and so I'd shoot across and pick up a bit for the kids and they'd follow me up there to share the loot! This one summer's day, about four o'clock, I went and had a wee look inside and I was just about to go into a van when the security guards came running out – they'd set me up! I legged it and as soon as I did, the police cars came round the corner and they were chasing after me – there were soldiers as well, running after me. I was quick and at 15, you think nobody can catch you. I'd started about 30 or 40 yards clear of this soldier but when I turned round 20 seconds later, he was only about 10 yards behind. He'd thrown his rifle and backpack down and he was flying, so I had to hit the turbo. Fortunately, I just took off and I managed to get away from him, but it was a pretty narrow escape!

I hadn't mentioned the soldiers and the rifles had I? That's another story.

CHAPTER TWO

....

LIFE AMONG THE TROUBLES

I suppose for all of us, when you look back on the way you lived – and how the world was –when you were growing up, there are all kind of things you can take from it. So much from back then seems so dated now – the cars, black and white television that only had a couple of channels, phones that only made calls and stayed put in the house! – but it's also about the way we used to behave, often without thinking about what we were really doing.

I've already mentioned that even when I was 13 or 14 years old, I still hadn't met any Protestants. They lived in one area of the city, we lived in another and that was the situation, even before the Troubles started. When you think back, it was quite archaic how we were brought up and what actually went on in Northern Ireland. At the time though, you didn't really notice it. As kids, you didn't realise the kind of segregation that was going on, but the truth was that it was a them and us situation. You'd go shopping in the city centre and you wouldn't have known what religion anybody was, but then you'd go home to your different parts of the city. Yet funnily enough, I had a dream as a boy that I'd meet a Protestant girl. At that time, it was taboo for a Catholic and a Protestant to marry – and yet that was what I did 18 years ago! Deborah came from another part of town and another background but there was no real impediment to us being together by then. But 30 years earlier, to be honest, we could not have got married. It wouldn't have been accepted.

The schools were segregated too of course. I'd started my schooling at St. John's, just off the Springfield Road, same as my brothers and sisters. Going to and from school, you'd probably end up in a wee fight or two every day! One half of the school was for boys, the other half for girls. I wasn't really into learning while I was there, I was a bit of a scallywag and never really wanted to pick up too much education. I was much more interested in playing sports and running around.

After that, when I was 11, I moved to St Thomas' Intermediate School, an all boys school on the Whiterock Road in Ballymurphy, which is where later on, in August 1971, there would be a number of killings when they brought in internment. The headmaster had to run that school really hard, rule it with the rod of iron, because the kids came from really bad areas. We're talking some of the roughest areas in Northern Ireland, like Turf Lodge, Ballymurphy, the Falls Road, so a lot of tough characters were thrown into the mix. You always got confrontations and that was an education in itself! Those places were all flash points whenever trouble started, they were right in the thick of it all.

I used to run or walk to school every day and initially I still wasn't paying a lot of attention to my education, but suddenly at 13 or 14, I got into learning. I was still living at my grandmother's house, and she had these encyclopaedias sitting on the piano. She must have paid a lot of money for them. I hadn't been interested because there weren't enough pictures in them. I was into the comics. I loved "The Beano", "The Victor" and all the Marvel Comics, "Superman", "Spider-Man" and stuff like that. As a boy watching "The Avengers" on TV, I used to think John Steed was really special to be able to fight off all those different villains.

But eventually, I picked up one of the encyclopaedias and started going through it. One piece would be on Greek mythology, then you'd read about geography, history or whatever. I started learning without even realising I was doing it and from there, I got more interested at school and I ended up getting my O levels and A levels. I was lucky because, for all that it was a hard place, St Thomas' was brilliant. It was a secondary and intermediate school, it wasn't a grammar school, but it had some cracking teachers.

The school had some real characters in it. The headmaster, Samuel McKeown, he didn't really teach that much because he was busy running things, but he was actually an Irish language teacher. He taught me for one year, and I really did enjoy the way he went about it. Seamus Heaney was a teacher at our school, which is pretty amazing when you think about it. As I was getting older, coming towards exams, getting more interested in education, I decided that I wanted to be an architect. I loved technical drawing because of a teacher called Brendan Doran. My next love after that was woodwork. Aloysius O'Loan was the head of the woodwork department and because I was good at it, we got on well.

I wasn't a completely reformed character – I still had that streak of mischief in me when the moment was right. When we came to do our Engineering Drawing exam for O level, there weren't enough drawing boards and T-squares to go round in the examination room, so they split the group into two and some of us had to do the exam after the others had finished. To stop us seeing what the questions were, we got locked in a classroom for two hours before it was our turn to take the exam. While we were waiting, we worked out that the same exam would be going on at St. Peter's school as well, about 700 yards down the road. What about if somebody went down and got the question paper so we could see it before we did the exam?

One of the lads was out the window, down the spout, across the lawn and down to St. Peter's, got the paper and then myself and two or three other guys did the exam on the board for rest of the class. Everybody passed - 25 out of 25. Mr. Doran always suspected there was something wrong with that exam! He said, "I know I was a good teacher, but there was at least eight or nine of those boys should never have passed that exam!" Gerry McMahon was one of the boys with me that day, he went on to do really well at school and ended up as the head of St. Thomas'. About ten years ago, we both went up to see BD, as we called him. We were chatting away, and then I said, "I have to tell you this. Remember that exam, the 25 boys that passed it? I have to tell you what happened." I gave him the full story and at the end he said, "I knew it!" Still, you have to give us top marks for ingenuity!

I was looking at being an architect as something I wanted to do in the future as I came towards my O levels, but everybody in Northern Ireland's view of what the future might be changed after August 1969 when the British Army arrived in Northern Ireland. From there, the Troubles hit Northern Ireland big time and things changed dramatically, almost overnight. There were buses and cars on fire in the middle of the road, you'd see bomb sites. As a kid, I used to go to the movies to watch war films, but this was on your doorstep, like living on a movie set. You couldn't quite comprehend what was happening, you'd go out and think, "Is this real?" Whenever there was a fight going on, all the teenage kids would be out to watch it and things usually just escalated from there. If the Army came into the area, everybody would be out on the streets, just to create a disturbance. That became second nature, it went on for years.

If I'm honest, I don't think anybody was able to steer clear of the Troubles, it became part of your DNA. If something happens at the bottom of the street or on the road, as a young boy, your inquisitiveness makes you want to go there. Before you knew it, you were throwing stones with everybody else, so you never totally avoided it. There were always people around who wanted to influence you too, older men in their 20s or 30s. "Boys, come over here!" They'd be teaching you how to make petrol bombs, putting sugar in, a squirt of Fairy Liquid, showing you how to tie it up. You were taught that very, very quickly.

To be honest, it did feel as if you were defending your own area against an invader. You could relate it to watching a Western and watching the Indians attacking the fort! Crazy how the brain works, but it was as simple as that. Some parents were so petrified that they wouldn't let their kids out the door, but I was naturally adventurous, I'd be roaming around, I'd always be in the thick of it. It was frantic, but it was exciting as well. I had a lot of devilment in me, I was inquisitive, I was really thirsty for information and knowledge. It was a learning curve and sometimes you learned the hard way.

The funny thing was that when the soldiers first came in, the people were really happy! Early on, there was a foot patrol of eight or ten soldiers and my mum asked them if they wanted a cup of tea. They were stopping and talking to people because I think they were trying to build relationships with everyone. But within about two months, if something sparked off trouble, the atmosphere would just change at the drop of a stone. The soldiers would hide in alley ways and keep their heads down for fear of getting shot.

There were a lot of sectarian murders on both sides, and that was horrible. It didn't matter whether you had any involvement with an organization or not. I would say that probably 90% of the people who died in Northern Ireland through the Troubles had nothing to do with either side. They

were just innocent people caught in the wrong place at the wrong time.
Like the vast majority, I hated the bombings. Bombs were going off all over
the place. I could never understand why anybody would plant a bomb in
a shop or an area that was going to be packed with people, to cause harm
and cause turmoil and cause conflict. It was literally throwing petrol on the
bonfire. It just escalated and escalated and at one stage, I thought there was
never going to be a solution. You just didn't know what was coming next.

There were soldiers everywhere, road blocks were going up, people were
throwing stones, then the stones became petrol bombs. The next thing was
they started shooting plastic bullets - you'd have Army snipers waiting to
see who was throwing petrol bombs and shooting them. I know people
who were shot and arrested and then thrown into jail for throwing
petrol bombs. But it's crazy how fast you can accept things and become
accustomed to them. You have to understand that Belfast was a tough city
even before the Troubles so, to some extent, we were ready to cope with
what came. After two or three months, it was the norm. "Oh, it's only a
burning car." You just had to accept the stuff that happened around the
Troubles, because really, there was nothing you could do about it. You were
stuck. Every morning, you'd wake up, and know that when you went out,
everybody would be going about their normal business. But there might be
new barricades up. There could be a burning bus at the bottom of the street.
Maybe no taxis on the road. You didn't know what was coming, so you had
to have a goal to focus on. Mine was to play my sport and to get my O levels
and A levels.

There were plenty of no-go areas and the Falls Road became infamous,
but it wasn't just the Falls, it was all the way up to the Whiterock in
Ballymurphy. Honestly, it didn't matter what area you were in. It moved
on to Andersonstown about a mile away, up where Casement Park was,
it just spread everywhere, all over Belfast. And then it was in Derry, all
the different parts of Northern Ireland, it was spreading like wildfire.
You'd watch the news at night and you'd go, "Oh look, there's Beechmount
Avenue!" These things were happening a hundred yards from home, and it
was on TV. There'd be foot patrols going through there, 16 or 18 soldiers, all
armed to the teeth, then suddenly, somebody in a balaclava would step out
of a side street and starting shooting at them with a machine gun.

Going to school, you'd be walking down the street and the soldiers were
coming along and they'd been given orders to stop and search you. Some of

the kids they stopped were 13 or 14 and naturally, that would wind up the people in the street, they'd start shouting, "Leave him alone!" That's how confrontations would start and it continued like that for years.

They used to do a census at the different houses. They would come to your house and they would take note of the names of your brothers and sisters, your mother and father. They had all the details, they'd been in the houses, they knew what colour wallpaper was in your lounge. They knew if you were telling the truth and that you weren't saying that you were somebody else. If you were stopped in the street and you said you were from our household for example, they'd say "Ok, what's your brother's name? What's your sister's name? What's your mother's name?" It was just constant harassment. It just chipped away at the people. Before then, as kids we really were unaware of how we were segregated, but that quickly made it all very obvious.

Nowadays, I'm fully in favour of integrated education, I think it's the way forward, having the kids all mixed in together, whatever their religion, that's the way they're going to learn to get on with each other. I was lucky, football took me away to England in the mid '70s and from there, I was away for the best part of 30 years. Living abroad in England and Spain and seeing all the other places I went, it opened my eyes to what the big world is all about. You stop being so narrow minded, you have a broader outlook, you learn to accept other people's opinions and other people's thoughts and what they believe in. I was very grateful that I had that opportunity. I wonder how I would have felt if I'd had those 30 years in Belfast instead?

Like a lot of the boys, I was a bit of a target for the soldiers when things turned sour. At 15 or 16, I was already six feet tall and I probably looked older than I was. You'd come out of school with your bag over your shoulder, and they'd be sitting there, waiting for you. The Saracen would pull up alongside you, the soldiers would grab you and drag you in. They'd do it to break the monotony, for a bit of fun for themselves. They'd open the doors and stick your head out the windows and stuff like that and encourage kids to throw bottles or bricks at you. They used to pretend it was for their own protection – if anybody shot at them, we would get hit first. It was pretty scary as a teenager. When they were finished with you, they would maybe give you a slap and a couple of digs and throw you out a few hundred yards down the road. That happened to me a couple of times, but it was going on all the time and it does make your hatred towards them really grow. "What was that all about?" It wasn't just the soldiers either. Lots of times the police would stop you and take you in for questioning. They really didn't do themselves any favours by picking up these kids coming out of school. I don't know what their job was, or what they thought it was, but picking on people randomly because they were 16 or 17 wasn't helping anybody.

There were times when it got more serious than just being taken for a ride for half an hour. I had my run-ins with them over time, it was just the rebel in me and the fact that I was so stubborn. If somebody pushed me too hard, I'd go the other way. The one time, I was coming out of school and they pulled me and a couple other lads. The usual, "Who are you? What's your address?" This was happening two and three times a week and I was getting pissed off. Then the women in the houses came out, "What are you doing with those boys? They've not done anything wrong." All the women in the street went and got their dustbin lids, and started to smash them against the pavement to make a noise. That just generated a big crowd, which isn't what the soldiers wanted!

They tried to take me off and I had a bit of a struggle with them as they tried to get me into the back of the Saracen. Once they got me in there and had the doors closed, then they were out with the rifle butts, they were punching me and everything, and that carried on until we got to the barracks itself, which was in Paisley Park. This was in the middle of the afternoon, about four o'clock. I was in a room with two soldiers sitting on one side of me, one on the other side, and one standing up in front of me. They were starting arguments and picking on me and all the rest of it. The one that was standing up, he had his hand by the light switch. Suddenly, he switches the light off, and the punches come in from everywhere, punching me in the face, in the head. The first thing that really hits you isn't the pain, it's the shock and then it was just pure anger from there. I was 17 years old and these four guys were laughing at me, they thought it was funny.

They'd put the light back on but I knew it was going to go off again. I'd already made my decision that I wasn't going to keep my face where they thought it was! So when the light went off, I moved my head to the one side and then I started throwing punches. I caught one of them with a right hook, right on the button. The lights came back on and they're all screaming and shouting at me and then this guy walks in. He was about five feet eight or nine. They were all Scottish soldiers but this guy was English, and he had a dressing gown on for some reason. He walked in and said, "What's going on here?" They all jumped to attention because it turned out he was the commanding officer. I had blood on my mouth and I had a black eye coming up as well. He wanted to know what was going on and one of them said, "Just interviewing this person sir!" He turned to me and said, "Right, you. Come out with me." Once we were outside, he said, "Tell me everything that happened." So I did and he said, "I'll deal with these four. I'll get you a taxi home." I said, "Fair enough", because I just wanted to get out of the place and get home. Obviously, his version of a taxi was a big armoured jeep! They drove me to Beechmount, which was not far away but as they got close to home, they asked me where I lived and said they'd drop me off outside the house. I knew if they did that, somebody was liable to open fire on them, so I got them to drop me before then.

There were times when it was funny though. Coming back from the football club one day, a few of us were walking down the Whiterock Road. Foot patrols used to be all over the place, they'd be hiding in gardens, 12 soldiers in a line in different gardens, and as you were walking past, one would jump out and say, "What's your name? What's your address?" There was a guy who was with us who was a bit of a comedian. They asked us our names, and he said, "Mickey Mouse." So the soldier said, "Right Mickey, you're coming with us to Disneyland!" and they threw him in the back of the jeep. I have to admit, I laughed all the way home afterwards!

While all that was going on, the bombs were going off too. I remember one night, I'd been to the cinema and I came back to my grandmother's house. We were just having a chat and a cup of tea and then, "bang, bang, bang, bang" outside! As soon as you heard the shots, you hit the floor, you knew what was happening. That gun battle went on until the sun came up the next day - I probably fell asleep at times, face down on the floor. You could smell the gunpowder from the bullets being fired. In the morning, we gradually started hearing noises and people talking on the street and the soldiers had gone. You could see the empty shells from the guns, where the soldiers had been sitting in the little yards at the front of the terraced houses.

I remember having a little giggle, because obviously one of the soldiers got caught short in the middle of the night. Back then, you used to put your milk bottles out at night for the milkman to collect the next day and one of the soldiers had had a pee in the bottle during the night! You'd have a laugh over things like that, gallows humour I suppose, but that all become the norm, which is the scary part when you look back. I think that had an impact over the long-term on a lot of the people who were growing up in that area. It was just surreal, unbelievable. You saw horrendous things happening but when you see it again and then again, it becomes normal. It isn't, it's anything but, but you become conditioned to it.

The way of living with it was imposed on you and you just had to accept there were places you couldn't go, things you couldn't do, that you had to look out for yourself. But week after week, it just went up another level and another level, it continued getting worse and worse for a long time. Pretty soon, it wasn't just people throwing bricks or setting fire to buses. People started dying, they were being murdered. And then you know somebody who's been shot and that suddenly really brings it all very close to home. People's attitudes, their way of thinking changed, we had to accept we were living in a war zone.

My attitude to it was to just try and be as normal as possible, keep going to school, keep playing sport, but it wasn't easy. It was a very difficult time for everybody. It had begun as a civil rights issue but then the IRA took over the situation, they came from out of nowhere and got a foothold because the people didn't trust the British government, nor Stormont, and definitely not the soldiers. That put everything into the melting pot. There were people who I knew and I'd find out one day they'd been shot dead as members of the IRA, they'd been shot planting a bomb or while trying to attack soldiers or the police. The killings just escalated and escalated. You always hoped that maybe next week, next month, something would change, something would be sorted, but it wasn't.

With all that was going on, as you can imagine, there wasn't much you could do on the Falls Road in terms of entertainment, and that only made matters worse for the kids. They were just so bored with nothing to do and that tended to make them even more likely to get involved in trouble. To try and counter that, the church would put on a big dance, every Saturday night in Clonard, and all the teenagers would go to it. There was no alcohol, but you could get crisps, a chocolate bar, a glass of lemonade. Even then, there were always fights happening there, guys coming over from Turf Lodge or Ballymurphy down to the dance, coming in from all the different districts. The guys loved the confrontation, so there'd be a fight and then they'd get thrown out by the bouncers – the priest would have that all organised! They'd stick one on you, give you a dig in the face and throw you out.

One of my friends was Brendan McCabe, he was a carpenter, he'd been working for about nine months, just turned 17. He'd just bought himself a lovely new suit, it was his pride and joy. He wore it to the dance the one night and when the usual fight started, somebody grabbed him by the jacket and it ripped. That started World War 3. About five of us got thrown out and Brendan said, "I'm not going, I'm waiting for the other guy to come out!" So we waited for him, he was from another area, and when he came out, Brendan said, "Right, me and you now!" The two were going at it in the middle of the street, but then a couple of cars came flying down the road. There was a screech of brakes and out jump these guys in balaclavas with guns.

"Up against the wall, IRA, this is our area, you don't fight here. We don't want you bringing the police and the soldiers down here. We catch you doing it again, we'll kneecap the lot of you."

Then they started to pistol-whip a couple of them. There were about six or seven of us there, and I'm thinking, "Oh shit!" I was standing beside this lad called Albert Cavanagh. One of the IRA guys comes over and he got pretty rough with me, he threw me against the wall, but in that situation, you just take it. Suddenly, one of the guys in the balaclavas says, "Hey Gerry, how are you?" I'm thinking, "You have to ask?!" It turned out to be a guy I went to school with, he was a top man actually.

He says to the others, "He's ok, let him be. You can go Gerry. Who are you with?" I told them I was with Albert and they sent us both off and then gave the other guys a bit of a hiding to make sure they didn't come back and start trouble in the area again. That was a narrow escape.

About three or four months after that, I heard a bomb go off, which wasn't unusual, but it sounded pretty close. It turned out that it was a mile and a half away, but all the windows shook. I was getting ready for a Gaelic football match at the time, and I went outside and saw smoke going up from an industrial estate in Boucher Road. I found out afterwards that two guys had planted a bomb, but the police turned up and caught them. As they were running away, the police had shot them. Definitely one of them died, because that was Albert Cavanagh. I couldn't believe he was involved in stuff like that when, three months earlier, we'd both been stopped by the IRA. He must have got involved just after that. But nothing happened in isolation in those days, it never just stopped there, there was also the knock on effect that it had. Albert's brother Paul was younger, he was only maybe 14 when Albert died, but he then got involved in the IRA a few years later, probably to get back at the police. In the finish, he was sent away to prison for his involvement in blowing up the Chelsea Barracks in 1981, he got five life terms.

The trouble just kept getting ramped up and up. One night, I was on the way to training for my Gaelic football team, St. John's, up at Corrigan Park, I was 17 at the time. I was walking from my grandmother's house and going across the Falls Road to catch the bus. They were the old double decker buses with the big pole at the back, and you used to step up on there to get on the bus. As it pulled up, I went to step on and as I got a foot on the bus and caught hold of the pole, I felt two or three arms grabbing me from behind and pulling me off the bus. It was the soldiers, so I said, "What are you doing? I'm going to football training."

They took the bag off me and searched it, but all it had in it was training gear, my boots and a towel. Then it was the same questions as every other time, "What's your name? Where you from?" They already knew all the answers, they just wanted to pester and annoy you. The next thing, a Saracen pulled up and took me away and it ended up that I was away for two days. They took me off to various different police stations and they asked lots of questions, but it was more about the people that I knew, trying to get information from me about them. It was a horrible experience because you knew that you were pretty much helpless and at the same time, you're just incensed that something like this can happen to you, just for walking down the street in your own country, for no reason other than that.

I ended up in the Holywood barracks, and I was stuck there overnight. All the while, my mum and dad and the rest of the family hadn't been told where I was or what had happened, because the law at the time said they didn't have to tell anybody anything, which again was scandalous. Luckily, somebody had seen me getting pulled off the bus by the soldiers and they passed the message on to the family. As a result of that, my mum and dad were trying to find out where I was, they were phoning round and just getting fobbed off. In the end, they contacted our MP, Paddy Devlin, and he started making inquiries. It took him probably the best part of a day to find out where I was. Then they released me and they took me from Holywood barracks and just dropped me on a roundabout in the city centre, "There you go, get home!" Thanks very much!

I found a newspaper clipping about it from the time that says I was thinking about abandoning my A levels because I was sick of the harassment we were getting at school. In the end, I carried on, but it was aggravation that we didn't need and that we didn't deserve. I'm not saying all of the people at the school I went to and all of the people in the area were innocent, of course not. The soldiers were trying to find out as much information as they could, but it was like trying to crack an egg with a hammer. They went about it the wrong way because all it did was poison people against them and it alienated the community against them totally. There was never any love lost.

The arrival of the Army was a big turning point because it made it so difficult to find a way out of the Troubles from there. In my opinion, Northern Ireland should never have had soldiers in the first place, because soldiers fight wars, they're not there to fight people. It was a political problem and I blame the governments at the time, and over the next 25, 30 years, for their mistakes and their choices. To imprison people without any cause was a bad decision. They were probably desperate because they weren't winning, but every time they made a mistake like that, I think it only strengthened the IRA, because people turned towards them as being on their side. That then triggered off other groups like the UDA and the UVF from the loyalist side, and they would do their things.

The governments made so many bad choices and internment especially was a big mistake. It meant that anyone could be arrested and held without trial, whether you'd done anything or not. They could stick you out in Long Kesh in Lisburn, which became the Maze later, or on the prison ship Maidstone, and you could be there pretty much indefinitely. It was a scandal and yet internment changed my life. Fortunately, I didn't have to get locked away for it to happen.

CHAPTER THREE

....

BLOOD, SWEAT & YEARS

Maybe all those stories would make you think otherwise, but honestly, I have only good memories of growing up, of playing in the school playground, getting into fights, doing the things boys do. I didn't really pick up on football, soccer as we called it, until I was maybe seven or eight years old, and then I used to play in the street, like all the kids did. Most of the boys I played with were Manchester United fans and of course, everybody in Belfast loved George Best, he was the hero – little did I know that in years to come, I'd be playing international football with him and get to know him as a good friend.

But going my own way as usual, I became a Leeds United fan. I absolutely loved them – it's funny that years later, my first league goal for Tottenham came against Leeds at Elland Road. You didn't get to see much football on TV then. There was only a couple of channels, I don't think "Match of the Day" started until I was about 10, so we were lucky to get to see anything much outside the FA Cup final to be honest. Leeds were some team in those days with John Giles, Billy Bremner, Peter Lorimer, who had the hardest shot in football, and Eddie Gray on the wing was fantastic to watch. My favourites were Allan Clarke and Mick Jones up front.

Soccer was a bit of a sideline for me, it wasn't my main sport growing up, it was more something that we played in the street because all you needed was a ball, whereas for hurling or Gaelic football, it was a bit more complicated! Even just getting a ball was hard. There wasn't much money around, so a number of people would scrape the cash together to buy one and then we all played with that. I remember looking out the window one time, I was about 15, and my brothers were playing out in the road with the rest of the kids. I saw the ball bounce into the garden of this neighbour we had, a guy who had come up from the country, I think his name was Dara. He came running out, took a knife and stabbed the ball and then threw it back. I thought, "What a dirty thing to do." The kids were distraught, about a dozen of them. It was a disgrace because it was another two or three weeks before they could get the money together to buy a new one. When they got that, my brother Kevin was straight out there again with a few kids and of course, the ball bounced and went into this guy's garden again. But Kevin was ready this time. He was so fast, he jumped the gate and grabbed the ball and then jumped back out just as your man was coming out the door, and he ran back to our house with it. A few minutes later, this guy is banging on the door. My mum and dad were both out at work, so I opened the door - I was already a big lad by then.

"Hello, can I help you?"

"Is your father in?"

"No, sorry, he's at work."

"Well, is your mother in?"

"No, she's at work as well."

"That's bloody typical of your family, you're a disgrace!"

So I hit him with a right hook and he flew back into the garden! I wasn't having anybody say things like that about my family. Then Kevin came running past me and he hit him as well! I said, "If you come back, I'll do it again!" He took off down the street.

I wanted to keep it quiet, so I said to my brothers and sisters, "Nobody says anything when mum and dad come home," and we never told them. About 12 or 13 years ago, we were at a party, a family reunion. We were talking about the old days and somebody said, "Do you remember that guy Dara? He was horrible!" My mum said, "I always used to say hello to him, and I remember one day he just completely ignored me and never spoke to me again." So Sinead piped up, "I know why mum!" I was there telling her to keep her mouth shut but of course, the beans got spilled!

Back then, I was more into Gaelic football and hurling, maybe because they were sports that came down through the family. My mother's side, the Gallaghers, they were all aggressive Gaelic footballers, they played hurling too, and a lot of them were very good. I had seven uncles and they all played Gaelic football for St. John's and for Antrim. I watched them every week as a boy and they were quite inspirational. Uncle Seamus especially I remember as being rough and ready on the pitch. He was really tough and he would compete, but saying that, they could all look after themselves. I even managed to play with a few of my uncles. I was in the same team as my Uncle Herbie when I was young, about 13 or 14, playing men's football in the lower divisions. When I got quite good, at 15 or 16, I made my senior debut at St John's with my Uncle Michael on the team.

I loved all sports though, that's what came naturally to me. I was good at running, I threw the javelin, did the high jump. In each year group you had had A, B, C, D classes and each had maybe 30 boys. The teacher would take you out and teach you javelin, long jump, shot put and then pick one or two to represent the class in the Sports Day competition against the rest of your year group. I was entered in nine events and I won eight of them and was second in the high jump. Jim Murray, who was eventually my brother-in-law, was in the same class as me, he was a good goalkeeper. Jim used to say, "Look, there's no point in anybody else turning up, because we know who's going to win it," because I was just so competitive.

After that first year, I couldn't be bothered with it because I didn't feel like I had anything to prove, so I never turned up. I'd just sneak off to the cinema because I was mad on the movies. But in the fourth year, the teacher said, "Armstrong, I remember you didn't turn up last year when you were supposed to. Make sure you're there tomorrow." No escaping that time! I was in for six events and won the javelin, the shot put, the sprints, the long jump and came second in the high jump again. Then there was an open competition in the javelin for boys a year or two older than me. The teacher stuck me in for that and I won that as well. It gives you confidence as a young boy to beat boys older than you are. I got used to playing against older boys and then men, both at hurling and Gaelic football and that forces you to develop quickly.

The Gaelic back then was much more physical than it is now, but there were some fantastic players with all the skill and technique you needed. There was a guy called Andy McCallion who played for St. John's and for Antrim. He could do everything, he was the best I ever played with. He was just a superstar. He was smaller in stature and had a low centre of gravity, two great feet. He could score free-kicks, could take goals, could go past people, he was an amazing player. He was really precise, but he was quick, he had all the techniques, great dummies, a body swerve that lost everybody, he had it all. He was the first All-Star from Northern Ireland. I was a different sort of a person to him. I was much bigger, more powerful, I relied more on my athleticism, but I still learnt from people like him.

Gerry Fee was one of my best mates back then. He lived in Logan Street and Gerry was another good Gaelic footballer, a good hurler, Peter Rafferty was another one, Paddy Duffin as well. We were all from the same area, we all went on to play football for St. John's, went to school together, grew up together, we were very close knit. There were a lot of big families like the Tohills and the McCabes, they were a big tribe, 11 or 12 people in the family living in a wee terraced house! Gerry McCann was a very good athlete, another brilliant footballer, I played with him in midfield. Jim Milligan was a great central midfield player and he won the All-Ireland with County Down. Gerry McCrory was another one who I was lucky enough to play with, so you learn lessons from everybody, especially from people who are better than you are. That's how you improve - along with good coaching.

I played against the Ward brothers, Barney and Jimmy, and they were much older than me. I was only 17, 18 and they were grown men in their mid to late 20s, really good players, but hard as nails with it. I was six foot one when I was 16 so they wouldn't have been bigger than me and they certainly wouldn't have been fitter than me and that was my advantage. They were very uncompromising and they would try and stop you in whatever way they could. They'd punch you soon as look at you! I remember Barney was sent to mark me in an Antrim final at Casement Park and I went past him one time too many! I dropped my shoulder to go one way and then went the other and he just threw a punch and caught me in the face. I kept going and played on, but I was thinking, "I'm gonna get that bastard in a minute!" I never really got the chance to get him back, but because the game ended in a draw, we had to have the replay the following week. At the start, they have two players from each side in the middle and they throw the ball up in the air and you jump and see who catches it. As it was thrown, I never even went to catch the ball. I just threw my fist and hit Barney smack in the middle of his nose. He went down and he was off the pitch 20 seconds later. It was brutal, but listen, he did it to me, so I did it to him!

A lot of my family always said I was a much better Gaelic footballer than a soccer player, which I wouldn't disagree with. At 15, I was playing senior football for St. John's and I won three or four Antrim titles. Then I played county level senior football for Antrim from when I was 17 and I won Ulster titles, Ulster under-21 titles, I played in an All-Ireland Under-21s semi-final, I played at Croke Park loads of times, so I had a good early career in Gaelic football.

I loved hurling too and I played it pretty well. I played for Antrim against Tipperary in the 1971 All-Ireland Vocational Schools final at Croke Park and that was a really big deal. Antrim's never won that title since and to beat Tipperary that day was special, because they're one of the best in the world. Back then, Croke Park held 100,000 people but there were probably only about 10 or 11,000 people in the ground at the start of the game. That was still a huge crowd for us, but you didn't see it because they were rattling around this huge stadium. But because Dublin were playing a National Football League match after our game, by the second half, there were 25,000 in there and people just kept on coming in for that game and to watch the tail end of our final. By the finish, there must have been 40,000 people in, so that was a really good experience.

They were exciting times and that kind of thing did teach me a lot about the crowds and about how to focus, which was one of the things I found difficult. I carried on having trouble with that at Tottenham and probably beyond that. The first couple of months, when I was playing in the first team, coming out at White Hart Lane in front of 40,000 people, 50,000 people, in the limelight, with the television cameras there sometimes, knowing your family and your friends are watching back home, I did feel the pressure. You don't want to let them down, you don't want to let yourself down, but focusing was the hard part for me in that first period. It was part of a learning curve and in every game I played, I learned something and I kept evolving and developing.

As far as hurling went, at that stage, I was one of the most promising young talents in the game. Hurling and Gaelic football were a big part of my growing up because they are properly competitive sports! They teach you how to be brave, because if you're not brave, you will get badly hurt. I've had lots of stitches in my head from getting whacked by hurling sticks, but it teaches you to committed. That made me tough, ready to mix it. Playing on a huge, muddy pitch, it built my stamina, and the strength and power. All of that became invaluable to me when I took up soccer.

In those days, there were very few players who went from Gaelic football to soccer, certainly not to the level that I did. Kevin Moran was one and we played against one another, but since then, there haven't been too many – Niall McGinn now is one. But there are certain sports that can help each other, you can learn lessons from one that you can apply in the other, not just from a physical point of view, but from a technical point of view. I do look at the discipline in rugby, the respect the referee gets - he doesn't get that respect in soccer. I don't know why. Both are tough games, but rugby's even tougher! But rugby has mostly been tough and fair where in soccer, players know what they can and can't get away with and they play up to that, especially now when a lot of the physical element has been taken out of the game.

Soccer was still a long way from my thoughts as I was doing my A levels. I played a bit, but it was definitely third on the list. Playing and training for Gaelic football and hurling took up most of my sporting time, so I just played soccer on the side. But as I've said, internment changed all that when it came into being in August 1971. That newspaper story I mentioned about me getting lifted by the soldiers was called "School Behind The Wire", and another part of it was about a pal of mine called Billy McKnight. Billy was studying for his A levels at St. Thomas' when the soldiers came and took him away, and that article talks about him having to sit his exams in Long Kesh. Billy was an intelligent lad, doing well with his education, but they locked him away without any trial, which was shocking.

It always makes more of an impression on you when something happens to somebody you know, and Billy and I had knocked about together quite a bit and we got into a few scrapes. Boxing Day was always a big day in my granny's house in Beechmount, all the sons and their families came together. It was a small terraced house but there were about 70 people in it! I was about 16, thinking, "I'm bored here," and I knew that Billy and a few friends were going up to Ballymurphy for a party, so I disappeared and went off there – there were so many people in the house, nobody was going to miss me.

We went off to the party there, had a good time and when we were leaving, it must have been about one in the morning. Billy was walking back with me but there were a couple of other lads who were driving back to Newtonards – one of them was Gerry McCrory who I mentioned earlier. They got in their car but it wouldn't start – turns out it had no petrol, they hadn't put any in. Billy says, "I'll get a hose and we'll siphon some off." Ballymurphy was a pretty dodgy place but I went over to this parked car with Billy. We stuck the tube into the filler hole and we were getting some out, but the guy there must have heard the noise. He looked out the window and saw us and he came out and chased us and we took off with a bit of petrol and the hose! That's the sort of stuff the kids did then. Eventually we got the petrol in the car and got the boys off and then we set off walking home – I got in about three and I walked in and nobody had missed me, there were that many people there!

Anyway, Billy ended up in Long Kesh, but he wasn't the only one to get that treatment either. A few of the lads from St. Thomas' were interned, and one of the knock-ons from that was that the school soccer team was missing a number of players. I remember the teachers coming round and saying they were short of players because they had the Sir Robin Kinahan Cup coming up, a tournament for the schools. I offered to play. The geography teacher, Mr. Purvis, he was running the team and he said, "You're a Gaelic footballer. You don't play soccer." He was actually a rugby player and yet he coached Gaelic and soccer! In the end, he told me to come along and play and he put me in as centre-half. We had some good players, there was a guy called Eamon Caughey who played for us on the left wing, he was really quick. It was a decent team, we all complemented each other, we were all hard working and we ended up winning the trophy. We played Carrickfergus High School in the final and beat them 3-1. I scored twice - I came up for the corner kicks. The first one was a volley and the second was a header.

I must have made an impression in what was a pretty big game as schools football went. At the end of the match, this guy came over and introduced himself as Jack Fullerton. I remember he had on this long overcoat, he looked the part. He told me he was scouting for Everton and asked me would I like to go across for a trial there? I told him I didn't really play soccer, it was only for this tournament and I wasn't really interested, but thanks anyway. Looking back now, turning down Everton as cold as that seems crazy. They'd won the First Division in 1970, they were a massive club, but it just shows how soccer was definitely third on my list of sporting priorities. Little did I know that a few months later, I was going to get suspended from Gaelic football!

CHAPTER FOUR

....

SLIDING DOORS

I started to get a little bit more involved in soccer after playing for the school. I started playing for St. Paul's Swifts and I was enjoying it. When you were used to the physical nature of hurling or Gaelic football, soccer was a bit more genteel you could say! Certainly, coming up against big centre-halves or centre-forwards didn't really hold any fears for me because I could hold my own on the Gaelic pitch, which took some doing. In that game, you couldn't back down, because if you did, you'd just get brushed aside and you'd be finished. There were always lots of conflicts in Gaelic games in those days, everybody was fighting, it was a really, really rough game, just relentless.

I enjoyed the challenge, the confrontation and people were talking about me as an up and coming talent in the game, but it all went wrong when I played in a minor Gaelic final against Cargin. Nowadays, I probably wouldn't have played because, as it happened, I had a plaster cast on my hand because I'd been in a fight the week before. I just covered it up with a glove. It was only a part cast, with two or three fingers sticking out and there was a metal strip to secure it.

We were a better team than Cargin were, so they sent these two guys out just to stop us playing. We were five or six points clear and we were cruising, so being physical was the only way they could stop us. One of my team-mates was a guy called Joe McGuiness and he had his arm broken. Catching the ball, their player kicked him as he caught the ball and he broke his elbow and he had to go off. Then the ball was on the ground and Brendan Heaney from our side and one of their lads went in for the challenge. Their guy came in and kicked him on the ankle and busted his foot, so he had to come off as well. It was getting a bit nasty and a bit of a brawl started. In the middle of it, I instinctively threw this left hook and caught their guy on the jaw – I broke it actually - and that sparked a real punch up. When the dust settled, I got sent off, which I suppose was fair enough, even in a Gaelic game!

What I didn't think was fair was that afterwards, I got a four week suspension. I played in the seniors for Antrim as well as under-21 and minor, so I didn't think I'd get a suspension at all, or if I did, it would just be a short one. But there was a lot of politics around the game in those days and they decided they were going to make an example of me because they didn't take kindly to the fact that I was playing soccer now. That was almost taboo, even if it was only with St. Paul's Swifts. They thought they'd teach me a lesson because they didn't want anyone playing soccer. I remember reading an article about Liam Brady, and as a 15-year-old, he was playing for the Ireland soccer team at the youth level. He didn't play for his school team at Gaelic because of that and so they suspended him. They had these rules that stated that if you played foreign games, which could be rugby, could be anything, and chose that sport over Gaelic, you were banned. They were very narrow minded, but I wouldn't have anybody dictate to me what game I was going to play. I went the other way, I turned against them. I was stubborn and it set me on a path that would take me to where I ended up. That ban happened for a reason because it was that that took me into playing soccer.

I needed to take it up a notch from the Swifts, so I joined a club called Cromac Albion, an amateur league team. All I wanted was to get a game because I had all this energy and now I couldn't use it up playing Gaelic football. I went there with a guy called Vincent O'Riordan, a left-back, he had a good left foot. We went down to the Black Bull, a bar in Belfast, which is where they used to meet before the games, and they would pick the team there. The manager was a guy called Sammy Watson, he looked like Arthur Daley, he had the coat, he had the trilby hat, the whole lot.

There were 17 or 18 players there, I had no idea what sort of team it was or anything like that, but in fact, they were one of the best amateur teams in all of Northern Ireland. Sammy didn't know me, he picked his team, the 12 players he wanted, and that was that. Some of them were picked because they had cars to ferry everyone about I think, it was funny how he did it! Then he said, "Sorry lads" to the rest of us and that was that.

I turned to Vincent and said, "What's going on here?"

He said, "Gerry, we're not getting a game today."

"I've got to get a game today."

"No, we're beat, nothing we can do."

We were walking back to get the bus up the Falls Road, heading towards Castle Street and a couple of guys on the other side of the road who knew Vincent shouted across to us.

"Vincent, we've got a game on but we're a couple short if you want to play?"

We were up for that. "Where do you play big man?"

"Oh, I'll play anywhere up front, just stick me in there."

So we played for this team called Old Park Celtic and they were playing the top team in the league, who were just above Cromac Albion. We beat them 4-1 and I scored all four goals. That night, about half past seven, I'd just had my dinner, and there was a knock on the door. My father answered it and this guy was asking for Gerry Armstrong, which is also my father's name.

So he said, "I'm Gerry Armstrong, what do you want?"

"Oh, sorry, it must be your son I'm looking for."

It was Sammy Watson. "Listen big man, I didn't know that was you in the bar today. You're playing for me next week, alright?"

That's how I ended up going down to play for Cromac Albion, but I only played three or four times for them as things turned out. One was in midweek, a Wednesday night, and there were two guys at the match, watching us. Afterwards, they came up to me and another lad and asked if we'd be interested in going and training at Bangor Football Club. It was

Bertie Neill, the manager, and he had his assistant, Billy Neill, the coach, with him.

He said, "A blue minibus will pick you up at the back of the city hall at half past six on Tuesday and Thursday nights if you fancy coming down?"

"I'll be there!"

So the next Tuesday, there were about eight or nine players who got picked up in the back of the minibus. I trained there on the Tuesday and Thursday, met the players and I really enjoyed it. On the Saturday, the reserves had a semi-final in the Steel & Sons Cup which was a big amateur cup competition in Northern Ireland. They were playing the Civil Service on their ground. Ralph McGoogan was the manager of the reserves and he said to me, "Look big man, these lads have worked really hard to get here, so I'm going to start you on the bench. If I get a chance to put you on, I will."

It was 1-1 with 15 minutes to go and Ralph said, "Big man, get yourself ready, you're coming on. Go out and get me a goal!" So I warmed up, couldn't wait to get on, bursting with energy and looking to make my mark. Within a couple of minutes, I got the ball and went past two or three defenders. Football was a very physical game back then, especially in Northern Ireland, maybe because we'd all been hurlers and played Gaelic football too. They had a big centre-half, he was a monster. He tried to take me out but I went past him and got a shot away. Their 'keeper saved it but it rebounded to one of my team-mates, and he stuck it away.

The big centre-half came over to me and growled at me, "You do that again and I'll break your fucking legs!"

"Oh, will you?"

So a few minutes later, I got the ball again and I went past a couple of players and the big gorilla came across and tried to take me out. I nipped past him and smashed it into the corner of the net. I turned round and the big lump was coming at me, so I dug out the right hook and he went down! Well, from there, everybody piled in, it was a free for all. When it was calmed down, I can still see it now, the referee was laughing as he was sending me off! I'd only been on seven minutes! I was thinking, "What did I do wrong?" I didn't even know the laws of the game at that point!

Bangor Reserves won the match 3-1 – I was suspended for the final of course! – and I went into training the following Tuesday. I went in the dressing room, which I loved because they were great lads. I can't remember if Tony Smith or Jim Thompson was the captain, but one of them said, "Here he comes Muhammad Ali, Cassius Clay!" They were all cheering and laughing, but I couldn't work out what the fuss was about - that was just normal stuff in Gaelic football. Anyway, I was told to go and see the manager and Bertie was very strict.

"What are you doing, you punched the fella!"

"Well, he said he was going to break my legs!"

"Ah, he didn't mean it."

"Well then he shouldn't have fucking said it!"

We had a bit of a chat and Bertie said, "Listen, you can make a good career for yourself if you listen to me and do what you're told, but you can't go around punching people!"

That was me told off. I got a dressing down, but within a few weeks, I was in the first team. He played me as a right winger because I was quick, but I was strong as well – if I couldn't go round them, I'd go through them! I started scoring goals and getting a reputation. Then I moved inside and there was a guy who I played up front with, Gordon Stewart, he was the top goalscorer. He was smaller than me, about five foot eight, a wee Scotsman, but he was a great finisher. I was the target man, I was going for everything. If they were shouting "Keeper's!", I was shouting, "No it's not!" And I'd be up with him, putting him off, jumping into him, putting myself about a bit and then Gordon picked up all the bits and pieces and scored goals. We formed a really good partnership.

I had plenty of rough edges that needed smoothing off but my fitness, my athleticism was second to none. I didn't want to be indoors, I wanted to be outside, doing things. The playground and the streets had been my training fields, I was always doing some sort of exercise without realising it, but as far as soccer was concerned, I never had any real coaching until I was 17 and got to Bangor. Looking back, I maybe lost out in terms of some technique and of understanding the game more earlier on, and perhaps I could have done better as a player if I'd had that coaching early on. I just wish I'd spent more time practising all my skills when I was a kid. If somebody had coached me when I was 9, 10, I could have been a bit better. But then maybe if I had been coached from the age of seven or eight like the kids are now, maybe I'd have lost some of that passion and hunger for the game.

I had a really good attitude in terms of wanting to play, to compete, to do well, in never pulling out of a challenge. I got all of that from hurling and Gaelic football. The biggest thing is, you have to enjoy it, whatever your sport is, and that gets the most out of you. I couldn't get enough sport growing up and I must have played some kind of sport every single day for school, for a club, in the street. That's how I stayed fit and got stronger. The other thing I had that has been so important for me, was my ability to think for myself, which I must have inherited from my family. That wasn't easy, especially growing up in Belfast with the influence of the church, then the Troubles, but my gut instinct was always what I worked by.

The church played a huge part in West Belfast and my mum had us going every Sunday. Because I was in the choir, I'd be there for two or three hours, singing away. As the Troubles were getting really bad, there was nowhere for the kids to go, so at St Paul's church in Beechmount, they tried to do something. There was a school attached to the back of the church, an old primary school that was closed down. We had the idea, could we not turn it into a youth club? All the youths in the area decided that they would go and work on it for free and get it up to scratch. Some of them were carpenters, electricians, painters, so we all went in and did a bit of everything, doing the place up with the blessing of the priests and the church. We worked on it for two or three weeks and then we were able to have a dance. Twice a week you could go to the club, and it was something for the kids in the area to go to and keep them out of trouble on a Saturday night and on a Tuesday or a Wednesday. There was no alcohol, it was always like Coca-Cola or Fanta or whatever, packets of crisps, there was music played and it was great for the kids.

I was always training for one sport or another by then, so I would do that and then on my way back home, I would go to the youth club as well. The first time, they did a special mass and the priest blessed the place and that was fine. A couple of weeks later, I was coming back from training and I went in there about nine o'clock, I had my kit bag with me. They always had a man on the door like a bouncer, just to make sure there was no trouble, and the priest used to be there as well. This bouncer asked me where I'd been and I told him I'd been training. He said, "You know you're supposed to go next door to the church and go to the novena and do the mass before you go into the club." I told him I couldn't do that because I'd been training and I was back too late. From there, it then became a prerequisite over the following weeks that the novena was your ticket in.

A few weeks later, I turned up after training and they told me I couldn't go in. Yet I'd been working on this place and had helped to do it up. I had a row with the priest and the bouncer and basically said, "You're blackmailing people. I go to church on a Sunday, I don't need to go on a Wednesday or a Saturday night. You can paint it whatever way you want, but I know what you're doing. You're blackmailing everybody." I wouldn't have it and I fell out with them over it. It was a huge row. My sister was about 15 at the time, and she heard it all and went home and told my mum – she wasn't too pleased! But that was part of growing up, becoming a man, becoming my own person. I didn't have anything to do with them for years, that was me and the church parting ways, because I had my opinion. I just thought they were very narrow minded. It was very silly. The church does a lot an awful lot of good for people, but on that occasion, I felt it was taking advantage, especially of young people who were vulnerable and easily pressured. It was like they were pushing me a certain direction and I can't have somebody who does any of that. I make my own mind up.

It all went to make me a committed person and someone who wasn't going to back down if somebody threatened me. When it came to sports, I just loved the competitive side of it. That all became pluses for me because when I went to Tottenham and saw the technique, the quality, and the skills of the players around me, I thought, "Oh my God, how am I ever going to get into this team with these players?" But you do because over a period of months, I got fitter, I learned a lot more skills. I worked on my touch, technique and control in the gymnasium with Peter Shreeves and I was working towards an end. Looking back on it now, we did a lot of good things in training. I didn't really see the plan, the bigger picture, but I just enjoyed it.

While I was doing all the sports, I was still working hard on my education. I did my A levels and passed them in engineering drawing and woodworking theory and that's when I went into the architect's office. I had the qualifications I needed and joined an architect's practice, McRandall's on the Malone Road. Danny McRandall ran it, it was a big company, and I was working there for about 18 months, but I didn't like it. I knew after about six or eight months that it didn't suit me, I found it boring, and I knew it wasn't what I wanted to do for the rest of my life. Ann, my girlfriend at the time, who later became my wife, was working in the housing executive and as a result of that, I got a job there in the commercial property section. I worked there until I went to England and joined Tottenham.

The work was really varied, going out to look at premises all over the country, measuring them up, putting a value on them, and then they go off for rental. If it was a new community, the first things that would go up was a Spar supermarket and a chemist, so you could see what were the essential things to people's lives and how things ticked. You would favour somebody who wanted to put those up when it came to planning permissions. But there would always be an off licence as well! The price on the off licence was always a lot more, like £1,200 a year, whereas the Spar would only be £650 a year, it was it was driven that way.

Frank McGrath was our boss. There was Josephine Love, Patsy, Jim Cunningham a lot of real characters, we just got on really well. There was a guy called Tom Haire, who went on to become a councillor on the Belfast Council. Tom and I used to go on location all over Belfast, on the Shankill Road, the Falls Road, we'd measure up shops, we'd go out to the countryside, it was great. Another guy joined us called John McKeown, he was more into the commercial property side of it, which was outside of Belfast, in Antrim, because the housing executive covered the whole of Northern Ireland. There was a lot of variety to it and I really enjoyed it.

You couldn't avoid the reality of life in Belfast amid the Troubles though. Driving around was a big part of the job, and fortunately, I'd taken my driving test when I was 17, at the Duncairn Gardens test centre in Belfast. My dad was a driving instructor, but he put me on to somebody else to teach me and then I put in for my test. Everything was going smoothly and I remember coming up the inside lane towards some traffic lights to make a left turn into Duncairn Gardens to end the test. I started to slow down because the lights had gone amber when I was about 10 or 20 yards away. There was an armoured personnel carrier on my right hand side. As we pulled up to stop, this guy stepped off the pavement about 50 yards in front and opened fire with a machine gun at the soldiers. I just floored the accelerator and went straight through the lights and they were definitely on red. I went straight through them. Everybody was ducking and diving all over the place, but I was away on the left turn, into Duncairn Gardens. It was instinctive, I thought, "I'm not getting caught in the middle of this!" and just did it. The driving examiner, I tell you, he shit himself! The test had been going really well, no mistakes but I just thought, "He's going to fail me now, I've gone through a red light." I pulled in, we got out of the car and he said, "Well done Mr. Armstrong, you've passed your test." Under any other circumstances, I don't think that would have happened. But that was Northern Ireland back then!

When I was working in the housing executive you used to get bomb scares every other day. That's all they were usually, just a scare, so we got a bit complacent. We had one call one day and as usual, we had to evacuate the building. I didn't rush down the stairs, I didn't hurry. I was probably one of the last people out along with a couple of guys, Sean McKenna and Gerry Judge, where everybody else had sprinted out as usual. I remember walking down the street to get to where the barrier was, but we didn't know that what they'd done was put a package in a post-box right outside the housing executive. I don't think it was a big bomb, but we were no more than 30 or 40 yards away when it went off. The next thing, you were face down on the road, you don't even realise it! Part of it was the shock and the noise as well, my ears were ringing for about 10 minutes. It scared the shit out of us! Next time there was an alarm, I can tell you we were first down the stairs and right out of the door! It was all part of your education on how to live in Belfast at that time. We were living in a war zone, but people are very adaptable in Northern Ireland, they're the greatest people that I know of for that. They were put under an awful lot of pressure, but they seemed to deal with it. No matter what, they seemed to cope.

When I was 18 or 19, I bought my first house. It was just a terraced place and the houses there didn't have indoor toilets, they had one out in the backyard. I was working at the housing executive at the time, so after I finished work, I'd go to the house, do a couple of hours work, painting or whatever, and then go off and stay with my mum. I'd got friends coming in and doing a bit of electrical work and that kind of thing while I was getting it ready to live in. It was about nine at night and I was ready to go to my mum and get my dinner. I decided to go to the loo first, so I went to go out the back. There was no electricity out there, but I'd put one of those little battery powered lights in the toilet that you press to turn on. I pushed the door and it only opened five or six inches. I couldn't get it fully open, I couldn't understand it. I put my hand in and managed to turn the light on and I had a look through the crack in the door. There were a couple of Armalite rifles and a box or two of ammunition in there and I just thought, "Holy shit!" If you were over 18 and that kind of stuff was found on your property, you were going to get done for it. No excuses, you were responsible. I had a family member who was heavily involved in all of that, and I went straight round to his. "What's going on here?"

"Ah, don't worry Gerry, we'll get it moved for you tomorrow morning!"

I was still training with Bangor on Tuesday and Thursday, playing on a Saturday, but with my suspension over, I was also back playing Gaelic football on a Sunday for Antrim and training on a Monday and Wednesday. The only night I had free was Friday, but that was fine. I didn't drink, the most I'd have was a pint of lager shandy, so I wasn't missing out on that. I loved training and playing and I was very fit and strong. That was all my focus was.

At Bangor, we won a couple of trophies, the County Antrim Shield was one of them in 1974/75. That was the first they'd won in a while and that was against Glentoran. It had already been arranged at the start of the competition that the final would be played at The Oval, which is their home. It was a great stadium and a brilliant pitch. We went a goal down early on, but we got it back level by half-time. It was a pretty tight game in the second half but with about 15 minutes to go, a free-kick came in and I managed to get above everybody and headed it into the top corner.

It still wasn't all over because there was about three minutes to go when there was a bit of a scuffle on the pitch between Andy Dougan who played for Glentoran and Ian Jeffrey on our team. The referee separated them, but this guy in the stand threw a flagpole with a Glentoran flag onto the pitch, and it hit Ian on the head, knocked him out. One of our players was an ex-policeman. He couldn't play in the game so he was in the stand as well and he tried to arrest the guy who had thrown it. From there, it kicked off in the stand as well as on the pitch and it was absolutely World War 3! We finally got the last three minutes played, but we couldn't get presented with the shield on the pitch, we had to go into the boardroom to get it. It was a great occasion though, and it was my first medal in semi-professional football. It was lucky I got one so soon because I wasn't going to be semi-pro for much longer.

CHAPTER FIVE

....

SIGNING ON

Combining all my sporting passions wasn't easy, especially as things started to get more serious on the soccer side of things. In the summer of 1974, Bangor went off to England on a pre-season tour, which was the first time I'd ever been on a plane. We played Morecambe, Hull City, Shrewsbury Town, teams at that level, from the Fourth Division and what would be the Conference now. I enjoyed that and I must have made an impression because Shrewsbury put in a bid for me at the end of the tour. Bangor weren't happy with what they were offering and they wouldn't sell me, which was ok with me at that stage, I was in no real hurry. But when we got back, Antrim dropped me from the Gaelic football side because I'd been away playing soccer. That was very much the way it was – the two sports didn't really get on, especially from the Gaelic side!

I did get back into the Antrim side and I'm glad I did, because it was a big part of my life growing up. Over my time I played in Ulster finals, I won GAA medals. My last big game for Antrim was an All-Ireland semi-final against Kerry at Tralee in August 1975. Kerry were the team. Paudie O'Shea and Pat Spillane were in that team, guys who went on to win five or six All-Ireland medals in a row. That was not long before I signed my contract with Spurs, so that was pretty much the end of it for me.

That pre-season trip to England must have done us good because Bangor had a very decent season in 1974/75, one that ended up with us beating Glentoran 2-1 in the final of the County Antrim Shield, which was only the second time we'd ever won it. I felt I was getting better all the time, I was scoring plenty of goals and there was a lot of interest in me by the end of that season. I was still a better Gaelic footballer than soccer player, but soccer was a way of making a career where the GAA sports were amateur affairs where you definitely couldn't be thinking of giving up the day job!

Things like that were much more important to me because by now, I was a married man. I got married very young, I was 19, and I married my first girlfriend, Ann. We'd not been married seven or eight months when we found out Ann was pregnant, and then we discovered that she was having twins, a boy and a girl, so we were thrilled about the prospect of being parents and starting our family.

Unfortunately, it was one of those things that was never meant to be. They were born prematurely, both weighed under two pounds and they both had breathing difficulties. The boy, Gerard Peter, he died after two days, and then the day after that, Jennifer Anne, she died too. That was a real kick in the teeth for us, it was absolutely soul destroying, to lose everything like that when we'd been thrilled by the idea of having the children. We were distraught about it. It was an horrific experience to go through when we were just kids ourselves really.

With all that was going on with the Troubles, then with that happening to us, it started to change my perspective on things. I didn't see any solution to the Troubles, I couldn't see how they were going to end, so the idea of maybe using soccer to go to England was a Godsend. I was really looking for a way out of Northern Ireland and to create a fresh start for us at that point from where we could have children again in the future.

That summer of 1975, there was some talk about Sheffield Wednesday coming in and making a bid for me – they'd just been relegated to Division Three, but they were still a big club and they were looking for a goalscorer to fire them back up the league. That came to nothing and I wasn't unhappy with that because I thought I could get a move to the First Division, because I knew a few of those clubs were starting to take an interest in me. Bertie Neill was telling a lot of people about how good I was and that I had a lot to offer, so a lot of clubs came to watch me early that season. There was Tottenham, Arsenal, Coventry, Liverpool, Celtic, they all sent scouts to watch Bangor and things really did start to hot up because I had a good start to the season and the goals were going in for me.

In the end, the most serious interest came from Tottenham and Arsenal and it looked as if it was going to boil down to me going to one of them. Arsenal especially seemed really keen. Gordon Clark was their chief scout, he'd been manager at West Brom and Peterborough before that. He came to virtually every game Bangor played early that season. He was always chatting to me and said they wanted to sign me, wanted to sort a deal out. Then in late September, Spurs asked me to go over to England for a trial and to spend four or five days training with them, which was really exciting. I went over with Johnny Jameson, who ended up in the World Cup squad with me in 1982, when he was at Glentoran. He was about three years younger than me, but he was a talented footballer.

We stayed in digs in Chingford with the Brett family, and we were told to keep it all hush hush. We stayed there for a few days and trained with the reserves, and then we went and played a match in Hendon against the RAF. We won by three or four and I got a couple of goals. I thought I did ok, made a bit of an impression. The guy who looked after me was in charge of the youth team at the time, and that was Peter Shreeves, who eventually went on to be the manager at Spurs a few years later. He was brilliant, a great guy, and he loved all that technical side of the game. Later on, when I eventually joined Spurs, he coached me in the afternoon and again in the evening down at the gymnasium. You didn't have to go back in the afternoons, but I wanted to because I needed to work on my technique because I was trying to catch up with the boys who had been there from the age of 15, 16.

The fourth day we were there on trial, we played a match, a half an hour game, where the first team were playing the reserves. Pat Jennings was in goal for the first team, Steve Perryman was there, all the star players were involved. It was very, very competitive from our side because all the reserve lads wanted to do really well, they wanted to prove a point against the first teamers, while the first teamers were just going through the motions a little bit. There weren't too many chances, but I managed to get on the end of one and scored what turned out to be the only goal of the game.

After that we flew back to Belfast and Bertie and Billy Neill were asking us how it had all gone. We told them we'd enjoyed it, the facilities were great and that they'd looked after us really well. I had a good feeling about Tottenham. I've read since that Arsenal asked me to go there on trial too, but I don't remember that to be honest.

Once we were back home, it was a case of waiting to see what happened. I heard nothing for five or six weeks after that, and so I just thought they weren't interested. Little did I know that Bangor were negotiating the fee and the details of the move with Terry Neill and Tottenham in the background. In the meantime, Arsenal had continued to watch me playing for Bangor and they'd come in with an offer after a cup match where I scored after about 13 seconds, the fastest goal there'd been in the competition – I don't think the scout had even had time to sit down before I scored! It didn't matter because after about 80 minutes, I scored again and we won 2-1. Bertie Mee was the manager at Arsenal and they were playing in Europe that season, so he was a bit busy, but Gordon told me that he wanted to come to see me. He said that if I moved to Arsenal, they'd sort me out a house, and make it all very straightforward for me. Most of the communication I had with English clubs was with Arsenal, so having heard nothing from Spurs, I thought they were going to be the club most likely to come in for me.

It was all just rumbling on, and nothing much seemed to be happening. Then one Sunday morning, I had a phone call at about half past eleven, and it was the vice-charman of Bangor Football Club.

"Listen son, we've got a big meeting today, I need you to meet me at the back of the City Hall in an hour. You're going to sign today."

He didn't say who for, so I just assumed that they'd done a deal with Arsenal. Him and his wife picked me up at the City Hall, took me to the Dunadry Inn hotel and there was Terry Neill, who was the manager at Spurs.

"I thought I was signing for Arsenal!"

"No son, you're coming to Spurs".

Bertie and Billy Neill were there, a lot of the board members, and I remember sitting down and negotiating the contract. Actually, Bertie did it for me. I was earning £24 a week at the housing executive, which was a decent wage, so I was doing ok at the time.

Terry Neill said, "We're going to offer you a one year contract with a one year option", which meant nothing to me!

Bertie said, "Could you not do a two year contract?" But they wouldn't.

Terry said, "We'll start you off at £60 a week." And I thought, "That's nearly three times what I'm making, this is great!"

But Bertie said, "No, that's not enough. You can pay him £70."

He was negotiating on my part and in the finish, we agreed £65. I was happy with that. I think Bangor were getting paid a £5,000 fee up front and then there were other stipulations they'd get paid £5,000 more if I got in the first team and another £5,000 more if I played international football. I know that Bangor also passed some of the money onto Cromac Albion as well which was great for them, and I was pleased with that because they'd given me my first push in soccer.

There was a bit of controversy about the move because Arsenal really weren't happy about what had happened. They were looking at making a bid as well, and they felt that Bangor had used them to bump the price up. Bertie Neill wasn't having any of that. He said that they'd told Arsenal that Spurs were coming over on the Sunday to try and do a deal and that he'd been told that Arsenal didn't work on Sundays and wouldn't be able to make an offer until the Monday, which sounds crazy nowadays when football is a 24/7 operation. Maybe it didn't hurt Spurs that Terry Neill had played at Bangor as a young boy either!

It was still sinking in that I'd signed to play in the First Division when I realised I'd got a problem. I had a Gaelic game to play that afternoon. That wasn't allowed anymore, so I had to phone the GAA guys, one of the committee members to say, "Sorry, I can't play at Casement Park today, I've just signed for Spurs!" That was me finished with the Gaelic football and about a month or so later, I was away over to London to start a new life. Well, not quite finished…

St. John's had got to the semi-final of the club championship, which was massive, and the game was taking place at Breffni Park. I really wanted to play and nothing was going to stop me, but obviously having signed for Spurs, the GAA weren't going to let me play – and neither would Spurs to be honest! So because I couldn't play under my name, I went under the name of Gerard Gallagher, my mum's family name. It was one of those games that got a wee bit tasty and I remember smacking this guy, right hook. After what had happened to me over the previous wee while, having punched somebody, I just thought I was going to get sent off, but the referee came over and booked me.

"What's your name?"

"Gerard Gallagher."

So I got booked under the wrong name in my last game for St John's!

That move to Tottenham happened pretty quickly after we lost the twins. It was a good time for it to come around after what had happened to us, it gave us a new focus. Northern Ireland was home, I loved being with the family and being at home, but opportunities like that come once in a lifetime. Part of me just wanted to know if I could become a professional, was I good enough to play? I only had a one year contract with a one year option. I wanted to give it a go, but it also gave us a new beginning, to get over to England and see if we could start a family afresh and make a new life and a new career. Fortunately enough, it worked out.

My mother was pleased that I was getting the chance to get out and away from what was going on. There were plenty of other ones at home that she still had to worry about! My older sister Mary, she had moved down to Dublin when she was 17 or 18 to get away from it. Later on, when I was at Watford and had moved to live in St Albans, my brother Kevin came over to live with me. He was an electrician and there wasn't much work at home, so he got himself a job and moved his family over from Belfast, lock, stock and barrel. Later on, a couple of my sisters moved over too, so they ended up following me to get away from the problems at home.

My dad moved back to Omagh in 1983 because they needed driving examiners, and that was good for him, going back to where his family was. He had eight brothers and sisters living in the country out there, so he moved my mum and my youngest brother and sister out there, away from Belfast, which is where most of the trouble was of course. But in reality, there was no escape from the violence anywhere in Northern Ireland during that period. Years later, on August 15th 1998, the Omagh bombing happened. I was working for Sky and for BBC Sport at the time. I used to go in and do a News 24 type show on BBC. They'd go to the sport at around quarter past the hour, and I did that with Chris Hollins. I was in there the one Saturday and slowly, reports were coming in of a huge explosion in Northern Ireland.

At that time, my mum and dad were spending a bit of time with me in England for a few weeks, and while they were over, the rest of the family that were still living over there, they went in and put a new kitchen in the house for them as a surprise, so they were all in Omagh. When the news came through that the bombing had been in Omagh, and there had been casualties, you get this horrible feeling run through you. They started saying they'd found seven bodies, then it was eight, then ten, it kept going up, and the number of injured kept going up. So when I was off the air, I tried to phone some of the family, but I couldn't get through, all the lines were engaged, so it was horrible, just desperately trying to find out.

Late in the afternoon, about five o'clock, I finally managed to get in touch with one of the family. Fortunately, they'd all been in the house at the time. They heard the bomb go off, probably half a mile away in the centre of Omagh. But what we didn't realise at the time was we had a second cousin who wasn't declared missing until the next day. She had died in the blast. That's the reality of it all and no matter how long it had all been going on, no matter how many times you heard about injuries and deaths, no matter how many times it happened to someone you knew, it always hit you hard, every single time something new happened.

I was lucky in the sense that I left Northern Ireland in 1975 at the age of 21. I've lived away from home for most of my adult life but in going back to Belfast to live in recent years, I see it from a different angle now. A lot of people who have lived through it, they don't see it, but the improvements are unbelievable. When I do see them, I actually make a point to say it to people, to say it in interviews, because I think you have to be positive. I don't think anybody will allow things to slip back into the way it used to be, even though you're going to find a small percentage, nationalists or unionists, who will always try to scupper it all and put their way of seeing things across. We'll see what happens over the next few months with Brexit and the border in the Irish Sea and all of that, but I think it could actually be a great opportunity for Northern Ireland because it's linked to Ireland, which is a country in Europe and the UK is not. We're unique within the UK in that we do have borders with a European country. I think it could be a benefit to Northern Ireland, and we need to look at it from a positive attitude - hopefully, it works out that way.

I was very definitely ready to say goodbye to the Troubles though back then. On Monday, November 10th 1975, I handed my notice in at the housing executive. I was now a professional footballer for Tottenham Hotspur.

CHAPTER SIX

....

GLORY, GLORY TOTTENHAM HOTSPUR

Heading for England and a new life was exciting, but daunting too. I'd watched Spurs play West Ham in a League Cup game a couple of days after signing for them, when I went over to London just to sort a few details out before heading over there full time. It was a pretty hectic game, very fast, good quality too, so it was an early sign of the level I was going to have to reach if I was going to play for the first team on a regular basis.

Tottenham were a good side at that time. They'd won the League Cup in 1971 and 1973 and the UEFA Cup in 1972, and then they'd lost in the final in 1974. They had Martin Chivers up front who had scored a silly number of goals over the previous few seasons, but he'd turned 30 and so they were looking to find a successor to him. Terry Neill was in his second season as manager there after the great Bill Nicholson had retired. He was looking to carve out his own team and style to try and take things forward, so they were in transition a little bit. But if you looked at the first team, they still had some great players like Martin, Pat Jennings, Steve Perryman, Willie Young, John Pratt, John Duncan and Ralph Coates.

Initially, I went over there alone, just to get settled into things at the club before Ann came over and we found ourselves somewhere to live. I started off in a hotel up in Finsbury Park for four or five weeks and I didn't really like it. I'd get the bus every morning to join in training wherever it was that day, either at White Hart Lane or at Cheshunt. Alfie Conn, who had joined the club around the same time as I had, was in the same hotel as me and he was ok with it, but he was a wee bit older and he was a first team player. I was a kid in the reserves, trying to prove myself. Alfie was a nice lad and we'd chat together and have dinner together sometimes, but he was in a different league to me, often we were we training at different times. For me, it got a bit frustrating being in the hotel.

After about a week, I remember telling Terry Neill that I didn't feel comfortable in the hotel, that it wasn't my cup of tea. He thought I should venture out into London a bit to see the city. "Why don't you go into the West End and see a movie or go to a show or something?" But I didn't really fancy that. I'd got talking to Chris McGrath, who was in digs in Edmonton, and I told Terry that I would rather be in digs with Chris and have a more normal family life than being in a hotel. That was a better fit for me, so they put me in with Chris, another Northern Irish boy, and we stayed with Mr and Mrs Walker in a flat on the Edmonton High Road, above the Tesco. They were lovely people, they looked after us really well, it was home cooked food and all of that! They had a son that had been at Tottenham as a youth team player but didn't get signed as a professional, so they were big Spurs fans and it was a nice environment for me to find my feet in. I felt more at home and I was there for a few months until we got our own house and settled down in Enfield.

That was all part of just me adjusting and getting used to training every day, getting paid to play professional football. Everything was a challenge and you sink or swim. I wanted to swim! I had a lot of determination. I was never the most skilful player on the park but I was probably the most determined, and that took me a long way. None of the coaches could ever accuse me of having a bad attitude because I always gave everything. Coming late to the game and playing amateur football brings you up a certain way. I would train even though I had a knock. I loved training. I loved playing football, so that passion would drive me on. I just wanted to play.

Going into the changing room was a real wake up call. Just looking at the other players who were on the fringes of the first team, never mind the regulars, was something else - the talent they had was crazy. One of them was a 16-year-old called Glenn Hoddle, then there was another one, Neil McNab. Seeing them up close, wow! And these guys were five years younger than me. Glenn could do anything with either foot. I couldn't do half of it with my better foot! He could control anything with either foot and then pass it over any distance and stick it on a sixpence. Neil would sit in the dressing room on the floor, put his hands on the ground and throw the ball up in the air and keep it up, right foot, left foot, right foot, left foot, just keeping the ball up. He would go 15, 20, 25, 30 times doing that. Glenn could just walk around the room, keeping the ball up. That was all a wee bit frightening in those first couple of weeks.

We trained every day and I would come in in the afternoons as well for extra training, just to work on my skills and technique. I was learning all the time, but looking at how good the other guys were, I was thinking, "I'm going to have a problem here!" But over six, seven, eight weeks, I started to see it differently. None of them were as strong as me nor as athletic as me, and your attitude then becomes a big part of it. I started realising that I had attributes that they didn't have and that's what I had to concentrate on. I had power, I had pace and I had a great attitude. I would never miss a chance to train.

You have to have faith in yourself, that plays a huge part in why some players come through and others don't. Some of us get lucky breaks too, but I do think you make your own luck to some extent. Certainly if you put the effort in, you get the rewards, definitely I believe that, and I've always preached that to my kids over the years. Every month, I could see there was a bit of progress. My first goal was to get fitter, then it was to be sharper, then to learn more about the game and ultimately, it was to aim for the first team.

I expected a lot from myself, but patience has never been my strong suit! With me, it has to be today, not tomorrow and definitely not next month! I was always happy to put the effort in, I loved working, I was determined. I only had a one year contract to start with, so I had to do an awful lot to prove myself – that was exciting in itself because I like a challenge. I did have to learn a bit of patience at Spurs because it did take me a few months to work out the attributes that I had that were different and that I could bring to the team. To start with, I was trying to do what Glenn Hoddle was doing or what the other players were doing, not what I could do. That was completely the wrong way to go about it.

At that time, John Duncan was a great goalscorer for Spurs. His brain told him where to go, where the opportunity was going to come, and he had the nous to sniff out a chance and be in the right place to score from it. I didn't have that ability at that stage, I had to develop it and you do that by playing with and against good players, better players. You might know you're faster and stronger than the centre-half, but sometimes the centre-half is cleverer than you. If the ball's coming up and he sees me jumping for it, he drops off. I end up flicking the ball on, but he's gone five or six yards deeper and says, "Thanks very much!" It was all about accumulating knowledge in that period because I'd only been playing for three years and obviously not at First Division level either. But I started to understand that I could win balls in the air that nobody else was getting near because I was more athletic and aggressive, I was more determined, and so that attitude side of things began to come into it and I could use that to my advantage.

I was very lucky because our coach, Peter Shreeves, was just great to train with. Peter did all the skills training, but there was always an end product, it wasn't just for its own sake. He loved people who would have the right attitude, who wanted to learn. By doing professional training, working on it full-time rather than three or four nights a week after work, working on the right exercises in the right way with top coaches, my fitness levels went up 10 or 15% straight away, just in the first month. I lost six or seven pounds as I toned up, and that meant I became sharper. Suddenly, nobody would beat me over 100 yards, nobody would beat me over a mile, I would never pull out of a challenge, and in that way, I started carving out my own niche. I wasn't the elegant footballer that Glenn was, but I was becoming valuable in a different way.

The physical side of it was no problem to me, the centre-halves over there really didn't worry me in that way. I'd played Gaelic football and hurling and when you come through that, anything that they want to do to you in soccer, I'd just think, "Bring it on!" The biggest thing is that you learn so quickly from being with better players. That stretches you and challenges you and you have to work harder to get to their standard. I was learning the game, reading the play, learning about movement off the ball, what runs to make, how to get into good positions, I was being taught how defenders think, how they want to mark you and what you need to do to get yourself free. I came into it all so, so raw, having hardly played the game other than in the streets as a kid, until I went to Cromac Albion and then Bangor. Now I was learning how the game really worked at top level, what was required of you mentally, in terms of tactics, what you needed to do for the team. It was a very big learning curve but I was hungry to put the time in to make sure I took on all of those lessons and became the best player I could be.

I wasn't short on company from back home which helped the settling in process. I was in digs with Chris McGrath and big Pat Jennings was a legend at Spurs of course. Pat looked after me. He was a Newry boy and he'd come and talk to me, ask me how I was doing, and later on, we ended up in the Northern Ireland squad together. We roomed together for about ten years on those trips. But at weekends, Pat was off with the first team and for that first year, I was mostly with the reserves!

I also became big mates with another of the young lads who joined the club, Noel Brotherston. He was a Protestant boy who was also from Belfast. We hit it off straight away and we were attached at the hip for a year or two before he moved to Blackburn. We had so much in common and we did everything together. In the summers, we played a lot of tennis together, which was a great way of keeping fit before we would have to go back to pre-season. On a Friday, we'd go ice skating, and you weren't supposed to do that, for obvious reasons! He talked me into going so I tried it out. I was sliding all over the place, I ended up on my backside quite a few times, but it meant my balance improved and as a footballer, good balance is so important. We played for Northern Ireland together later on, he was with us in the squad in Spain in 1982. Sadly, he died very young, he was 37, but he had a heart problem that nobody knew about. He's sadly missed.

After four or five months, I was starting to do really well in the reserves and in training. Towards the end of February, Terry Neill put me in the first team squad and we travelled up to Everton on the Friday. I was on the bench at Goodison Park – there was only one substitute in those days. I didn't get on during the game, but it was a great experience to be so close to the action in front of a full house. It was a clever bit of management from Terry to give a youngster like me that bit of experience and the chance to see what the First Division was really about. Once you get that first taste, you want more of it and it just made me work even harder in training. A month after the game at Everton, I got a late call-up to join the Northern Ireland squad for a friendly in Israel – I'll tell you more about that one later - so that was a real confidence booster. I played in a couple of testimonials and friendlies for Spurs before the end of the season, scored a couple of goals, so it was a solid start to my time there. I was pleased with how things were going.

It set me up for a fresh opportunity because at the end of the season, Spurs were setting off on a world tour. With a few of the senior players going off to play in the British Championship and so on, I got the call to be in the touring party along with a few other youngsters like Glenn, Steve Walford and Mickey Steed. I was thrilled at the thought of it but looking back, nine games inside four weeks, genuinely playing all over the world, was a real stretch for a lot of the players after a long season. As we were to see the following season, I don't think it did the team a lot of good in the long-term, though it was really good for me on a personal level.

We flew from London to Toronto and played the Toronto Metros-Croatia, where Eusebio was playing. They were a good team that went on to win the Soccer Bowl a few months later. We beat them 1-0 and the next day, we travelled to Los Angeles. We had a couple of days there, a lot of the players went around Disneyland and then we had a night at the movies before we got a connecting flight the next day to Hawaii. We stayed briefly there and then went on to Fiji and stayed in Lautoka before we played a game there on May 1st. I remember scoring in a 4-0 win over the Fijian Select XI. We had a couple of days training there as well. I do remember a few of us lads running on the beach and suddenly an hour later finding that our shoulders were absolutely burnt - the skin I've got coming from Northern Ireland, it burns very quickly!

Then we had two games in New Zealand in three days, in Auckland and Wellington against the local FA XIs. They were very physical in both games and we picked up a few injuries. Don McAllister had to fly home early with a cartilage problem, we picked up a few other injuries and because we hadn't got a huge squad with us, you had to just play through it if you could. From there we flew to Sydney and played there against Victoria, then we drove up the coast to play in Newcastle, it was two or three hours on the coach. We played games in Adelaide, in Melbourne and in Perth after that. Perth was the last one, against Western Australia, and I think we were all pretty happy when the final whistle blew. It had been fun, but it was pretty exhausting. It still wasn't over because it was a long haul home too. From Australia we flew to India, to Mumbai, and we were there six or eight hours. Then we got another connecting flight to Milan and then finally back home.

We did get a few days off in amongst it too, and we young lads learnt a few drinking games! One was called Captain Bluff. You had to recite these words, then tap the table with one hand and then the other, then stamp your feet, and do it all in the right order, then you had a drink from these big schooners of lager. If you got it wrong, you still had to have a drink but then you had to start all over again and keep on doing it until you got it right and then the turn passed to somebody else. There were a few drunken players on that trip, including myself!

In all, we were away for a month after a long, hard season. A lot of the players were shattered, we were just wiped out on the plane coming back. You think you'll be ok three or four days later, but you're not. We only got maybe three weeks off and then we were back in for pre-season training and most of us hadn't recovered. We'd set off going west, out to Canada, and we ended up coming home from the east! The trip, all that travelling and then the lack of a proper break, it all took too much out of the team. So maybe the money was good for the club in the short-term, because I'm sure it made some cash and promoted the club in new places, but it was a poor decision to go in the end because we didn't come back in the best shape and that had a knock on effect into the following season. Hindsight's a wonderful thing! It sounded exciting before we set off, getting the chance to see these places all around the world that I'd never been to before, but by the time we got to New Zealand, we were already shattered and we were only halfway through!

It was a good learning experience for people like myself and Glenn, just coming into the professional game and learning what it was like at that level, seeing how the boys trained and lived. Guys like Steve Perryman, Martin Chivers, John Pratt, Willie Young, they'd been playing a long time, played a lot of games, lots of experience and it was good to learn from them. Steve was the captain and he was just a dream to play with. He led by example. He was really thoughtful too, there was nothing he wouldn't do for you. He would keep the players onside, but if anybody was out of order, he would sort it out. A lot of the time, the manager didn't have to get involved. Nobody would question Steve as a captain, he would sort it out and the players would back him because he had the authority.

Just as we were back into pre-season in early July, Terry Neill left to go to Arsenal as manager which was disappointing – and a bit worrying – for me given that it was Terry who signed me from Bangor. The club appointed from within. Keith Burkinshaw got the job after being a coach under Terry. At least he had seen me play and knew who I was, but obviously, he was the man I had to impress now. I was feeling more settled now though. I'd done well on the tour, we'd bought a house in Enfield towards the end of the previous season and were busy getting things as we wanted, and then I scored some goals when we went on a pre-season tour of West Germany. Things were really positive.

In fact, they couldn't have been any more positive because on August 21st 1976, I made my debut against Ipswich Town at Portman Road in the first game of the season. That was a great experience. I ended up playing against Allan Hunter, who I now knew from that Northern Ireland trip, and Kevin Beattie. What players those two were. Allan was brilliant in the air, he read the game so well, he was great in the tackle. Then Kevin was just as good, but so fast as well – I thought I was quick before I came up against him! I did ok but it was a bit of an eye opener. I soon realised there were some really good players in the First Division. Ipswich were a good side at that time, with players like John Wark, Mick Lambert, Keith Bertschin, George Burley, Mick Mills. We lost the game 3-1, we missed a couple of chances, made a couple of mistakes at the back and we paid for it - we conceded a couple of late goals to lose the game. That was a good introduction to that league, especially learning how small the margins were. I really enjoyed it, getting out there and playing after the best part of a year with the club. I was learning how to be a part of the Spurs team. It was a momentous occasion for me making my debut and because of that, it meant that Tottenham had to pay money to Bangor more money too, which was pleasing for me. They deserved it for bringing me through.

I was doing good business as a tour guide by then as well, because half of Belfast was coming over to see me! Billy and Bertie Neill, who were my coach and my manager at Bangor, whenever they had a chance to come over on a free Saturday, they'd fly over and I'd get them tickets for the game and take them on the tour at White Hart Lane, showing them how it all happened. Then I had Frank McGrath, my old boss, Jim Cunningham, and lots of other housing executive people that came over to see me. That's the sort of bond I had with people. The people in Northern Ireland are like that, you make friends and they stick with you. Those were good days. I think they were quite proud of the fact that I went on to become a professional footballer, and then went on to play for the country. They knew me, we'd worked together, played football together for the housing executive in charity matches and things like that, so that friendship endured. It was good for me as well, to stay rooted in that community, even though I was over in England now.

Not everything was great though because as a team, we were having a
hard time of it. At the start of that season, we drew a lot of games that we
should have won and lost games we should have drawn and that put us in
trouble right from the off. Personally, it was a good season for me, I played
21 games, got my first few goals for the club and for me, it was progress.
I was 22 then, it was my first season playing at that level, it was a process
of educating myself in how to play First Division football. But the bigger
picture is always the team and things just wouldn't go our way. I felt we
were a good team, we played some good football, but results wouldn't
come. Our away record especially was very poor. Everybody kept saying
we were too good to go down, but that kind of talk is a load of nonsense.
That said, I will always maintain that the real reason we were having such
a struggle was that world tour the previous summer. It just took too much
out of everyone.

We got relegated against Manchester City, in the last game but one in the
season. I remember Glenn Hoddle was in tears, because you convince
yourself that you're going to survive. We lost 5-0 that day at Maine Road
and everybody in the dressing room was totally gutted. That was a massive
blow because they hadn't been relegated since they came back to the First
Division and won the league with the push and run team in 1950/51. You
do feel guilty as a player when you've been a part of a relegated side and
that's really the case when you're at a big club like Spurs that's expected to
always be in the top division.

But you go away for the break in the summer and you have to pick yourself
up and come back in ready to put it right. It was a difficult time, but the
board stuck by Keith Burkinshaw as manager and the players were happy
with that because everybody liked him, we all wanted to play for him and
to get back up as soon as we could to put things right. The club used it as
a chance to change the squad around a little bit as well. A lot of players
moved on, the likes of Martin Chivers went, Neil McNab moved around
that time to Manchester City, Steve Walford went to Arsenal. But the one
we never saw coming was when Keith sold Pat Jennings, and to Arsenal of
all clubs, in August 1977. We couldn't believe it and it turned out to be a
massive mistake. Keith thought that at 32, he was getting too old, but Pat
played another seven or eight years for Arsenal, he won the FA Cup, he
qualified for two World Cups and went past 1,000 games. Keith has always
held his hand up and admitted he got that one wrong! Barry Daines was a
good goalkeeper to follow him, but he wasn't in the same class as Pat – not

many goalkeepers ever have been. Pat Jennings was the best goalkeeper in the world for five or six years, without a shadow of a doubt. When he went, I was absolutely gutted because he was a good friend as well as being the safest pair of hands in the game. I just felt it made the job ahead that much harder. We knew that if we didn't go straight back up, things could get difficult for the club, so that pressure was there right from the start.

Away from the football though, it turned out to be a great summer. Ann was pregnant and on August 1st 1977, our son Ciaran was born in the hospital, with mother and baby both doing well. It was such a relief after what we'd gone through before that Ciaran was healthy and we were both thrilled. My brother Kevin was staying with us at the time with a friend and I picked them up from the tube station. I was telling them that she'd had the baby, they were both doing really well, and Kevin said we ought to go and have a wee drink to celebrate. Where we lived in Enfield, there was a local bar, the Salisbury Arms, run by an Irishman called Pat Dunn, I think he was from Tipperary. Even after the introduction to those drinking games on the Spurs world tour, I didn't really drink still, I'd just have a pint of shandy, but it was good craic in there with Pat. My dad had sent me over a bottle of poitín, perfectly clear, inside this lemonade bottle. I'd told Pat about it before and he loved the stuff, so because this was a very special occasion, I got this bottle of poitín and took it with us. We had a few drinks, and I opened this bottle and poured it out. My God, it was strong stuff!

About an hour or so later, we headed off home and I left the bottle behind. Pat must have just left it up on the counter and a bit later, this guy came in with his girlfriend. It was a really hot summer's day. "Can she have a dry martini and lemonade and I'll have a pint of lager shandy please, I'm dying of thirst!" So Pat picks up this bottle that he thinks is lemonade and he pours it into half a pint of lager and then he puts a drop into the martini and asks her if that's enough. She tasted it, "No, it's too strong, can you put a bit more lemonade in please?" Meanwhile, her boyfriend picks his pint up and knocks it back and then ends up grabbing his throat and falling on the floor – they all thought he was dying! I got a call from Pat an hour later, "You bastard! That poitín, I've nearly killed somebody in here!"

A few days later, we went out to Sweden to play in the Nolia Cup at the start of August as our pre-season warm-up and we suddenly had a problem at centre-half. Willie Young got himself injured and we didn't have any other centre-halves fit. Keith came to me and asked if I fancied playing at the back against Royale Union. He said, "You're fit, strong, good in the air, it might be another way into the first team for you." The opportunity to play was great and so I was willing to give it a go. I played there alongside Steve Perryman, and he's only about five feet nine, but he read everything and he was telling me what to do through the game. He knew the game inside out, he anticipated things. He'd tell me when to go and attack the ball and I won it most of the time, but even if I didn't, Steve would drop off and pick it up behind me. Up against us was this centre-forward who was six feet six, built like a brick shed, they were calling him Garth, like the comic strip. I had to go and pick him up, and we had a real ding dong battle, but he was too slow. I was too quick and too aggressive for him and even though he was six inches taller, I was winning everything in the air, and I was winning everything on the ground as well.

Playing with Steve was all good education for me, trying to catch up on all those years I'd missed by coming into football so late. Every season, I learnt a bit more about the game and about myself. After the match, Steve said, "Big man, you could play centre-half for about 20 years!" It's a totally different experience, everything is happening in front of you. When you're centre-forward, you've got your back to goal, you've got the defenders behind you, you're trying to make the ball stick, you're trying to send the defender one way so you can go the other, it's a much more complicated job. I found being a centre-half dead easy. I was quick, I'd already shown at Spurs that nobody would beat me in a sprint, there was no way I was pulling out of any challenges, so it suited me in that way. But it was too easy, I didn't want to play centre-half – there's no glory there!

We won that game and then we played Leicester City in the semi-final. We'd just been relegated to the Second Division and they were a top flight team, they had Keith Weller, Alan Birchenall, Frank Worthington up front, they had a bit of class. Steve Perryman said to me before the game, "You're marking Frank. Don't let him turn, he's got a great left foot, he's played for England, he's a good player." But I made sure Frank didn't get a kick and we won 2-1. Afterwards, Keith came up to me and said, "You're my new centre-half, you're the best one we've got at the club." Keith did a lot for me and gave me my chance, I owe him a lot, but after that, he really saw me as a centre-half and that was the one thing we disagreed on! But I ended up playing loads of times at the back. Because I was versatile, I was the sub a lot of times in the days when you only had one sub. I came on to play centre-half, up front, right-back, midfield, anywhere. Because I was athletic,

I became a bit of a utility player and Keith would put me on anywhere down the right or through the middle. I even went in goal when we were on tour the once as well! Over time, that versatility worked against me and I didn't play as many games at centre-forward for Tottenham as I would have liked. But it was part of my education and playing in different positions helped me out later on in my career. At that time though, I think it was easy for Keith to make me the sub every week, knowing that whatever injury we got, I could come on and do a job somewhere on the pitch.

It was a really tough year in the Second Division. It was such a competitive division with teams like Stoke City, Sunderland, Burnley, Crystal Palace as well as Bolton and Southampton who were the ones making the running. Glenn Hoddle came of age that year and had a huge season for us. He was 18 or 19 at the time, he scored a dozen goals for us. There were times he was unplayable. Steve Perryman was so important too, not just as a leader but because he wasn't afraid to mix it when he had to on the pitch, and you need that in the Second Division, you need to be able to put your foot in. Playing alongside him sometimes, if he told me to take somebody out, I'd take them out! You took one for the team, got your booking if you had to. If somebody is going to go past you and is probably going to score and you take them out before he gets into the penalty area, that's something that is always going to be a part of the game. There is the brutality of the game, some call it professionalism, but you're always going to get that. One of the reasons I like watching Messi is because they kick him and he just gets up and gets on with it, doesn't make too much of a hue and cry about it, and he's what? Five foot seven? That was very much the mentality when I played. There was no diving either. It's embarrassing now when I work on Champions League games for TV to see the lengths they go to just to win a match. I think there's a right way and a wrong way to do it - and that's the wrong way.

As we got towards the end of the season, four teams had broken away from the rest, but only the top three went up because this was before the play-offs. It was between Bolton, Southampton, Brighton, who came really strong at the end of the season, and ourselves and we played all three of the others in our last five games. I remember there being 50,000 at White Hart Lane against Bolton in early April. We won that one 1-0 and then we had to go down to the south coast to play Brighton the week after. We lost 3-1 there, which opened things up with another three games to play. There was a bit of doom and gloom the following week because we lost at home to Sunderland which meant we were third, but only one point ahead of Brighton. Then Steve Perryman scored the only goal against Hull in the midweek to set up the last game, which was away at Southampton.

We both needed a point to be sure of going up. We were in the tunnel before we went out, and Alan Ball was in their team, and he was saying, "A draw does us both ok lads, don't forget!" Then in the first five minutes, they had a couple of chances and we were throwing ourselves at the ball to block it, so they were quite obviously happy to set about winning the game! Chris Nicholl had a chance from about six yards out to win it for them – thank God it fell to Chris, because he hammered it over the bar on the volley. It was a really tough game but thankfully it finished 0-0. Brighton won their game at home and had we slipped up, they'd have gone up instead of us. Bolton went up with 58 points, then Southampton with 57 and we were on 56 with Brighton, but we had a much better goal difference. We went off from Southampton straight on to Truro to have two or three days out on the golf course and then in the bar to celebrate, because it had been such a draining season. But we'd done it.

Winning promotion that year changed everything for Tottenham – and, as it turned out, for English football.

CHAPTER SEVEN

FRONT TO BACK

Winning promotion was a real achievement for everyone at the club and, for those of us who had been there when the team went down, it felt like we'd redeemed ourselves and put a few things right. We'd only been away from the First Division for a season so now we could just enjoy a break in the summer and watch the World Cup from Argentina before getting back to work. We all sat at home watching that amazing tickertape World Cup. It must have been a great atmosphere, all that paper floating around, falling on the pitch and then Argentina went on and won the competition at home with all those great players who we just assumed we wouldn't see again until the next World Cup four years later. Little did we know!

Getting over the line and winning promotion changed everything for Tottenham because after that World Cup, Keith Burkinshaw went out and signed two World Cup winners, Ossie Ardiles and Ricky Villa. That was huge, having those two come to join us at Tottenham, because there hadn't been many foreign players in the game at all at that stage. It was a really brave decision from Keith because it hadn't been done before. We were newly back in the First Division and it was a risk – but it certainly paid off. He loved good football and wanted to see his team playing that way.

It was the first time any club could go out and make any signings like that because foreign players had been banned in England since 1930, unless they served a two year qualification process first, living here without playing. That meant that English football was very much a domestic game at that time, featuring players from the four countries of the UK and Irish players too. At Spurs in goal we'd had Pat Jennings from Northern Ireland, then it was Barry Daines who was English and Mark Kendall from Wales. John Gorman and Gordon Smith at full-back were Scots, Willie Young was another at centre-half, John Duncan as well up front. Graeme Souness had left just before I arrived because he wanted to play more games and so he moved up to Middlesbrough. Alfie Conn was another Scot. Jimmy Holmes was an Irish full-back, myself and Chris McGrath were from Northern Ireland.

Chris Hughton came into the side a bit later on too. He was a terrific full-back, good pace, decent on the ball, he liked getting forward. I roomed with him quite a few times, a very nice lad, committed to his football. He got his call up for the Republic of Ireland because he had an Irish grandmother, from Limerick. That was when they were really starting to look around for players who could qualify through their grandparents. I got a call from a friend the one day, "Have you seen who's playing now? Tony Galvin!" Tony was from Yorkshire! The only thing he has that's Irish is a donkey jacket! Seriously though, it was great to see them both playing international football because they worked so hard at their game and they deserved that reward.

In training sometimes, we used to have a game in the gym - and it was a concrete gym – and you'd have Northern Ireland, Scotland, Wales and Ireland versus England. It'd be something like Willie Young, John Duncan, myself, Pat Jennings, Terry Yorath up against Steve Perryman, John Pratt, Glenn Hoddle, Terry Naylor, Barry Daines. It was no holds barred. We kicked lumps out of each other, nobody pulled out of tackles. It was so committed. But I'll tell you what, we were all best mates. It was just that we were totally committed and that's an attitude that I don't always see now.

There was a lot of player development going on within the home nations in the 1970s and they were getting their opportunities at big clubs a lot of the time. I think they've suffered from the way that has dropped off in the last 30 or 40 years in particular, with the influx of players from abroad. Certainly it's made it more difficult for the likes of Northern Ireland. Our Football Association has had to work much harder in the last 15 or 20 years to develop our own talent because we never have enough to choose from.

If they are playing, often you're picking players for international football who play in the second or third tier. The foreign players have brought a lot to the game but the way it is now, I do think it's stifling the development of homegrown talent. The very best will always get through in the end, but there are a lot of very good young players who struggle to get a game.

That change came about in 1978 when clubs were allowed to bring in players from wherever they wanted. It was Keith Burkinshaw and Tottenham who really opened the floodgates. We'd come back in for the start of pre-season and we were out playing a couple of friendlies in Belgium and Holland when we heard about Ossie and Ricky joining the club. We were away in a training camp and we were staying three of us to a chalet. They arrived to join us while we were out there and they were put in the same chalet as Peter Taylor, who is one of the funniest guys. Ossie spoke a few words of English when he arrived but Ricky didn't speak any.

Pat Weldon was our first team coach, so he was doing the warm up with us every morning, a few stretches and that kind of thing, just to get you loose and ready to start work.

"That's it Ricky, have a bloody good stretch."

So Ricky looked up at him and smiled and said, "Bollocks!"

Peter Taylor had been teaching them all the swear words, so within a couple of days, Ossie was at lunch and he said to the manager, "Keet, pass the fucking salt." Everybody was in hysterics - I ended up having the same done to me when I went out to play in Spain a few years later!

They were great lads and having them in the squad was a big lift because they were fantastic players, genuinely world class. While we were on pre-season, I do remember looking at Ossie and he was so small, such a slight figure. I must admit I did start wondering if he was going to be able to handle the way English football was so physical. I thought he would find it difficult, he looked too small for the English game, I thought he'd get blown away. How wrong was I! When he played, nobody could get near him. He had lovely balance, he could roll with the tackles and keep going. He just skipped over challenges, his anticipation, his understanding, his vision were all incredible, they had him prepared for the tackles and took him away from them. He could see passes that nobody else would see and then he could actually play the ball to the spot he wanted it to go – and this was in a totally different climate to Argentina and on those English pitches that hadn't got any grass on them after November and could be mudheaps or be frozen hard. I learned so much from watching him. It was an education, seeing how he used his technique.

He didn't have quite the same vision when he got in a car though. Being the stars of the show, the two of them had sponsored cars, one was a Rover, the other was a Marina. One day at the training ground, Ossie turned up with the back of his car all bashed in. He told us he'd had an accident and so I explained that if somebody hit him from behind, it was their fault and that the other guy's insurance would have to pay for it all. He said, "No, not their fault Gerry. I wait at traffic lights. Then I start again in reverse!"

Ricky was more obviously physically built for the game here, but on top of that, he had such technique and skill that he could just twist and turn past people. The goal he scored against Manchester City in the FA Cup final was exceptional. I don't think a British player would have even tried that, but those are the kinds of things overseas players have brought into our game. They have a different view on the game and how to play it. Ossie and Ricky, they gave so much encouragement to the younger players, they were great people to learn from. Certainly I was learning from the people who were better than me. You looked at them, you saw their technique and you just worked harder to be like them.

We saw their potential very early on. I scored a goal in a 2-2 draw with Chelsea at White Hart Lane, right at the start of that first season back in the First Division, three games into it. We went 1-0 up when Ossie did brilliantly down the right hand side and cut it back for me. I took it on my chest but as it bounced in front of me for me to hit, John Duncan was in the box as well. He was very alive to what was happening and he pivoted and smashed it in the roof of the net. Chelsea went straight up the other end and equalised. Glenn had got caught in possession on the edge of the box and they scored from it.

Then Ricky and Ossie played an unbelievable one-two between them and that got Ricky away to the by-line. He went to cross it with his left foot but the defender came across to block, so Ricky pulled it back onto his right foot and played a slide rule pass into me, to come onto it at the edge of the box and hit on the volley. It just flew in past Peter Bonetti. That was the sort of stuff they produced week in, week out and that type of football was new to this country. It was mesmerising. Keith Burkinshaw was the man who made it happen, he could see the possibilities.

We played some brilliant football under Keith, he was a great manager, but he was an even better coach, I think he was different class at that. He was good at dealing with players as people. He loved Glenn Hoddle, and in the days when people were complaining and saying he couldn't tackle, Keith would always play him. Ron Greenwood said Glenn Hoddle couldn't tackle and that's why he was left out of the England team sometimes. I can't believe he only got 50 odd caps for England. He should have had 150! Glenn had great vision. Even now when I talk to him, he's always thinking outside the box, he's an innovator, he sees something that others don't see. It's great, attractive football that he tries to play. He played some great football when he was at Swindon and when he went to Chelsea, and then when he took over in England. Glenn had had some amazing times and it's a shame he hasn't had more opportunities as a coach or as a manager over the years.

As I said, Keith loved good football, that's why he bought Ossie and Ricky, but it could go wrong sometimes. Four games into that new season, we got absolutely hammered by Liverpool, 7-0 at Anfield. I was on the bench, and we had a midfield of Hoddle, McNab, Ardiles and Villa. Technically, every one of them was different class, but they hadn't got that steel that Graeme Souness or Jimmy Case had on the other side. Liverpool had that real balance, which is why they were the best team in England and in Europe as well at that stage. To play them and get that lesson from them, it was a huge wake up call. John Pratt was the one real workhorse that we had and it became pretty obvious that we needed to put him in there somewhere. Again, that was part of my education for when I went on to become a manager myself. You can't play Maradona, Messi, Best in the midfield all the time, you need to get somebody who'll go in and do a job and hold things, dig in, win the ball, make the tackles, so that they can go and play. John was straight into the team for the next game and he did his job. We went on a good run and only lost one of the next nine. Graham Roberts came in and played that role later for Tottenham. He made all the tackles, won the ball and gave it to Glenn, gave it to Ossie, the lads who could play.

Signing Ossie and Ricky really raised the profile at Spurs and we had a couple of decent seasons, back in the top division, finishing in mid-table.

I didn't get a lot of football in that first season back, 1978/79, and Danny Blanchflower, who was then my manager with Northern Ireland, made a bid to sign me for Chelsea that season – he was manager there for about six months when they were struggling at the bottom of the First Division. I turned it down – it was a pretty big offer – but I can't remember why now! I think it was because they looked certain to be relegated, which they were, and having won promotion the previous season, I didn't want to go straight back to Division Two. I wanted to stay and fight for a place at Spurs because I was settled there and we'd had another addition to the family – our son Brendan was delivered safe and well on December 22nd 1978. With that in mind, I was happy to stay where I was.

It worked out because in 1979/80 I really felt that I started to establish myself in the team. I played 30 games in the First Division, played nearly all the cup games as well, most of them up front with Chris Jones. We had Colin Lee on the books as well, Tony Galvin was coming through, he was a late developer because he was also studying at university, he got a degree in Russian. He was great for Spurs on the wing, he went past people so easily, two good feet. Mark Falco was another making his way into the team at that stage, Terry Gibson was getting a few games up front as well, so there were a lot of strikers around at the time at Tottenham.

Then in the summer of 1980, Spurs went back into the transfer market in a big way again and they signed Garth Crooks and Steve Archibald. That was the point where I started to think I had to move on, because they spent really big money on those two and so obviously, they were going to be first choice up front. As the next few months unfolded, I could see that if I was going to get games at Spurs, it would only be as a defender and I didn't really want to do that. I didn't mind playing on the right hand side of midfield, but it was becoming obvious that Keith saw me playing at the back and that made my mind up for me that it was time to move on.

I was 26 by then. I needed to be playing regularly and I wanted to do it up front. By then, I had an international career to think about.

CHAPTER EIGHT

....

"I'M PLAYING UP FRONT WITH GEORGE BEST?"

When the Troubles began in Northern Ireland, the segregation that had quietly been a part of the country came more to the forefront. People took their sides and the division between people became more obvious. That was carried into the way people felt about the Northern Ireland football team too, certainly in the 1970s, though things would slowly change as that side grew in stature towards the end of the decade.

It was definitely true that a lot of people from the Falls Road, from that side of Belfast, wouldn't have followed the national team because they'd have looked upon it as being a British team or a loyalist team. I never felt like that at all. To me, it was an unbelievable honour to be picked to play for your country. What higher honour could you have as a sportsman? And just think of being a player in that era, getting the chance to mix with the likes of Pat Jennings, Martin O'Neill, and to actually go out and play on the same pitch as the great George Best! I think there were other people that would have scorned that and looked down on it, and I know they were upset that we were standing for "God Save The Queen" before the games and all of that. It was a time when lines were being drawn because of the Troubles and there were staunch republicans who wouldn't have any of that, but to play for my country, I was proud of that achievement. Then once you get into the squad, you get to know the players, it becomes like every other team. You're all in it together, you have fun as team-mates, you enjoy that camaraderie. However much I loved playing for my various club sides, playing for Northern Ireland was the pinnacle and it was the most enjoyable experience of my career.

I got a very early introduction to it, probably earlier than I would have expected. I had only been at Tottenham about four months when I got my first call-up for the squad. It was a friendly match out in Israel in March 1976. Back then, there was no international break. You'd have club matches on the Saturday, then you'd join up with your national team on the Sunday, play on the Wednesday and then be off back to your club. Because of that, there were always a few injuries on the Saturday before and, especially late on in the season, a few club managers were also reluctant to let players go off to play for their country when there might be a big league match the following Saturday. Because it was a friendly as well, a few players pulled out, so that gave me the opportunity.

Terry Neill put me forward to Dave Clements, the Northern Ireland manager at the time, and he brought me in. At Spurs, even from early on, I trained most of the time with the first team and the reserves, so I had three or four months where I was getting into the routine, getting fitter, I was working really hard every afternoon on the training side of it. I think with the call up, Terry was giving me a reward because he'd seen the progress I was making. He said to Dave, "Look, this guy potentially is going to be a future international, you could take him with you as cover, just to have a look at him and get him bedded in." I wasn't aware of that at the time, I was just chuffed to bits to be invited. It was a good learning curve for me to meet the superstars who were playing for Northern Ireland so early on.

When a couple of players got injured on the Saturday and pulled out, that night I got a call to report to Heathrow the following morning to join up with the squad. I was still in digs with Chris McGrath at that time and he was in the squad as well, so he drove us both over to Heathrow on the Sunday to meet up with everyone and then fly out. I vividly remember arriving at Ben Gurion Airport. There had been a bomb attack there not long before and there was shrapnel and everything stuck in the wall. Derek Spence said, "Oh look, they know we're from Northern Ireland, they're trying to make us feel at home here!"

I sat and watched as we drew the game 1-1. Warren Feeney scored the goal in his only game for Northern Ireland - later on, his son went on and played plenty of games and scored a few goals for us as well. It was after the game that things got interesting. We weren't flying back until the following day, so we had the rest of the evening to ourselves. We went back to the hotel, got changed and we were told that there was a really good nightclub run by Mandy Rice-Davies and her husband that was a great spot to go to. There was Pat Rice, Pat Jennings, Sammy Nelson, Jimmy Nicholl, who had made his debut that day, Derek Spence. We all headed off there.

We were there in our suits, standing around having a quiet drink, and Derek was up dancing with this girl. This guy came in and he must have been her boyfriend, because he definitely didn't like it. He went to hit Derek, so Jimmy went across and said, "Hold on, hold on, what's the problem?" This guy grabbed Jimmy and threw him onto the floor and then he went for Derek. I just instinctively stepped in and I caught him with a right hook. The shit hit the fan big time then! They were coming in from all angles. Me and Derek were pinned in the corner, I was hitting anything that moved, but all the time I was thinking, "There's three or four other lads here, they'll come and join in." No. Not a hope in hell! Next, the police came in and I got arrested. I could see Pat Rice, Pat Jennings, Sammy Nelson all standing to the side, in hysterics, just laughing at me. The Israeli police came in and arrested about seven or eight people, including me and Derek. It was handcuffs, the whole lot. I was thinking, "I've not even made my debut for Northern Ireland and that's me finished already!"

We had a big stroke of luck though. On the Sunday before the game, Pat Jennings had won the PFA Player of the Year award. He went to the dinner in London on the Sunday night and then came out to the game a day after us, he flew in on the Monday. He was always very cool and in control of things was Pat. While I was getting arrested, Pat disappeared away and then came back with this guy Rafi, who had picked him up from the airport on the Monday and brought him to the hotel. Rafi was a massive Tottenham fan and he was heavily involved with the government, quite a wealthy man. He came over and started shouting at this big policeman, and then he points to me. "Tottenham Hotspur! Get those handcuffs off him!" So I said, "What about my mate?" They let Derek go as well, but all the other local lads, they were all arrested! Pat Jennings said afterwards, "Big man, you were unbelievable!" But it was just my nature, it was how I was brought up – if your mate's in trouble, you go and help him out.

I was on the fringes of the squad for a while after that, building my experience. Early the next season, in the October, we played the Netherlands in Rotterdam, our first World Cup qualifier for the 1978 tournament. We were in a group with the Dutch, Belgium and Iceland, only one qualified, so the odds were very much on the Dutch. We had 22 of us who met up to train in Coventry over the Sunday and Monday, then the manager, who by now was Danny Blanchflower, selected 18 from us to fly out for the game. The big story was that George Best was back in the fold for the first time in about three years. He'd come back to England to play for Fulham, so of course, he was going to be straight back in the side.

It meant I got the chance to train with George Best and to see him at close quarters. That was just amazing. Even at that stage, later in his career and when maybe he hadn't been taking the best care of himself over the years, his control of the ball, his ability, it was phenomenal. If George was playing now with his sort of talent, he would be a super-superstar because you wouldn't ever get the ball off him. He never got the protection that players get today, plus the quality of the pitches today is a massive improvement on back then, the quality of the boots, the footwear, it's all totally different. He didn't get the benefit of that. People forget how brave George was too, playing in the days of the tackle from behind, against people like Ron Harris, Tommy Smith, Jack Charlton. He'd take it and just get up. I preferred that way of playing if I'm honest - people would make tackles and if you got hit, you could make a tackle back. You wouldn't roll over three or four times. If you can roll three times in a row, there's nothing wrong with you! I've never changed my opinion on that. Back then, you didn't want to show you were hurt, that was a sign of weakness. Now, it's a way of getting a decision.

The other thing you noticed when George came into the squad was that everything changed, the whole atmosphere around us. People came from everywhere to watch training when they found out he was there. They just wanted to be around him and the team and I discovered just how tough it must have been to be George Best and to have to deal with everything that went with that.

Jimmy Nicholl, David McCreery, Sammy McIlroy were all playing pool in the hotel between training sessions and I was sitting watching them with George, just having a chat. This guy came over and said, "I'm on next."

They told him, "We're playing doubles here. You have to have a partner."

He says, "Okay, me and George will play."

George didn't know the guy and said, "Sorry, I don't want to play."

Anyway, the game finishes and this guy puts his 50p down and says, "Right, George, come on, let's go."

George tried to appease him, "Look, I'll play the first shot but you're on your own after that." So he played the first shot, then everybody played their shots and it came round to George's turn again.

This guy said, "George, your turn".

"I told you I'm not playing."

Chris McGrath was with us and watching all this and he gets up and says, "Look, he's told you, he doesn't want to play." There was a bit of a row between Chris and this guy, but there were no punches, just an argument. The next day, I remember the front pages of the paper: "George Best in fight in hotel". Everything was blown out of all proportion. George hadn't done anything, but he was painted the villain when it was all down to some idiot who wanted to tell his mates he'd played pool with George Best.

Getting the chance to be around the likes of George was an incredible privilege and I suppose, looking back, you can see just how it was that some players went off the rails a little bit, because you were left to your own devices a lot of the time. Nobody back then talked about diet, what you ate and drank, any of that kind of thing. As I've said, I didn't drink, the most I'd have was shandy – it wasn't until I met George and the boys in the international team that I first had a real drink. They introduced me to vodka and tonic, and I hated it! To this day, I've never drunk it again, but as a 22 year old in that company, you do feel under a bit of pressure. I was the youngest in the party, we were sitting in the hotel in Coventry, and it was me, George Best, Pat Jennings, Allan Hunter. Some company!

George says, "Hey son, go and get us a wee drink," and he gave me a fiver – it shows what you could get for £5 in 1976! "What do you want Pat?"

"I'll have a vodka and tonic."

"I'll have one as well. What about you Allan".

"I'll have the same."

"So, three vodka and tonics then?"

"No, four, one for you as well."

"I don't drink vodka and tonic!"

"You do now son!"

But just being there, listening to these guys talking about their exploits, winning leagues, FA Cups, European Cups, it was something else. These guys were top of the tree and there's me coming in after a year at Spurs and mixing with these guys. It was hugely exciting for me and a great learning curve being around them.

I had to wait a little bit longer to get my debut, but it eventually came in a friendly in Cologne when we played West Germany, the reigning world champions, on April 27th 1977. Danny Blanchflower told me the night before, "I'm playing you up front with George Best." I said, "Are you kidding me? I'm playing up front with George Best?" Happy days! I remember watching him as a kid do his stuff in the European Cup final and in other games for Manchester United and I thought all my dreams had come true, because George was everybody's hero. I was tense and nervous before the game of course, because they were the toughest opposition you could face.

They had world class players all over the pitch, but for the first 25 minutes, George was brilliant. I just got the ball and gave it to him. He was nutmegging players and playing one-twos off their shins, it was amazing. The German fans loved it. They were just in awe of his ability. He was just an artist. Steve Perryman talked to me about him once and he said he was the best player he ever came up against. He said he was always thinking, "How do I play against him? How do I stop him? I never really found an answer." George was so comfortable on the ball. He didn't even have to look at it, it was an extension of his foot. He just looked at you and waited on your movement before he made his move.

It was great for me to make my full debut, I was so proud of that. I played 65 or 70 minutes and then I got substituted, but what an experience and what an opportunity to learn so much about the game at the absolute top level in such a short space of time. We played pretty well too, we kept them at bay for an hour but then once the first goal went in, the second followed and it was a bit of shellshock after that, it was damage limitation. We ended up losing 5-0, but it was a great experience to play in that game.

From there, I was in and around the team. I played the next game against England when we lost 2-1 in Belfast, then Belgium was my first World Cup game in November 1977. I scored twice in a 3-0 win, and that was really the start for me as a regular. The first one was from 20, 25 yards out and it flew in the top corner. David McCreery was really brave, the ball had bounced up and one of the Belgian players put his foot up, but David stuck his head in and the ball fell kindly for me. I took one touch and it flashed into the top right hand corner. Then in the second half, I broke clear from the halfway line and went past one defender and, as the keeper came out, I pretended to shoot but came inside on my left foot and stuck it past the defender getting back on the line.

Danny Blanchflower was putting his imprint on the team by then. He was fantastic, but he was a bit like a Cruyff, if they score three, we'll score four, he had that mentality - only Cruyff was manager of Barcelona! In football, especially international football, you have to be a little bit careful, you have to have a bit of common sense. You can't go all guns blazing, you have to have a little bit of a balance.

That Belgium game was the last one in the group. We finished third behind the Dutch and Belgium, but what we did start to do was get some really good results in Belfast. As well as beating Belgium, we beat Iceland and only lost to a late goal against the Netherlands. That was important to us, not just in footballing terms, but because we'd had a period where because of the Troubles, it was difficult for us to play in Northern Ireland, especially in the British Championship. We were having to play home games in Liverpool, so when we were given the chance to play at Windsor Park, we wanted to capitalise on it.

That became even more important when we got to the draw for the European Championship qualifiers for 1980. Again, only one team went through and we were in a five team group with England, Denmark and Bulgaria. The last country in there with us were the Republic of Ireland and of course, that got people really excited because it was the first time the two countries had met in any kind of game.

The game in Dublin was the one that kicked the qualification group off for us in September 1978 – they had already drawn 3-3 in Denmark. They had a really good team, John Giles was player-manager, Liam Brady was a brilliant footballer, they had Frank Stapleton, Don Givens, David O'Leary. On paper, the Republic of Ireland team looked better than us. It was a massive, massive game and naturally enough there was quite a bit of tension in the build up to it amongst supporters and in the media, but honestly, the players were all fine about it, apart from the usual nerves about an important game.

I remember Danny Blanchflower saying in the press beforehand that having an all-Ireland team would be great, the way it was in rugby for instance. John Giles said he had no problem with that, so Danny said, "I'm older than John and I'd be quite happy to step to one side and let him manage the team!" This went back and forth in the papers for a while, but the two associations were never, ever going to come to an agreement that they would have one association again. It's a nice idea but you have to accept that there would be problems that nobody could really get around. Where would you have your games? Do you play them in Dublin or Belfast? It would be complicated enough nowadays but back then, at the height of the Troubles, there was definitely no chance of that happening!

The first game was in Dublin, a really tight game as you'd expect. Danny had us very well organised for that one, it definitely wasn't one for going gung ho, and we came away with a 0-0 draw. I had one chance at the far post, I headed it back across goal and it landed on top of the net. Don Givens had a couple of chances, Pat made two or three great saves. A draw was probably the right result on the basis of the game and we were happy enough with that. It was a stalemate but we didn't give anything away and we had a point on the board.

Afterwards, I remember I was trying to get away quickly, to get back to London and to get back into training with Tottenham on the Thursday. Bryan Hamilton and Chris Nicholl were the same, looking to leave from Dublin rather than go back to Belfast and then travelling from there. Danny was happy for us to do that. The Republic of Ireland team was taking their bus back to their hotel, and because we all knew each other, they told us to jump on board and they would give us a lift, because they were going past the airport on the way back. Inevitably though, some of their fans saw these Northern Ireland players at the front of the bus and started throwing bricks and bottles at us! That's the sort of mentality there was at that stage, and it was all ramped up because it was the first time the two Irelands had ever met.

England were always favourites to qualify from that group, which they did comfortably enough. We went over to play them in the following February, at Wembley. Our preparation wasn't exactly perfect, because Danny had forgotten to book a room in the hotel for us to have our team meeting before we went down to the game. So instead, he said, "Ok lads, everybody just come down to my room." It was a standard room, two single beds in it, with 17 players piling in! We were all sitting on the edges of the beds and big Chris Nicholl sat down on one where there were already five or six players. As soon as he sat down, the leg on the bed broke and it all collapsed!

Danny had something like a Subbuteo pitch, it was magnetic and he had these counters stuck to the board. He had the England team lined up, and then he put counters representing us on the board. He was trying to show us some tactics ahead of the game, what he wanted from us. Danny could get carried away because he was a very eloquent man and at one point, he was waving his arms around. He turned and hit the board with his elbow and it went flying, all the figures fell off, so we were all in hysterics again, it was like "Fawlty Towers". So he said, "Forget the board and the magnetic men. I've looked at this England team and I've looked at us and on paper, England is four goals better than us. See, if we only lose 2-0 or 3-0, it's a moral victory!" We were all looking at each other, "Did you actually hear that?" We were laughing, but we were going into the game with a smile on our face. You know what the score was that night? We lost 4-0.

We had to play England again in the British Championship that summer, and that one was in Belfast. It was a bit closer but we lost 2-1. That was the game when I kicked Terry Cochrane up the arse - and he was my own team-mate. I thought we were playing quite well that day and I remember running after Dave Watson. He had the ball and I caught him. Dave turned away from me, because he knew I was going to make a tackle and as he did, me and Terry Cochrane bumped into each other. He says, "Get out of my way there!" Wee Cocky used to wind his own team-mates up, but I wasn't having it that day, so I booted him up the arse! The referee saw it and didn't do anything. Brian Moore in his commentary said, "Gerry Armstrong appears to have kicked Terry Cochrane up the backside." I was quite spontaneous like that!

The return game with the Republic of Ireland was the last one in the group. England were already through by then, but we'd done ok. We'd beaten Bulgaria home and away, beaten Denmark in Belfast, and we were level on points with Ireland, seven each. They had a game left after the one in Belfast, away to England, so we needed to win if we wanted a chance to finish second in the group.

There was a lot of security around the game again and I think Gerry Daly got hit by something thrown from the crowd, but given how big a game it was, it went off pretty well. That was probably helped by the fact that we won the game 1-0 with a goal early in the second half. Sammy Nelson went running down the left and he went to cross but checked back on his right foot and crossed from there. The trajectory of the ball was going towards their goalkeeper, Mick Kearns, but I had already started my run and I was very committed, so I managed to get in first. I got across him and although it was going away from me, I threw my head at it and got on the end of it just ahead of the 'keeper and I headed it past him. That was the first goal between the two Irelands, a really big goal, and it won the match. Pat made some terrific saves in that game, just underlining what a fantastic goalkeeper he was. Not only did he make difficult saves look so simple, but he would radiate calm throughout the team, especially the back four. Even if you were under the cosh, you could look at Pat and know that it would take something special to beat him.

We came in after the game, absolutely delighted to have won but then we got this thunderbolt from Danny. "Well done everybody. I just want to let you know that I'm packing it in." That was a real blow because Danny was such a fantastic man. I loved him to bits. He'd done a really good job with us too. We never had huge playing resources but he found a way of playing that suited us, especially at Windsor Park where we started to be a real force. In international football, because qualification is over so few games, if you can win your home games, you're giving ourselves an opportunity to achieve something. Danny wasn't quite there because maybe we were too open away from home, but he put in a lot of groundwork, not just on the field but off it too, because he formed a real tightly knit group who would fight to the finish for each other

Danny was always trying new ideas. I remember him at training, before we were playing Holland, and he decided he was going to take the wall away at free-kicks. "We don't need to have the wall 10 yards away, we've got Pat Jennings in goal! Step back 15 yards." So we did and Sammy Nelson smashed one over the wall and into the roof of the net. Pat says, "Get that wall closer, ten yards is plenty far enough away!" It was a really happy camp that Danny created. He went out on a high and rightly so. He was a great man, but he was too attack minded for us away from Belfast. We had to keep clean sheets to win games and when Billy Bingham came in, it was a different philosophy.

What Danny did was to start developing a team that came together over a couple of years. Boys like myself, Billy Hamilton, Jimmy Nicholl, David McCreery all began to get established around the same time and that added to players like Martin O'Neill, Pat Rice and Sammy McIlroy who were a wee bit older, then Pat Jennings who was the senior statesman. We had a good blend of ages for Billy Bingham to build on when he took over in March 1980.

Billy wanted a bit more discipline than Danny in terms of the way we set up and how we defended and we took to it. The British Championship in 1980 was a really important week for us because that was the start of what would happen across the next six years in terms of going to World Cups and all of that. It didn't look that promising at the outset because we were missing the Arsenal players – Pat Jennings, Pat Rice, Sammy Nelson – because they were playing in the Cup Winners' Cup final, which they eventually lost to Valencia on penalties. But it gave opportunities to other players, including Mal Donaghy, who could play anywhere in the back four. Tommy Finney played some games in midfield, he was a hard man in there, he could look after himself. Jim Platt did well in goal, so it meant we started to find a few more players who could add to the squad and give it a bit more depth.

We beat Scotland in Belfast in the first game with a Billy Hamilton goal and then we got a 1-1 draw at Wembley, so because of the way the other results had gone, we knew that if we beat Wales in Cardiff on the Friday night, we would win the title. My old pal from Tottenham Noel Brotherston scored the only goal, a fantastic goal midway through the first half, and we won the match and the competition outright, which was the first time Northern Ireland had ever managed to do that – Ireland had done it in 1914 - and we did it in the centenary year for the association as well. That was a real achievement. It gave us real confidence and belief and a lot of the players grew in stature as a result. We started surprising people because supposedly we were a weaker team, but it was a team that had a lot of belief, a lot of heart, a lot more ability than people gave credit for. We just loved playing for each other and supporting each other and we grew as a team. That was the beginning of finding our way to the World Cup in 1982.

Before all of that though, I had to find my way out of Tottenham.

CHAPTER NINE

....

TAYLOR MADE

Early in the 1980/81 season, it was becoming obvious to me that my time at Tottenham was coming to an end. I had a great time there, I was grateful to the club for giving me my first chance in professional football and I loved working for Keith Burkinshaw. But we had a fundamental difference of opinion on where I should play for the team and with the signing of Garth Crooks and Steve Archibald, I could see my days up front were numbered.

There were quite a few clubs rumoured to be interested in signing me ahead of that season, including Arsenal, Birmingham, Ipswich, Aston Villa, Luton and Fulham. Keith wasn't interested in selling me because he still saw me as doing a job for him at the back and as being a very handy sub who could play in most positions on the pitch. But I was 26, coming to my peak years and I wanted to play up front every week.

It would have been nice to get it done over the summer but Spurs weren't ready to let me go. I wasn't in the team very much and I'd only made four appearances as a sub by the time they finally agreed to a move in November 1980. In the end, I went to Watford and the reason behind my decision was the chance to play for Graham Taylor, simple as that. He said to me, "You've got so much potential that hasn't been harnessed and utilized", so I took a gamble and left a big club like Spurs for a much smaller one, in the Second Division, never been anywhere near the top division in the past. But I was excited by Graham's plans, I thought they had potential too. It was going to get me more first team football and it was going to get me playing up front, which is what I wanted to do. Graham also told me that he had been trying to sign me for over a year, which was a nice thing to hear.

As soon as I went to Watford, I felt like I fitted in and that I could offer something to the team, it was a great move for me at the time. Graham explained how everything was going to be done as a team, how we were going to play, why it was going to be successful. He laid it all out on charts and graphs. This is long before anybody was using stats, which is the basis of so much nowadays. Graham made sure he had stats on everything. He had people watching matches and tracking the events in games, so he knew how many crosses we put in, he knew how many shots we had had, he knew how many free-kicks, how many corner kicks, how many goals you scored from them. So as you built up that database of information, you could see if you were scoring a particularly good number of goals from corner kicks. In that case, you play to get more corner kicks because you knew you were going to score from them. It was pretty logical and when he would show it to the players on a graph over seven or eight games at a time, it all made sense and the players started believing. Graham started putting his theories to us and we all bought into it. He was very much ahead of his time in that way.

His man management was a great strength. Graham was very good at teaching you to play to your strengths. That's exactly what I did at Watford, more so than I had at Spurs I'd say. He got me to focus more and he certainly got me a lot fitter. He was really good on the discipline, he made sure you did things right, there was always a right way and a wrong way to do it. When you joined the club, you had to buy into his vision. It was a very family orientated club too. All the kids were looked after in the family enclosure, none of that had ever happened before. Elton John, as chairman, was the figurehead, larger than life. He barely missed a game. He was great fun and again, he played a massive part in fostering that family atmosphere about the place.

When you're part of something, on the inside, you can see all that's happening, how it's taking shape. Very early on, I knew Watford were destined to go up into the First Division. Graham had that in his sights and once he set his sights on something, he was going to achieve it, but that was a long way off when I joined the club in November 1980. Watford had won two consecutive promotions from the Fourth to the Third and then to the Second Division, but they were finding life a bit tougher at that level. They finished 18th the previous season and when I arrived, they were in the bottom six or seven, just above the relegation zone, but there was still just over half the season left.

Pat Rice came in to join the club the same week that I did, to bring some experience and leadership to it and that was a big statement from the club, bringing in players who had played a lot of First Division football. Les Taylor came in as well, a midfielder from Oxford United and he was another good player who made his mark. Pat was brought in not just as a player, but as a captain, for him to be the leader on the pitch. Straight away at the first training session, Graham said, "Pat is joining us here from Arsenal, he is going to be the new captain of the club." He was there to lead by example. He was always vocal and he would keep people right, same as Steve Perryman had. If he said, "This is what's going to happen now," then that's what happened, as simple as that.

Pat said later, "I thought I was going for an easy life, finish my career off. Bloody hell, the last three or four years I had there, it was the hardest I've ever worked! It was the fittest I'd ever been, but we had so much fun out of it, and got so many rewards." He did a great job. Watford was a different kettle of fish to Arsenal or Spurs, starting from scratch with players who had no recognition, but they weren't in awe of the other teams or players. Before games, we were just told, "Listen, they've got two legs, you've got two legs. It's who wants it the most." There was no fear, that was the attitude all the way through.

At Watford, it was as if I went back to the start again. At Tottenham, we'd travel on a five star coach, you had waiters on the coach who would serve your food, you'd have your starter, your main course, your dessert, and you'd have a drink on the way home. Arsenal were the same, as were all those big clubs. I remember sitting with Pat Rice the first week we went away. The bus turned up and it wasn't a five star bus! It wasn't even a four or three star bus, it was just a coach that took you from A to B. There were no tables, it was just seats. There was a cardboard box at the front and it had packed lunches in it, a sandwich and a can of drink, like Fanta or Coca Cola, and an apple or banana or some other bit of fruit. That was your meal on the way back from the game. Ricey would say to me, "Back down to earth here Big Man!" It was hilarious. But it does get you into a routine where you have to work hard and you dig deep. It's about character and Pat had a lot of character and determination. He captained that Arsenal team, they won league titles and FA cups and then he went back again with that same attitude to coach the youth team and develop a lot of big stars before he went on to be Arsene Wenger's assistant.

He was right about the fitness side of it as well. You had to be fit to play in Graham's team. We were like athletes, we could run and run. The longest cross country we'd do at Tottenham would have been about a five or six miler, but at Watford, we were doing nine or ten miles in pre-season. Pre-season would only last for like 10 or 14 days at Tottenham, but pre-season was every week at Watford! If we had a day off in midweek, he'd have you up Cassiobury Park in Watford. Everybody was timed, so they could see what you were doing in the summer, when you were doing it again in September and October, and then November, and they could tell what your fitness level was. That's an early version of what they're doing now in terms of blood samples and all of that. That was their way of finding out whether you were fit enough, because he could check your times.

I could see myself getting fitter by the day. I did so many crossover runs with Luther Blissett and Ross Jenkins it was unbelievable, but the benefits were soon obvious. It wasn't just physical fitness, it was mental fitness too. We were really focused, we knew what we wanted to achieve and how we were going about doing it, what was needed from us. A manager has to be able to get that across to players and get them to buy into it and believe in it.

Graham was very good at that, but it was also the right time for me too. I probably hadn't understood it so well when Keith was doing that at Tottenham, because I was younger and I was still so raw and inexperienced in the ways of professional football. By the time I got to Watford, I knew what it was all about. At Watford, I think that was when I first realised what a disadvantage it had been to me not to be coached more as a youngster and how much difference it might have made to have a coach like Graham take me under his wing at 13 or 14 and teach me the basics. I watched how hard he worked with Nigel Callaghan, John Barnes, Neil Price, young boys like that who went on to play in the first team, and if I'd had that when I was younger, I'm sure it would have made a big difference to my all-round game.

Things came together pretty quickly and after Christmas, we started climbing the table to finish the season in ninth place. Over the last 20 games, we became very difficult to beat. We won nine and we only lost four so not only were we well clear of the relegation zone, it gave us plenty of confidence going into the new season.

The first pre-season I did there, in the summer of 1981, we went to Scandinavia to train. We were woken up at six in the morning, and we had to be straight down to the foyer in tracksuits and running shoes. The training ground was about a mile away, so we got the bus there. We did a 12 minute run round the track, 200 sit ups and then Graham said, "Because you've taken the bus here, you'll know the way, so you can run all the way back to the hotel." Then you'd get a shower, have your breakfast, then at 10 it was back on the bus and back down to do the second session which ran until about half past twelve. Everything was done with the ball in that session, but we were running with it, working hard, it was very effective. I loved it. The coach took us back to the hotel for lunch, then we'd rest and around three o'clock, we'd have a third session, unless we had a game that night. It was three sessions, or two and a game, every day for a week. Then he would start to ease off and begin to concentrate on how we were setting up, our set plays, that kind of thing. Every single player bought into it and we were really convinced that we were going up that season, 1981/82.

Everybody could sense something special was possible as early on as that, and we were all buzzing. I remember one of the days in pre-season, we'd finished our lunch and I was laying on the bed, reading a book, thinking I could chill out for another half an hour before the third session of the day. I could hear this noise in the corridor and I went out to see what was going on. It was Kenny Jackett, Luther Blissett, Barnesy, Nigel Callaghan and all the boys playing cricket. They were bowling and hitting the ball down the corridor of the hotel. That was part of the appetite we had. Imagine, you've done your second session and you're waiting for the third one to start in less than an hour, and they're still playing cricket. That was all down to Graham and his staff, John Ward, and then, later on, Steve Harrison.

Steve was the left-back when I joined the club, but he left briefly during the summer of 1981 to go to Charlton, but pretty soon, he was back at Watford as part of the coaching staff. Eventually, he went on to be Graham's coach for the England team. He was great fun, there was never a dull moment with him around. Even on the 10 mile runs, you were breathing out your backside, but you still had fun with Harry. He became a coach and he was still infectious, because again, he wanted it to be done the right way, he wanted you to train hard and he felt that you'd only do that if you were enjoying it. He had a great work ethic, but Steve was the funniest guy, just unbelievable. We went out to train one time, and it had been raining, there was surface water all over the place, you're not looking forward to it that much. Steve came out with his hand over his face. "Oh no. I've got a bit of dirt in my eye." He goes to Steve Sims and says, "Would you get this out?" So Steve said, "Move your hand so I can see". He moved it away and he had a worm up his nostril! The players were in hysterics. Then he pulled the worm out of his nose and he would eat it.

He had a party piece, which I saw once, and he was renowned for it. Everybody would gather in a hotel room and then Harry came out of the bathroom with a dressing gown on. John Ward used to say, "Ladies and gentlemen, the Great Harry will now perform his amazing feat". Me and Pat were saying, "What is it?" And the rest of the lads were laughing, "Oh, you'll know what it is in a minute when you see it!" He got a chair and he stood on it and then he got on top of the wardrobe. John put a pint glass on the floor. "The Great Harry will now shit into this glass from the top of this wardrobe!" So Harry was there trying to shit from the top of the wardrobe into the glass on the floor. I cried laughing, it was ridiculous. Harry was like that, he was a crazy, crazy guy. But he was a good coach, he had a good rapport with the players. He was also part of the entertainment to keep people laughing and smiling.

Before the season kicked off, we would have a party at Elton John's house on the Sunday before. It would happen every year, religiously. The players would all meet at Vicarage Road, get into the cars and head to Elton's place in Windsor, a convoy of 30 or 40 cars. They came to the security gates, you had to have a pass to get in, then you'd get in there and he'd have it all lined up. There was music, he had big plant pots full of sweets for the kids. He had a five-a-side football pitch, he used to land the helicopter on it. The first time Pat Rice and I went, he wasn't there when we arrived, but we were told he'd just arrived at Heathrow. Then this helicopter comes and lands and he gets out, a big Stetson hat on, it was just surreal. There was a girl sunbathing by the swimming pool, that was Kiki Dee, she was staying with him.

Elton was class, he'd have a drink and a chat with everybody, not just players but the people who worked in the office, the groundsmen, everybody was there, it was great. It was a big family. Whenever he had a concert, we would order our tickets through the club, 40 or 50 players and their families would be there. Then afterwards, backstage, we'd go and see Elton and have a bit of craic. The Christmas parties, you had to do fancy dress in bad taste. Elton came dressed as a pregnant nun! Roy Claire was our kitman, an ex-paratrooper. He came dressed as an Argentine general just after the Falklands, which didn't go down too well! I loved that part of Watford, that we worked hard but didn't take ourselves too seriously off the pitch, and that was down to Graham Taylor. He instilled that and those players are still very close knit. Every last one of them will tell you what Graham Taylor did for them, because he was Mr. Watford. Even to the extent when I was with Northern Ireland at the World Cup, Graham would phone me up, "Gerry, proud of you, you're doing great. When you run at them, they don't know what to do. Keep running at them, take them on. They shit themselves, they're so petrified of you. Just keep doing what you're doing." That was great, having him give me encouragement as well.

One of Watford's real strengths was that there was a conveyor belt that ran through the club, delivering really good young players for the first team on a regular basis. If you can have that core of homegrown talent at a club, then it creates a special atmosphere about the place. The team spirit at Watford reminded me a lot of the feeling I had with the international team. Everybody fought and worked hard for each other and that's what you need if you're going to get success. Graham put a guy called Tommy Walley in charge of the youth team. Tommy was smart but he was tough as nails, a real character. He had an unbelievable attitude, he just was an out and out winner. He wanted people to run through brick walls, he wanted them to be fit and he wanted them to be brave.

He worked the boys physically and mentally and the number of star players who came through because of Tommy, we're talking dozens. John Barnes, Kenny Jackett, Nigel Callaghan, Neil Price, Gary Porter, Charlie Palmer, Jimmy Gilligan, it was an incredible run. Paul Franklin was coming through, Steve Terry was another, and these lads suddenly just went from being youth team players to first team players. Tommy's youth team beat Manchester United 7-6 over two legs in the 1982 FA Youth Cup final, which was unbelievable stuff, up against Mark Hughes, Norman Whiteside and the rest.

The important thing then though was that Graham would give the boys a chance, and that doesn't happen at some clubs, especially today when it's easier for the big teams especially to go out and buy a ready made international from somewhere. But Graham was brave enough to stick John Barnes into the team as a 17-year-old, at the start of that 1981/82 season. Barnesy was like a breath of fresh air and one of the best players I've ever played with. He'd go past people, he could cross a ball with his left foot or his right foot, he could play down the middle, played as a centre-forward on occasions, could take free-kicks, everything. He was an amazing boy and to watch a player like that come through, he reminded me of Glenn Hoddle.

Two footed players like Barnesy are special. George Best was two footed, you wouldn't have known if it was left or right footed. George is up there on a pedestal. He could head a ball, George could tackle, George could dribble, his balance was unbelievable, he would turn defenders inside out. He scored goals with his left foot and his right foot. He played on terrible pitches for most of the season, he had lumps kicked out of him, but he was just sensational. On top of that, he was a nice person as well, great fun to be with. Going back 20 odd years, we old boys were playing charity matches and George wanted to play, but he got to the stage where he just couldn't play, he'd got thrombosis in both legs. That comes from being kicked.

George used to roll with it, and just keep going, his balance was unbelievable. But that's what you did in those days, you carried on, there was only one sub in games so you couldn't come off unless you could barely walk, and if you didn't play, you lost your appearance money, so players had to get out there. I remember in my last year at Spurs, Terry Yorath broke his toe and you'd naturally think he'd be out for weeks. But no, an hour before kick-off, the doctor would come in and inject Terry with a painkiller straight into the big toe and he would go out and play. Players don't have that attitude or that mentality any longer, but in later life, they won't have the problems that players of my generation and before have had, from getting cortisone injections and playing through with injuries.

Off the back of pre-season, we were flying at the start of things and in the league, we won nine and drew one of the first 12 games, which really established us in the promotion picture. We won away at Newcastle and at Chelsea in that spell and it was us and Luton that were leading the way at the top of the division. Graham wouldn't let you get complacent though, he would just keep turning the screw right through the season. He was a great motivator. I remember one day, I wasn't feeling particularly well, I had a bit of a cold, but I decided to run it off and train anyway. I did the cross country and as usual, it was all timed and recorded. I was about 25 seconds outside my time and finished seventh or eighth, when I was used to finishing in the first three. Graham called me over afterwards, "Gerry, I need a word. I've just looked at your time, you're well outside your average." So I explained about the cold but he said to me, "Listen, I'm telling you now, if you don't finish in the first three of everything you do, you're cheating yourself and you're cheating me." That was how it was there, no excuses, you had to hit the highest standards every time you did anything, and that was a great discipline.

Fitness, attitude, psychology, you have to put all these pieces of the jigsaw together to make things work. With Graham, it might be chucking it down, but you're not wearing tracksuit bottoms! You don't do it on Saturday, you're not doing it today. If we had the first team v the reserves, everybody had shin guards on, because there were going to be tackles! Nobody ever pulled out of a tackle. Nobody. That mentality, that commitment, it set up a mindset. We were at the stage where if it was a 60/40 ball in the other guy's favour, I fancied myself to win it. He created that mentality and as a result, you become more confident, you have more belief in yourself. Those are the teams that become winners. Winning is a habit just like losing is a habit.

In that era in the '80s, Liverpool won trophy after trophy, but they never trained as hard as I did at Watford. What they had was the additional level of pure talent and their own confidence. Martin O'Neill talked to me a lot about his time at Nottingham Forest, playing in the European Cup final. They went off and had a party in Spain, enjoyed themselves, didn't do that much training for two or three days away. They came back, flew over to play the game and beat Hamburg, John Robertson scored. That would be looked upon as unprofessional now, but it actually worked! Getting your mind into the right place is as important as what your physical state is sometimes.

Graham understood that and he liked to try and take us away for a few days in mid-season when he could. He looked at those trips as team building because of the camaraderie and the stories and the laughs. The players used to have so much fun. There were always incidents, there was always fun, always good craic. In October or November the one season, we went to the Isle of Wight for a little break. We all had to wear Watford hats, like the fans would wear, and you weren't allowed to take your hat off. If you did, you were liable to a fine and the fines went towards a party on the last day. It was just a three or four day break with all the players and the people who had the guest house that we were staying in were all Watford fans.

We did a wee training session, trained pretty hard, and then the lads were given a free night to go out. There's the likes of Luther Blissett, Ross Jenkins, John Barnes, Pat Rice, Les Taylor, we were all there and we went into the bar. Most of what they had was ales and I'm not into that, so I said I'd have a glass of wine. The boys said, "We're drinking pints here!" So I said, "Give me a pint of wine then!" So I was drinking a pint of wine while they were drinking pints of beer. I got a few pints of wine in me and we were coming out, having a bit of a laugh, but obviously I'd had a lot more to drink than the others, the wine was much stronger. We were walking through the town and we saw this place that looked like a wee office, just a couple of steps and a door, but it was the police station wasn't it? Me being me, I kicked the door of the police station and ran off, so all the rest of the boys had to leg it after me - it was the fastest they ever moved! I just about remember getting back to where we stayed and I was in a room with Les Taylor and Pat Rice. The next day, I remember waking up and saying, "Jesus, what was I drinking last night?!?"

We just had a sink in the room, no bath, no toilet, so Les gets up and goes over to have a wash in the sink. "What are you doing?' says Pat.

"Just going to wash my face in the sink here to wake up."

"I wouldn't do that if I were you. Gerry pissed in that last night!"

We had a bit of a blip in the league around December and into January, but we had good cup runs as well. We got to the quarter-final of the League Cup, we beat Manchester United and West Ham in the FA Cup, which all showed the progress we were making. We'd dropped to third place but we had three or four games in hand on a lot of the teams around us. We played Derby County in midweek late in January and we beat them 6-1, I scored twice, and we went on a great run from there, we only lost another three games to the end of the season, one of those on the last day.

We played Chelsea at home a couple of weeks after the Derby game. Sebastian Coe was somebody I knew through my accountant, a big Chelsea fan and they were banned from going to away games at one point. My accountant phoned me to see if I could get him tickets. They turned up and John Barnes absolutely roasted their full-backs, went past them for fun. Afterwards, I went to the players' lounge to see them, and they were congratulating us on the win, raving over Barnesy. In the players' lounge, you had to pay for your own drinks but whenever we had had a good performance, Elton would sometimes stick his head in and say, "Well done lads, all the drinks are on me." He comes in and he sees Sebastian Coe. "What are you doing in here?" Seb was a bit panicked then, pipes up, "I'm just with Gerry!" "That's ok then", and off Elton goes. I think Seb thought he was going to throw him out!

By late April, we were in a really good position with five games to go. We needed another eight points from those games to be certain of going up, so the pressure was on. It was such a big thing for Watford to go up, the first time in their history, so you could feel the tension. Northern Ireland had a British Championship game against Scotland at Windsor Park, scheduled for a Wednesday night, the last week in April, but Watford had a rearranged game at Crystal Palace on the Tuesday. It was a must win game for Watford to try to make sure of promotion. Graham had said to me, "Look, Gerry, I need you. You'll have to play for us." I was happy enough with that. It was 32 games in a row that I'd played for Northern Ireland, which was a record, but I was ok with coming out of the squad. This game for Watford was more important.

I played against Crystal Palace, and we beat them 3-0. I remember going down the right hand side, chasing after the ball. The linesman, I don't think he kept up with me, because when I crossed the ball, it was probably two or three inches past the by-line - and we scored from it, 1-0. About 15 minutes later, I hit one from 25 yards that flew past the goalkeeper and from there, we'd got the game won, job done. Coming off, Graham came over and put his arm around me and said, "Well done Big Man, that was brilliant tonight. By the way, I booked a flight for you for tomorrow morning, out from London Heathrow. You're joining the squad for the game tomorrow." I ended up on the bench, Billy Bingham used that game to play Bobby Campbell, but it was great to be there, meet up with the lads. That was Graham. You'd do anything for him because of the way he treated you.

Watford drew at Charlton at the weekend and then on the Tuesday night, we beat Wrexham 2-0 at Vicarage Road, and that sealed promotion. We lost eight games that season out of 42, we only conceded 42 goals which was the lowest in the division, and we scored 76 and only Luton scored more. I remember coming off the pitch and celebrating. There was a great photograph in the local paper of myself, Luther Blissett and John Barnes picking up Graham Taylor and throwing him in the bath with his clothes on. We went to celebrate in the boardroom and there was a bit of a party. Elton wasn't there, he was doing a concert in Scandinavia that night, but he came off from the concert and phoned the club, spoke to the manager, to the other directors and then he spoke to every single player to congratulate us. "Can't wait to get home, you've done me proud," he said. We all looked upon him as a friend.

I was in cloud cuckoo land. We'd just got promoted to the First Division. I was looking forward to playing in the World Cup in Spain that was coming up in a couple of months. It couldn't get any better could it?

CHAPTER TEN

....

BRITISH CHAMPIONS

Like any footballer, one of my biggest ambitions was to play in a World Cup finals. For Northern Ireland, we'd only seen a team get there once, in 1958, but as we started qualifying for 1982, there was a chink of light. The tournament had been expanded from 16 teams to 24 and so that meant 13 European teams, plus the hosts, Spain, would qualify. Most of the groups had five teams in them, but initially we were in a four team group with Scotland, Sweden and Portugal but then those countries were asked if there were any issues in adding Israel to the group. Because of the political difficulties, they were going to be added to European qualifying, and all the nations involved were happy enough with Israel making it five. Two teams would qualify and with the way we were becoming very hard to beat at Windsor Park, we felt we had an opportunity, we were confident we could go and do something.

Qualifying started early, in March 1980, when we went out to play in Israel, a return to Tel Aviv, but there were no problems in a nightclub this time! We felt it was a good chance to really kick qualifying off with a strong result and to be perfectly honest, we didn't think it was going to be tough a game for us. When we got there though, it was roasting hot, they were a really fit side and made it hard for us, so a 0-0 draw wasn't a bad result. In fact, we got a bit lucky because as the second half went on, we were struggling until the floodlights failed with about 15 minutes to go. If they hadn't, I think we'd have been in trouble because we had underestimated how hot and humid it would be. We were all breathing out of our backsides at the time, and they were full of enthusiasm. But then the floodlights failed and gave us a ten minute breather, a chance to get some water into us, and we regrouped. We could even have won the match in the last five minutes, Sammy McIlroy had a good chance. We walked away with a 0-0 draw and we were a bit disappointed but we thought other sides might find it difficult out there.

From there, as I've already said, we went off and won the British Championship at the end of the 1979/80 season. That created real belief, because that's strong opposition. England were just off to the European Championships in Italy, Scotland had been to the last two World Cups. It was a big achievement and it was also the centenary of our Football Association, so it was a big deal all round. We were presented with medals to commemorate it, it felt like a special time, and of course, that proved to be the start of things for us. We went off on a tour then to Australia, and the bond got stronger because you're all having fun together, but we didn't lose any games either. We played Australia three times, won twice and drew the other one, so all of that set us up nicely. We knew that a lot of our players were coming to the right age, towards our peak years and we had a confidence about us similar to what we had at Watford going into 1981/82.

Billy Bingham was a very astute manager. He'd been at Everton for a while and after leaving there, he went to Mansfield Town and I remember going to play them with Spurs in the Second Division. We were a very good team at that level, going for promotion, and we thought that we'd beat them comfortably, but it was a really tough game for us. We got a draw, 3-3, and we were losing until Glenn Hoddle scored a fantastic free-kick. But from that, I knew Billy had all the attributes you needed to get the most out of a team. When he took over with Northern Ireland, he brought his ideas in and the team started to grow. We didn't have a huge pool to pick from, maybe 35 or 40 players who were playing, right down to Division Two or Division Three football in England, some boys in the First Division, some in Scotland, but that meant we couldn't chop and change and we became very close knit.

Billy inherited some good players from Danny Blanchflower too. Sammy McIlroy, David McCreery and Jimmy Nicholl had won the FA Cup with Manchester United. Martin O'Neill had just won the European Cup with

Forest. Billy Hamilton was coming through, Pat Jennings was as good as any goalkeeper in the world, we had a decent side. Then Billy started to change a few things in terms of keeping it tight at the back and becoming a more compact team than we'd been under Danny, and that worked so well for us. Billy was very meticulous, in terms of defending. Everybody had people to mark and he made that very evident to all of us. He looked at the players he had and said, "This is how we're gonna play".

He changed a lot of things. He brought in John McClelland, who he knew from his days at Mansfield Town before John went up to Rangers. He had a really bad injury, he busted his ankle, it turned 180 degrees. John then spent six months recuperating, and when he came back, it was the January, February of 1982, so by the time the World Cup came around, John was in peak condition in terms of full fitness. He had a great World Cup, and he came in and replaced John O'Neill. That was a clever change, because McClelland had more pace and alongside Chris Nicholl, it worked really well. Chris was a big six foot four guy, won everything in the air and John would sweep up behind. Mal Donaghy from Luton came into the picture to replace Sammy Nelson who was getting on a bit, so Billy started evolving the team. David McCreery was the anchor man in midfield, Martin O'Neill and Sammy McIlroy became the other midfield players alongside him, along with probably Tommy Cassidy. He played Noel Brotherston a lot as a right winger. Sammy played on the left and Martin and David in the middle. Noel was a very skilful, tricky winger, and he worked hard, he was a good athlete. He played a lot of the qualifiers.

Coming off the British Championship win, the next game was Sweden at home. In the first half especially, we just blitzed them and played really well. Jimmy Nicholl scored an absolutely fabulous goal, we played some very good football. We were 3-0 up at half-time, which was how it finished. Now it looked like we were off to a pretty good start, especially because Sweden had drawn at home to Israel and lost there against Scotland, so it seemed they were struggling to get out of the group already. Confidence started to grow and Windsor Park felt like it had become a fortress. Nobody came to Belfast and got an easy game. We had great camaraderie, we just loved to meet up, the stories would be flowing and we enjoyed being a part of the team and seeing our mates. We were looking forward to every single game, you couldn't wait to get there because the craic was always good and also because on the pitch, you could see how we were evolving under Billy. We were a very hard working team and we created a bond, a brotherhood.

103

We came back down to earth a little bit in the next game because we lost 1-0 in Lisbon and that made things a bit more complicated. Portugal had already got a draw in Scotland, so they were off to a very good start. By the time we played again, in March 1981, they'd also beaten Israel at home. That March game was at Hampden Park and we played pretty well against the favourites. Billy Hamilton put us in front with 20 minutes to go but John Wark equalised for them. Even so, it was a really good result and set us up for the one that really mattered now, Portugal at home the following month. Having lost out there, we had to win in Belfast.

It was a really gruelling game, nothing much in it, but with about 15 minutes left, I managed to score the only goal and from there, we saw it out, which was becoming a speciality for us, we didn't give a lot away. Winning – or not losing - becomes a habit, whatever level you're at. Go back to the great Liverpool side in the '70s and '80s, they ruled England and Europe and you talk to those boys and every time they went out on the field, they believed they would get the right results. You have the confidence and the belief in yourself and your mates. We had that at Watford when we won promotion and then finished second and we had it with Northern Ireland.

After the Portugal game, there was a celebration in the penthouse of the Europa hotel. The whole team was in there and Sammy Nelson and Pat Jennings were involved in a conversation with a couple of guys. It was getting a bit out of order and I went over, I tried to defuse it. I said to them, "Come on, lads, we're celebrating here, I'll get you a drink." And one of the guys was a bit naughty and said, "Go fuck yourself, Armstrong." So I hit him and the bouncers came running in, and all hell was let loose!

The frustration then was that we went to Sweden and lost 1-0, which let them back into the picture a little bit. Jimmy Nicholl gave away a penalty, he handled the ball. He was so wound up by playing behind Terry Cochrane that he lost his composure! Sweden then beat Portugal so at the end of the 1980/81 season, it was a really tight qualifying group. Scotland were on top with eight points from five games, then it was us and Sweden, both with six points from six games. Portugal were a point further back, but they'd only played five times.

Scotland did us a favour by beating Sweden at Hampden and then on October 14th, they came to Belfast for an afternoon game, which was only the second time they'd come over to Northern Ireland since 1970 because of the Troubles. We'd still got a chance. We were brilliant and again, Billy had us so well organised. We played some fantastic football and gave them a really hard time. We should have won that match but we just couldn't put the ball in the back of their net. Scotland were happy to go away with the 0-0, believe you me and that basically sealed their qualification. We went back to the hotel, pretty down at the time because we thought we were all but out because that night, Portugal were playing Sweden. If they won in Lisbon, they'd have the same points as us but with a game in hand.

I really couldn't see Sweden beating Portugal but Martin O'Neill said, "Listen, we're not out of it yet." Martin was very much a philosophical type of a person. He said, "Sweden's a decent side, they're not bad, they could cause a problem." Martin disappeared to his room to listen on the radio. After a while, he came back up. "Just to let you know, Sweden's 1-0 up." Then after half-time, he came up again. "It's 1-1 now." So off he goes again and then after a bit, he's back up. "2-1 to Sweden and they're hanging on." We listened in to the last few minutes and they did hang on, which meant if we beat Israel at home, we would qualify for the World Cup. That was just unbelievable, from rock bottom to the top of the world in a couple of hours.

In between those games, Israel hammered Portugal 4-1, so they were coming to Belfast in a bit of form! There was a month to wait for the game and everybody in the country was looking forward to it, the chance to go to a World Cup for the first time in 24 years. The tension was unbelievable. The night before, we were in the hotel, Pat Jennings was my room-mate as usual. We always had a cup of tea last thing and we'd stay up till about half 11, 12 o'clock and put the world to rights, having a chat. I remember going off to bed and Pat wasn't feeling great. He said, "I've got a terrible headache. I'm worried it's a migraine." I don't know if he was worrying about the game and the pressure of it, but at one in the morning, Pat phoned the doctor and he came to the room with Billy Bingham. Pat got an injection to help him get some sleep. They disappeared about quarter past one in the morning. I got into bed and 20 minutes later, I was asleep, so was Pat. We woke up the next day at nine o'clock to go and have our breakfast and get organised. He was feeling good now, so we just went about our business and got off to the stadium. When we got there, it was an unbelievable atmosphere. It was the biggest crowd I've ever seen at Windsor Park. It was only supposed to hold 40,000 people but there must have been 45,000 in that day. They were just packed in like sardines.

The first 10 or 15 minutes were tense, but then we got the set play, the free-kick. It was a crossover, one we'd tried for years and it hadn't ever worked for us, it was always blocked off. I went to the far post and then as I was coming back, Billy Hamilton made a run forward. As he made his run, I walked in front of the defender who's marking him and that gave Billy a couple of yards so that he could maybe get a free header. The ball was delivered somewhere just inside the penalty area by Noel Brotherston. As Billy got up to head it, I tried to gamble on where I thought his body shape meant he was going to put it and lo and behold, he headed it straight down at me, on my left side, on the volley. I pivoted and hit it with the left foot and it flew into the back of the net. The fans went crazy. Then we started passing the ball about, we were playing much better. We were a lot more composed. They never really had any chances, we were a good team to close up shop and not give the opposition too many chances. Billy gave us the platform by making it solid at the back. We only conceded three goals in eight qualifiers. That is incredible. If you keep it tight, you're always in with a chance.

Then when the final whistle went, Windsor Park went crazy, and I mean crazy! We did one lap of honour, two laps of honour, three laps. They were throwing scarves and flags and everything. It was just an unbelievable night. We packed up and went back to the hotel to celebrate. We were going to the World Cup!

CHAPTER ELEVEN

....

THE SPIRIT OF '82

Qualifying for the World Cup finals for the first time since 1958 gave the people something to look forward to – and that was so important in Northern Ireland at the time, given that the Troubles had been going on for 12 years or more by then. Lifting the spirits in the country was great, but the funny thing was that it wasn't just the people in Northern Ireland who were pleased for us and were going to follow us, it was the whole of Ireland, and then obviously Northern Irish and Irish people all over the world as well. Over the six months or so between qualifying and the competition itself, it became obvious that a lot of people were going to be backing us and the excitement started to build.

When the draw was made in January '82, that just knocked it up another level. There were six groups of four and the top two in each group progressed into another group round, four groups of three, the winners going on to the semi-final. We came out against Yugoslavia, who had come top of their qualifying group which included Italy, Honduras who, I'll be honest, we knew nothing about and the host nation, Spain. Obviously they were big favourites to go through the group and so the immediate feeling in the press and among fans was there was no chance we would qualify from that group. We knew we couldn't have had it much tougher, but we also felt that anybody that wanted to beat us would have to play well and they'd know they'd been in a game at the end of it. We weren't going to miss the opportunity. Billy Bingham was a brilliant manager, instinctive, but he had that experience of having played in a World Cup, which helped as well. He had lots of different ideas, and they worked. He picked the right team for each game through qualifying and it had seen us through. That was one of his big strengths for me.

We didn't have a particularly good build up for the World Cup in terms of results. We only had four games after qualifying, which were the three British Championship games and a friendly in France. We lost three and drew with Scotland at Windsor Park. That didn't really matter because we were using those games to get ourselves organised and there were a few things Billy Bingham wanted to look at as well. I played on the right wing a couple of times, he had that idea in his head already. I think he was thinking he could maybe play Bobby Campbell and Billy Hamilton, two big, strong battering rams, up front and then use my athleticism, pushing on from the right hand side. But another of Billy's great strengths was his flexibility, he was always open to changing things if a better option came up. It came from out of nowhere really because at the end of that season, a young boy called Norman Whiteside emerged from out of nowhere to play his first game for Manchester United. He only turned 17 in May '82 but Billy brought him into the squad at the last moment and that changed things. Eight or nine positions were more or less set in stone – Pat Jennings, Jimmy Nicholl, Sammy McIlroy, Chris Nicholl, David McCreery, Martin O'Neill, myself, Billy Hamilton - but Billy kept his mind open about other positions and Norman did so well in training that he forced his way into the team and started every game in the World Cup.

We trained really hard in preparation, we were determined to go there in the best possible shape and to maximise every opportunity we had. We set up our training camp in Brighton, at Sussex University, and it was really hot, 75 or 80 degrees. We basically did a pre-season there, Billy's training schedule was unbelievable. He brought a 10,000 metre runner in, the guy was the south of England champion, and he took us running across the Downs. We trained every morning and every afternoon. In the morning, we did all our physical work and then in the afternoon, we did the ball skills, the crossing and the shape. It was a really tough schedule but it was a great place to be. Everybody was into it because it was our first World Cup and honestly, we all thought maybe it was going to be our only World Cup.

The team had been evolving over a couple of years, but Billy made other changes even in Brighton, on top of introducing Norman. He brought in Bobby Campbell at the expense of Derek Spence, which I thought was a mistake. For me, Spence should have been in the squad. He had played a big part in our qualifying but he took the risk on Bobby because he was big and strong, and he was scoring goals for Bradford City. He thought that maybe he could do us a turn, so he took a gamble on Bobby, which didn't work out. In 1986 he actually admitted that, he told me, "Sometimes as a manager, you make good decisions and sometimes you make bad decisions. And that was a bad one!" I could see where he was coming from, but that didn't help poor Derek who was looking forward to finishing his career at the World Cup.

One really significant change in the team itself was John McClelland coming in for John O'Neill at centre-half. That was a good decision because he had a fantastic World Cup, which isn't to say that John O'Neill wouldn't have done the same. But of course, the massive one was Norman Whiteside. As the youngest player ever to play in the World Cup finals, and making his international debut at the same time, it was a huge decision, but Billy rated Norman from the start. Norman gave us good balance. It was incredible to watch somebody so young mature so quickly, and because Billy had such belief in him, it meant he could move me around.

As I said, in the lead up games to the finals, he'd dropped me into a deeper lying role on the right side of midfield and that worked to my benefit. A lot of the opposition sides were expecting me to play as a centre-forward but I played a deep, wide role in front of Jimmy Nicholl. I made these runs that gave me a chance to show my athleticism and use my power and pace. If Norman hadn't emerged, I'm not sure he would have done that. He might have had to carry on with me up front alongside Billy Hamilton. But Norman was brilliant, he had a natural left foot, he was a strong target man and he could score goals. So the shape of the team changed just before the World Cup and that surprised a lot of teams.

People underrated that squad as well. Mal Donaghy and I had both just got promoted to the First Division that season, when the Second Division was much stronger than the Championship is now. Pat Jennings was at Arsenal. Sammy Nelson had played there and now he was at Brighton who had just missed promotion. Norman Whiteside was at Manchester United, David McCreery, Sammy McIlroy and Jimmy Nicholl had all played there, Chris Nicholl was at Southampton, John McClelland at Rangers. We had Martin

O'Neill, who was very much a philosopher. He is a smart, smart boy, a deep thinker. On the pitch, he knew how we could take advantage of certain situations. He looked at the weaknesses and the strengths of the teams we were playing, and he always had a game plan. That's why he was such a successful manager. He would tell you that he learnt from every manager, Billy Bingham, Brian Clough, whoever.

The truth was that we had a good side, we all knew our strengths and our weaknesses, but we didn't quite have the depth in the squad. We had four players from the Irish league who were part-timers, which was incredible at a World Cup. The first 15 names were strong, but injuries gave us problems. George Dunlop was the Linfield goalkeeper and he came as a third choice behind Pat Jennings and Jim Platt, as an Irish league player. Jimmy Cleary was an outstanding footballer for Glentoran. Johnny Jameson, who I'd played with at Bangor, he was at Glentoran too and he was a very talented left or right winger. The other one was Felix Healey at Coleraine, a good midfield player, good athlete who struck the ball really well with both feet. What an opportunity, as semi-professionals, to be in the World Cup squad. They weren't used to doing full-time training but as we prepared for the competition, you could see them develop and they were so hungry to be a part of it. It reminded me a little bit of my early days at Tottenham and how I progressed after going full-time.

We flew out to Spain and we based ourselves in Valencia. The Sidi Soler was a fantastic hotel, right on the beach and everything was perfect. Billy organised all of that and it was the ideal place to operate from. Before the games started out, I must have had a few minutes to myself because I recently found a postcard that I sent home: "Looking forward to the first game. We might need a few of mum's candles to get a result!" I don't even remember sending it!

Looking at that first game, I'm not surprised I thought she'd have to light a few candles for us. Yugoslavia were the first opposition and that was a key game because we felt that second place was going to come down to us or them. Yugoslavia were a very good side. We looked at their qualification, they finished above Italy, who eventually won the competition, and scored 22 goals – we wouldn't score that many in five years! We knew they were technically a good team. The opening game of the group was Spain versus Honduras and that was a surprise, it ended in a 1-1 draw, and that really opened things up. Talking amongst ourselves before our first game, Martin

O'Neill said, "Honduras is the team we can beat. If we get a draw against Yugoslavia, then we'll only need a draw against Spain, and we can do that." That was the plan from the outset, but plans sometimes go awry!

Going into that opener, the big news from our camp was that Norman Whiteside was going to start, making his international debut. Norman still holds that record as being the youngest player ever to play in the World Cup. Pele sent a video to him and said, "Congratulations and well done. I hope you have a fantastic career ahead of you!" That was a really great gesture from him to do that.

Against Yugoslavia, we were nervous in the first 15 or 20 minutes, but we settled down. The heat was unbearable, the humidity. It was 90 degrees at eight, nine o'clock at night, we were all sweating like crazy, but the belief in the camp was really good. We understood our jobs and we defended really, really well. We suffocated the life out of them to be honest and they began to get frustrated the longer the game went on. They couldn't break us down and then despite the conditions, as the game went on, we were the fitter side, the work we'd put in in Brighton really started to bear fruit. The last 20 minutes, we were the better team and they were on the back foot. We were the ones that were looking to win the game, but to be honest, a 0-0 was a great start for us. We would have settled for that before the game.

We had flown up to Zaragoza for the game and we flew back straight afterwards on a private plane, back to our base in Valencia. We were told by Billy Bingham that we couldn't leave the hotel. We were allowed to have a couple of beers in the hotel bar, which was fine, and we just chilled out. But one of the television guys, Jackie Fullerton, and his producer, Terry Smith, they were going into Valencia for a night out. They were leaving about half 12, because in Spain, everything's on late, open until four and five in the morning. They were going to have a couple of hours in one of the clubs for a drink and a bit of craic. And, of course, Jimmy Nicholl and Billy Hamilton decided they were going to go with them.

It was nothing over the top, they were just having a quiet couple of beers and chatting away, but somebody recognised them in the club. All of a sudden, the Spanish press turned up, trying to get photographs and Terry, being a television producer in Northern Ireland, he knew straight away that it would be all over the news. He managed to sneak the boys out, but it still hit the papers the next day. Going to training, there was questions being asked by the press, who were all staying in our hotel, Irish press, English press, the whole lot. They were trying to find out what had gone on but they'd heard that one of the players involved was Nicholl. But we had Jimmy and we had big Chris Nicholl. Chris was a fantastic pro, he only used to drink Coca-Cola, that was as far as he went. The press were asking Billy all the questions and so after training, he takes Jimmy to one side.

"I need to have a word. There's a story here that Nicholl was at a club last night."

"No boss, wouldn't have been me."

Then he went to Chris. "No, it wasn't me boss."

Jackie Fullerton was the lead television reporter in Northern Ireland, and Terry, his producer, who'd been with him, said, "Jackie, this is big news, you've got to do an interview." It was hilarious, because Jackie got hold of Billy Bingham and says, "Billy what about this press story that two players were out drinking in a club in Valencia?" And Billy said, "It's a lot of nonsense Jackie, that's just the local press trying to wind us up because we're in the same group as Spain." We were crying laughing, because we knew Jackie was trying to keep a straight face through it all!

I do feel sorry for players now because if they cough or sneeze it's in the paper the next day. They're certainly more in the limelight. We were much closer with the press then, they were like friends, we had good relationships with them. We were quite happy to help people. Harry Harris was at the Tottenham Herald or whatever the local newspaper was when I was there. I used to give him stories, little bits and pieces of what was going on, who was doing well and who wasn't. It was the same with the international football, you make friends with a lot of the press guys and they were very supportive. They weren't looking for a headline story that would put them on the front page, just a bit of a steer on the team news so they wouldn't look silly with what they were writing.

The press guys were really good with us. We were all friends, we knew every press man except for the English guys who were given the job because it was a chance to go to a World Cup. They loved the fact that we were just a down to earth bunch of lads who would have a couple of beers but not go silly, who would give 120% on the pitch and do the right thing. There were people queuing up to come on our trips. I think that bond was set up in the late '70s under Danny Blanchflower, who was a great journalist himself, and then Billy took it on to another level.

Spain played again before we did, this time against Yugoslavia, and they won the game 2-1, which really set us up perfectly for the Honduras game. Win that and Martin was right, a draw with Spain would see us through.

It was looking really good when we got an early goal. It was a set play and the free-kick came in and hit the crossbar. I was following up, which I had been coached at Watford to do for everything, and I was just in the right place at the right time to head it in from close range. That was 1-0 after about ten minutes. Shortly after that, I could have wrapped it up. I had a good run from the halfway line, I went past one guy and then they had a big centre-half called Costly. He was square on to me. I remember shimmying to go to the left. He moved and then I went right and hit the shot from just outside the box. I thought it was in, but it hit the inside of the post and came straight back out and into the goalkeeper's hands again. If that had gone in, it was all over because we were well on top in that first half.

Unfortunately, they came back and equalized on the hour, a guy called Laing, a very good header of the ball. They were very well organized and they were more comfortable with the heat and the humidity, which affected us. We were very fit, but we weren't always comfortable with the conditions, we weren't used to it, and I thought that became a disadvantage. It finished 1-1 and that left it wide open for the last game against Spain. They had three points, ourselves and Honduras had two, Yugoslavia had one point. We knew that we had to win to qualify, but we weren't too down about that. Funnily enough, drawing with Honduras might have worked in our favour because we knew we had to beat Spain, a draw wasn't enough, so that clears the mind. We'd watched Spain's games and we thought they were ok, but we knew they were under massive pressure and we could exploit that. After all, nobody was expecting us to win.

That day before the game, Martin O'Neill was talking us through how the game was going to play out, like he was an extension to Billy Bingham. Martin was his general. He took over once we crossed the line. He was very much a leader. After our last training session, we were sitting by the pool and he said, "We know what's going to happen. They're the favourites.

They want to prove a point and send out a message to the competition, so they're going to come out all guns blazing in their own backyard. They'll be looking for an early goal. We'll do what we're good at. We get everybody behind the ball, and we'll play them across the park and not let them get in behind. After 20 odd minutes of them hammering us, we'll turn the crowd against them. Then we will get chances and we'll take one of them. We'll beat them 1-0, that's how it will work." We all bought into it. But we didn't plan for Mal Donaghy getting sent off!

We were allowed an hour by the pool after training and then we had to go in to get out of the sun. Nobody was allowed to sunbathe for too long, but Tommy Cassidy had fallen asleep on one of the sunbeds. We got about 20 cans of beer and piled them all up around Tommy. A load of Spaniards came in and they were all pointing to Tommy. I don't know what they were saying, but it couldn't have been good! The lads had set him up nicely! It was fantastic fun to be part of that squad and the boys. Jimmy Nicholl was behind a lot of that stuff. Jimmy loved the craic.

That's why those relationships lasted. I speak to Pat Jennings, Billy Hamilton, Jimmy Nicholl, Sammy McIlroy, Norman Whiteside and all those boys pretty much every week. That's why everybody wanted to be in the squad. It was a pleasure to go off to the international team. We were one big unit, so much so that the 22 players who went to the World Cup did a deal at the start to split the money from the pool equally. It didn't matter whether you were playing, on the bench, not on the bench, you were all part of this squad, you were part of this team and that was great for the team spirit. We were never going to score a lot of goals, we were a bit like the Italians, really hard workers, depending on each other, closing down, we pressed a lot and physically we could look after ourselves. Then we would create two or three chances and stick one of them away.

Spain always liked to play in Seville or Valencia when they wanted a big, hostile fan base behind them, which is why all three of their group games were played in Valencia. We only had about 600 fans over from Northern Ireland and the rest, about 49,000, were Spaniards. But we had nothing to lose. You turn up and say, "We're giving it 100%, leave nothing behind, leave everything on the pitch." That's what we did.

We were happy to keep it at 0-0, that was the first job. But in that first half, they became a very physical side from that frustration of not being able to score in the first 20 minutes and the fans getting on their backs, just as Martin had predicted. We were not an easy team to play against. We challenged for everything, but every single decision, the Paraguayan referee gave it their way. David McCreery was our anchor man in midfield and he was magnificent on that night, he was the key. He used to run everywhere, he was brilliant at getting his foot in and he could break up and start attacks. He used to intercept everything. He never crossed the halfway line normally, but he went on a run, he went past everybody. He got into the opposition half and he went to go past Alexanko and got body checked. It was definitely a yellow card. You could hear David yelling when he hit him. The referee gave a free-kick, but never booked him, so we knew we were up against it, here we go!

Just before half-time, Sammy McIlroy get kicked from behind and he retaliated - Sammy get booked but the player who kicked him didn't. There were stud marks down the back of Sammy's leg, he was in a bad way for three or four days afterwards. He was limping and eventually had to come off early in the second half, and Tommy Cassidy came on for him. Just after that, Martin O'Neill was down near the corner flag and had lumps kicked out of him, but no booking again for their player. We hadn't really had any chances, but we just stood our ground and at the break, it was 0-0. We were doing our job.

The messages at half-time were just to keep doing what we were doing, that the longer it went on at 0-0, the more frustrated they'd become and the more players they'd commit forward. Then we just had to wait our moment and exploit the gaps. That moment came a bit earlier than we expected. A couple of minutes into the second half, I read a pass that Gordillo was going to play just inside our half and I intercepted the ball. I took it forward and then fed Billy Hamilton who had peeled away on the right. He shrugged off a challenge and went off into space and knocked this low ball in, towards the edge of the six yard box. Arconada, their goalkeeper, came for it but he only parried it away and it came towards me – I'd carried on my run into the box. I concentrated on keeping it down and smacked it into the back of the net.

I saw big Norman and Billy both running towards me with their arms up, but my first reaction was that the referee was going to find some reason to disallow it with the way the decisions had gone, and so I was looking for him. Then I could see him blowing the whistle and pointing to the halfway line and giving the goal. Happy days! That's when I celebrated. It seemed to take a lot longer than it probably did. That was our chance and we'd got our goal. Now we had something to hang on to and that's what we were good at, hanging on and making it difficult for the opposition. "Right, let's get behind the ball, do what we've prepared for."

It was going fine, then just on the hour, we were down to ten men when we lost Mal Donaghy. He ran over to chase a ball with Camacho and there was some pushing and shoving but nothing much, nobody went down. Mal basically bumped into him, Camacho turned round and Mal put his hands up to push him away, on the chest, that was all. Camacho said something to the linesman, he passed that on to the referee and I thought he was going to book Mal, like he had Sammy. Then he pulls out a red card - the referee was just looking for an excuse to send one of our players off.

I couldn't believe it. Nobody could believe it. Mal still can't believe it! It was never a red card in the world. Again, that builds up a determination, "OK, they're trying to cheat us out of it now." So from then on, that really was backs against the wall. David McCreery played left-back, I dropped into central midfield. Norman dropped into left midfield and we left Billy Hamilton on his own up top. That's when it got really interesting, because they threw everything at us. We held firm. We worked and covered every blade of grass. About 20 minutes to go, Billy took off Norman who was struggling to get through 90 minutes at his age, he'd tire after about 65, 70 minutes, and we brought on Sammy Nelson, a real left-back. That meant that David McCreery could go back in the middle of the park along with Tommy, myself and Martin and we played one up front, Billy Hamilton. The balance was better, and they got so frustrated, and never really had any other opportunities.

We just got behind the ball and made it difficult for them, gave them absolutely no space at all. They didn't really have that much to offer until three minutes from the end when there was a ball lobbed over the top. Chris Nicholl thought Pat Jennings was coming to take it, Pat thought Chris was going to head it, and they both hesitated. The ball bounced and the guy that was the Pichichi, the top scorer, that year in Spain was called Quini, he was in there looking for it. Typical Pat, he saw what was happening, and he came out and flicked it with his right hand over the head of Quini and then caught it with his left hand and rolled over onto the ground. That was the real danger moment, we were holding our breath

– but that was Pat Jennings in goal. No problem! Pat tells me there was no misunderstanding and that he knew exactly what he was doing all along, that he knew he wasn't getting to the first bounce and he wanted to make sure that he could take the ball without getting near the striker, in case the referee might give a penalty. That's why he was the best goalkeeper in the world.

With that save, that was them done, we knew it was going to be our night. Martin went down the left hand side after a long ball, he got it into the corner flag and he started playing keepy-uppy with the ball, which was unbelievable. I thought he was going to get volleyed again.

Then the whistle went and everybody went crazy. I remember John McClelland running with his arms in the air, Noel Brotherston ran from the dug out straight to me, jumped on top of me and hugged me. That's the picture that sticks in my mind. Then Billy Bingham was on the pitch, all the lads were congratulating each other. Our few hundred fans went absolutely crazy. It was brilliant. One of the best nights of my life, I have to say. Looking back, I think we really did intimidate them just with the hunger we had. Down to 10 men, we were just so resolute, so determined, our attitude was brilliant. Everybody worked so hard for each other. It's got to be the best performance ever from any Northern Ireland team. Certainly I can't remember any results like that anywhere else. That squad was something else. That team spirit, if you could bottle that, you'd solve a lot of the world's problems.

I was coming off laughing and smiling and the doctor came over and along with Sammy Nelson and Tommy Cassidy, they picked me straight away for the drugs test – I suppose they hoped I'd fail it! They took me away to the testing room and I could not have a pee to save my life. I was that dehydrated. You lose between eight and 10 pounds of body weight in one game with the humidity. Next day you have it all back on again, once you get a couple of bottles of water inside you just to replenish it. They were running water, they were giving me drinks but I couldn't pee. Sammy was hilarious because he came in and the guy was saying about "pee pee". He gives you that plastic bottle and says, "pee pee". So Sammy said, "Watch this." And Sammy pretended he was going to shit in it and the guy is shouting, "No, no caca, pee pee!" The security guys and the Spanish players who were getting tested, they were crying laughing. I remember eventually getting back to the changing rooms and there was nobody left in there. I was going to get a shower but the lads were all on the bus and they were waiting for me, so I just stuck my tracksuit on and away I went. Getting on the bus, the boys were all cheering for me and off we went to the hotel to have a party. It was brilliant, we were in cloud cuckoo land, just enjoying ourselves.

I went up to my room to get changed and came back down and there was Billy Bingham and the press, all at the bar. We couldn't get a drink because the press were in front of us – same old story! The atmosphere was great. We had a lot of fans who had followed us back to our hotel, and the guys were all loving it. They were all singing and cheering, it was two, three in the morning and it was in full swing and then Billy came over. He had been in great form, but normally he would go to bed early. But he came over and he said, "I need to speak to you Gerry, Sammy, Pat, Jimmy, Martin."

I said, "What's wrong? There's nothing can be wrong on a night like this."

But Billy's face was like thunder. "You will not believe what's wrong. Our secretary has just told me that he didn't think we would qualify, so he has our tickets booked tomorrow to go back to London." We had a bit of a giggle over that.

I said, "Well, you'll have to change them in the morning because we're going to Madrid."

He said, "Well that's only part of the problem. The other part of the problem is we have no hotels to stay at in Madrid because he didn't think we would qualify. And we fly there in the morning." It was absolute chaos. We ended up getting a terrible hotel on the runway of the airport in Madrid. That's where we had to perform from, from there. That was where we were stuck. We had to hurry, but the hotel we got was not good. That was all still to come though.

I really didn't want to go to bed after the Spain game, it was one of those nights you wanted to last forever. I remember sitting on the balcony in the room and watching the sun coming up with Pat Jennings, having tea and toast. We'd had a few beers but we didn't have a lot of people who drank that much in our team. We were just quite happy to have a couple and just socialize together. It was great to see all the boys celebrating and making a bit of history, we wanted to remember that, to savour it – and we had more games to come now of course, so nobody was getting carried away.

I remember listening to Malcolm Brodie's typewriter, he was a Belfast Telegraph journalist and he wrote for all papers all around the world. He must have had copy to do at one o'clock in the morning, two o'clock in the morning, three o'clock for various deadlines. It was going to Australia, New York, it was going everywhere. He was typing away a couple of balconies down. In the end I had three or four hours sleep and then got up, still buzzing because of the result and the way we were all feeling, there was a big smile on everybody's face. I came downstairs and Billy said to me, "Have you seen the foyer? There's hundreds and hundreds of telegrams from all around the world. You've got to go and read them." So we went and started reading the telegrams. They were coming from the Taoiseach of the Republic of Ireland, the Catholic Archbishop from Dublin, from Omagh, the Reverend Ian Paisley had sent one. Later on, we met him at Stormont and he said, "I don't know any of you, but I know you all know me!" I thought that was hilarious. Players respond to that, we like a bit of craic, we never take ourselves too seriously.

The telegrams were coming from everywhere, all denominations. Billy said, "Have you heard the news? Street parties on the Falls Road, the Shankill Road, Sandy Row, doesn't matter if it's Catholic or Protestant areas. They're celebrating." That's when Norman Whiteside's mom was invited by my mother to go from the Shankill Road to the Falls Road to have tea and sandwiches with her! The camera crews were all there and milking it, it was incredible. What it did was it broke down all the barriers, and we thought it was great. We didn't realise it, but that was the start of something. The politicians had been trying for years to bring the communities together, but football had done that in that one World Cup. What we did and what those players achieved for our country was just unbelievable. It's great to know that we did that.

We were isolated from everything of course, we didn't really know what was happening because this was pre-internet and mobile phones. I remember phoning home from the hotel to be told everybody was partying. A lad from West Belfast had scored this goal that put Northern Ireland through and it was turning out to be probably the biggest night there has been in our football. People were having parties down in Dublin. Irish people were having parties all over the world and we didn't know about any of it, we were oblivious to what was going on. You couldn't write the script, beating

Spain in their own backyard against all the odds, and ending up doing it while playing with 10 men. We made it happen because we had that belief in ourselves and we had that determination and the organisational skills.

I've always said that as a result of it all, I learned a big lesson, that sport can do an awful lot of things that politicians can't do. Sport can break down all sorts of barriers. I'm still working on that with Co-operation Ireland, to produce future leaders, from Galway, from Dublin, from Belfast, from everywhere, teaching them about team building. Sport played such a big part in my life, but it makes a huge difference to everybody's lives, because they all support their country, it's something to focus on. That's a sense of identity. These are all 17, 18, 19-year-olds. Their country is in their hands, they're the future.

I still look at that photo of my mum with Norman's mother, "the orange and the green" was the newspaper headline, her coming over from the Shankill Road to the Falls Road for a cup of tea. We didn't realise the impact that World Cup had when The Troubles were still in full effect. What I also didn't realise until recently, when I was going through her things, was that my mum had kept in contact with lots of people who had phoned her and written to her to congratulate her after I'd scored that goal. The letters are incredible and there's a list my mum wrote down of all the different people who phoned and where they were from. She got letters from the Shankill Road, from Castlereagh, Sandy Row, places you wouldn't expect in Northern Ireland, and then from people all over the world. I think that tells you what we did in terms of bringing everybody together. That's part of the spirit of '82 for me.

There was another letter I found from the mother of a boy who was in a coma, he lived in Kells, just outside Ballymena. We were asked for a taped message that they could play to him, so myself, Martin O'Neill and a couple of other players recorded something for him. A while later, my mum got a letter thanking us because he'd recovered and they felt the voices on the tape had helped get through to him and bring him back. If you're a footballer, a sportsman, a celebrity, an entertainer or whatever, if you can use your position and your fame to do something like that to help people, it's great to be able to do it. It's a great feeling that we might have been a little part of saving somebody's life.

My mum was amazing. Where she got the energy and the time to do all

WBA V MANCHESTER UNITED WITH BRYAN ROBSON IN THE BACKGROUND

WITH MY PAL PAT JENNINGS AT THE GEORGE BEST STATUE UNVEILING

THE ARMSTRONG FAMILY

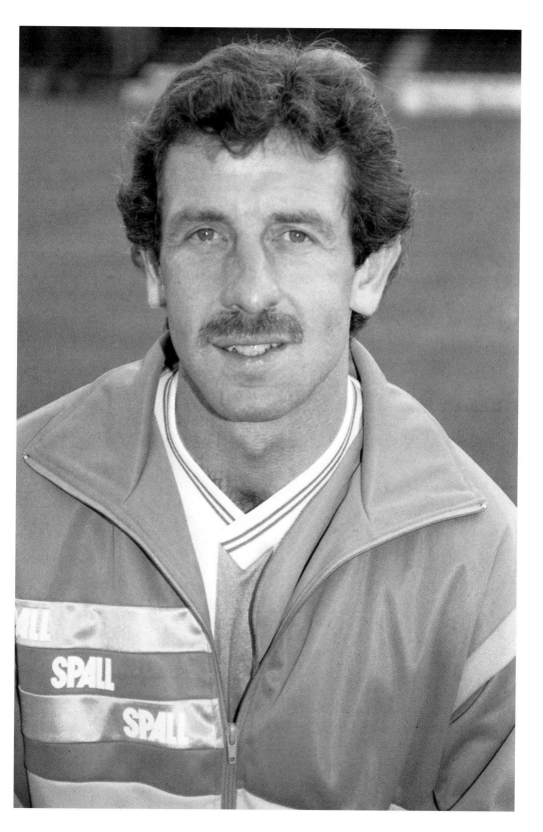

IN MY BRIGHTON DAYS!!

RISING EARLY AS TERRY HURLOCK AND KEVIN BREMNER (MILLWALL) LOOK ON
STEVE GATTING AND DALE JASPER (BRIGHTON) READY TO ASSIST

OUR BEAUTIFUL WEDDING DAY CEREMONY IN HUA HIN, THAILAND

CAITLIN'S HOLY COMMUNION IN HOLYWOOD

ON THE ATTACK AGAINST CRYSTAL PALACE

TRYING TO BEAT LARRY MAY AT VICARAGE ROAD V LEICESTER

MY ARRIVAL AT REAL MALLORCA, LUIS SITJAR

BRITISH CHAMPIONS AND CURRENT HOLDERS. WHAT A GREAT BUNCH OF LADS

Back row left to right the two Gerrys McElhinney and Armstrong , John McClelland, Pat Jennings, George Dunlop, John O'Neill, Mal Donaghy, Paul Ramsey, Billy Hamilton, front row Nigel Worthington, Jimmy Nicholl, Norman Whiteside, Billy Bingham, Martin O'Neill, Steve Penney, David McCreery & Ian Stewart

TRAINING IN MADRID BEFORE GAME V AUSTRIA.

MY GOOD FRIEND DEREK WADE AND AN ESPANA 82 OFFICIAL

FREE MASONS DINNER IN LONDON WITH MY TOTTENHAM TEAM MATES. OSSIE ARDILES IN A STRANGLEHOLD. JIMMY HOLMES, JOHN LACY, DON MCALLISTER, JOHN PRATT, PHYSIO MIKE VARNEY AND KEITH BURKINSHAW SPURS MANAGER

DEBBY IN HER MODELLING DAYS

ENJOYING OUR WEDDING DAY BANQUET (WOW HOW BEAUTIFUL IS MY GORGEOUS WIFE)

ME AND MY GIRL. MARIANNA 6 MONTHS OLD

DEBBY ONLY 2 MONTHS TO GO AND BLOSSOMING AT A FAMILY WEDDING IN DINGLE

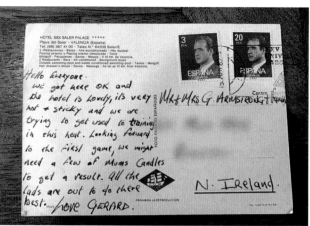

SIDI SOLER HOTEL VALENCIA

Hello Everyone.
We got here OK and the hotel is lovely, it's very hot & sticky and we are trying to get used to training in this heat. Looking forward to the first game, we might need a few of Mums Candles to get a result. All the lads are out to do there best. Love GERARD.

Mr & Mrs G. Armstrong + family

N. Ireland.

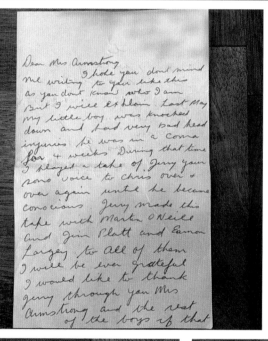

Dear Mrs Armstrong
I hope you don't mind me writing to you like this as you don't know who I am But I will explain. Last May my little boy was knocked down and had very bad head injuries. He was in a coma for 4 weeks. During that time I played a tape of Jerry your sons voice to Chris over & over again until he became conscious. Jerry made this tape with Martin O'Neill and Jim Platt and Eamon Largey to all of them I will be ever grateful I would like to thank Jerry through you Mrs Armstrong and the rest of the boys if that

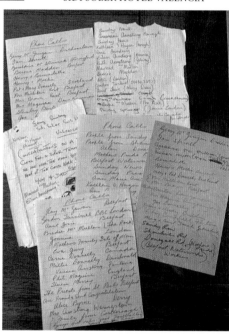

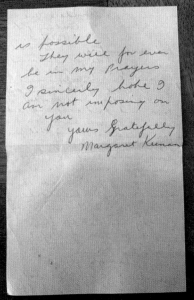

is possible
They will for ever be in my prayers
I sincerly hope I am not imposing on you
Yours Gratefully
Margaret Keenan

Dear Mum & Dad,
Having a great time

We went to the match on Thursday we enjoyed it the atmosphere was brilliant we were speaking to Gerard before and after the Match he has got a great suntan — all the players have. Give our love to wee Paul, Julie regularly misses him she hasn't stopped talking about him Paula sends her love too! We hope to see you all soon. (P.S Hope Jeannie is keeping OK). Love from Us all xxxxxx

Me & Mrs G. Armstrong

HOW LUCKY WAS I TO HAVE SUCH A WONDERFUL
MOTHER, SHE REPLIED TO EVERY LETTER AND
PHONECALL WE RECEIVED THROUGH THE WORLD
CUP, SHE HAD A HEART OF GOLD AND PROUD TO CALL
HER MY MUM.

JOHN O'NEILL   DAVID McCREERY   TERRY COCHRANE   GERRY McELHINNEY   PAT JENNINGS   SAMMY NELSON

N. IRELAND

BACK ROW (L to
Tommy CASSIDY.
Billy HAMILTON.
Noel BROTHERST
Mal DONAGHY.
Chris NICHOLL.
John McCLELLA
FRONT ROW (L
Jim PLATT.
Jimmy NICHOL
Sammy McILR
Martin O'NEIL
Gerry ARMST

1980 BRITISH CHAMPIONS CENTENARY YEAR IFA.
TOMMY CASSIDY, BILLY HAMILTON, NOEL BROTHERSTON, MAL DONAGHY, CHRIS NICHOLL,
JOHN McCLELLAND ,
FRONT ROW LEFT TO RIGHT
JIM PLATT, JIMMY NICHOLL, SAMMY McILROY , MARTIN O'NEILL (CAPTAIN) & MYSELF

Northern Ireland share honours but may still lift championship

WALES 1
NORTHERN IRELAND 1

Pat Jennings gave Northern Ireland a World Cup scare as their British championship finale against Wales ended in stalemate at Swansea.

Gerry Armstrong who scored with a powerful header to beat Southall.

Boxing curb

ARMSTRONG IS SET FOR WATFORD IN £200,000 DEAL

NORTHERN IRELAND striker Gerry Armstrong could be on the move today, leaving Tottenham and £200,000 deal to join Second Division Watford.

By TONY STENSON

FANTASTIC NOEL BROTHERSTON GOAL WINS
BRITISH HOME CHAMPIONSHIP IN OUR
CENTENARY YEAR - ON MY BIRTHDAY

ON THE MOVE

ST. JOHN'S GAC 1973 CORRIGAN PARK

DE LA ALEGRIA...

DEPORTES EL DIA
DE BALEARES
Nº 121 / 19 MARZO

Ayer se disputó en el Lluís Sitjar el partido más increíble que presenciarse pueda. Cuando a los 25 minutos, Gerry Armstrong impulsaba el esférico al fondo de las mallas visitantes, ni él ni nadie de los presentes podía imaginarse lo que iba a ocurrir a continuación. En décimas de segundo se pasó de la alegría al drama, siendo treinta las personas que vieron que ser hospitalizadas, a raíz de la caída de una pared del Gol Sur en la que muchos aficionados se fueron al fondo del foso que rodea el terreno de juego.

El fútbol se escondió tras el telón de la catástrofe y el escándalo, que fueron los que privaron el que había venido a denominarse el entro de la jornada. Un resultó contusionado

■Más de tr

THE DAY I BROUGHT THE HOUSE DOWN

OUR MEN FOR SPAIN '82

"Nobody Frightens Us In Our Group"

GERRY—HAPPIEST IN GREEN SHIRT OF IRELAND

IN these days of mobile, jet-paced forwards—like England's Trevor Francis, Tony Woodcock, and Kevin Keegan—Northern Ireland's number one striker is a throw-back to the good old days.

The big, strong, brave, and direct leader who typified the British style.

Gerry Armstrong is the man. The qualifications fit him like a second skin.

He's big—over 13 stone. He's strong. He's brave. And nobody who has seen him put his head down and go for goal would call him anything but direct.

What people sometimes overlook is the surprising control of the ball he can show when the confidence is flowing.

Unfortunately, Gerry has had little chance to develop that confidence at club level.

In the last four years he has never had a run of more than 16 consecutive matches for 'Spurs, and very often he has had much shorter stays in the first team.

best chances, but the heat took its toll, and we had to rely on Pat Jennings, in the end, to keep a point.

"We came off completely shattered. I've never played

Born in Belfast, Gerry joined 'Spurs from Bangor in November 1975.

With Steve Archibald from Aberdeen, now with 'Spurs, Armstrong could find himself

FIGHTING TALK AHEAD OF ESPANA 82

DANNY'S TOPPERS

Bulgaria .... 0 N. Ireland 2

Warning blitz by Armstrong and Caskey

GERRY ARMSTRONG, on offer at Spurs, doubled his transfer value to £300,000 with a goal that swept Northern Ireland to the top of Group One in the European Championship here tonight.

The Irish are now two points clear of England with their first away win in two years—although England still have a game in hand.

A downpour ruined the game as a spectacle. It was a tough hard running match and two Manchester United players shared the midfield glory—David McCreery and Sammy McIlroy who was replaced in the second half after a knock.

Pat Jennings was in his usual outstanding form and stand-by skipper Bryan Hamilton recovered from a poor start to prove one of the most dangerous Irishmen.

The goal that clinched the game came nine minutes from the end. Billy Caskey, on his debut, flicked on a corner kick from substitute Chris McGrath that had been nodded on by Chris Nicholl.

Armstrong's goal was a magnificent boost for the Irish. It came after only 17 minutes and was a typical Armstrong goal—all courage and pace.

ALEX TONER in Sofia

He gave his shadow Gruncharov a two-yard start, beat him and tapped the ball in after sidestepping the goalkeeper's challenge.

Armstrong had an easier chance 10 minutes later but shot wide from 12 yards after being put through by McIlroy. It

was an incredible miss from an unchallenged position after scoring such a superb goal.

Ireland were hard pushed after the goal and at one stage looked like surrendering the lead.

Instant pressure almost brought a Bulgarian equaliser. Stankov shot over the bar as the referee ignored a linesman's offside flag.

Stankov's break was only one of three anxious moments for the Irish. Jennings had to dash off his line twice to clear breaks from the dangerous little winger Gouchev and striker Gelaskov.

Hard-working Sammy Nelson was also unlucky not to get on the scoresheet when Goranov managed to scramble a free kick from him over the bar.

But Ireland's control in the second half was such that innings was forced to make one real save—a weak shot from Panov, who was marked out of the game by O'Neill.

Then came Caskey's clincher and the start of the shock waves sweeping across Europe to the England camp.

Bryan Hamilton, skipper for the day, said: "This is just another stop on the road Danny Blanchflower has planned ahead. As captain I'm very proud of the lads. And what a bonus for an old guy like me to be part of it."

GOAL-DEN BOY . . . that's Gerry Armstrong as he slips the ball home beating a full-back and the goalkeeper for Ireland's first goal against Bulgaria.

Skipper Allan left to ponder future

ALLAN HUNTER the Ireland and Denmark in

BEATING BULGARIA

ON THE RED CARPET WITH DEBBY AND MY DAD, JERRY Sr.

BACK ROW LEFT TO RIGHT
DEREK McKINLEY, IAN McFAUL, KEITH ROWLAND, JIM MAGILTON , DARREN PATTERSON, PAUL KEE,
GERRY TAGGART, IAN DOWIE , GARY FLEMING, MYSELF AND JOHN McVEY
FRONT ROW LEFT TO RIGHT
PHILIP GRAY, GEORGE O'BOYLE , MICHAEL HUGHES, STEVE MORROW, BRYAN HAMILTON,
NIGEL WORTHINGTON, KEITH GILLESPIE, KEVIN WILSON, GERRY McMAHON

FAMILY. BACK, LEFT TO RIGHT: BRENDAN (SON), AISHLEEN (DAUGHTER), DEBBY, MYSELF, CIARAN (SON), FRONT: MARIANNA AND CAITLIN (DAUGHTERS)

MOMENT OF HISTORY SCORING THE WINNING GOAL AGAINST THE REPUBLIC OF IRELAND

NORTHERN IRELAND
VERSUS
REPUBLIC OF IRELAND

Wednesday, November 21, 1979
at 2.30 p.m.
WINDSOR PARK, BELFAST

THE EUROPEAN
CHAMPIONSHIP

OFFICIAL PROGRAMME
50 PENCE

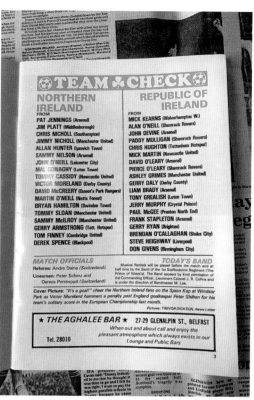

⚽ TEAM ☘ CHECK ⚽

NORTHERN IRELAND FROM	REPUBLIC OF IRELAND FROM
PAT JENNINGS (Arsenal)	MICK KEARNS (Wolverhampton W.)
JIM PLATT (Middlesbrough)	ALAN O'NEILL (Shamrock Rovers)
CHRIS NICHOLL (Southampton)	JOHN DEVINE (Arsenal)
JIMMY NICHOLL (Manchester United)	PADDY MULLIGAN (Shamrock Rovers)
ALLAN HUNTER (Ipswich Town)	CHRIS HUGHTON (Tottenham Hotspur)
SAMMY NELSON (Arsenal)	MICK MARTIN (Newcastle United)
JOHN O'NEILL (Leicester City)	DAVID O'LEARY (Arsenal)
MAL DONAGHY (Luton Town)	PIERCE O'LEARY (Shamrock Rovers)
TOMMY CASSIDY (Newcastle United)	ASHLEY GRIMES (Manchester United)
VICTOR MORELAND (Derby County)	GERRY DALY (Derby County)
DAVID McCREERY (Queen's Park Rangers)	LIAM BRADY (Arsenal)
MARTIN O'NEILL (Notts Forest)	TONY GREALISH (Luton Town)
BRYAN HAMILTON (Swindon Town)	JERRY MURPHY (Crystal Palace)
TOMMY SLOAN (Manchester United)	PAUL McGEE (Preston North End)
SAMMY McILROY (Manchester United)	FRANK STAPLETON (Arsenal)
GERRY ARMSTRONG (Tott. Hotspur)	GERRY RYAN (Brighton)
TOM FINNEY (Cambridge United)	BRENDAN O'CALLAGHAN (Stoke City)
DEREK SPENCE (Blackpool)	STEVE HEIGHWAY (Liverpool)
	DON GIVENS (Birmingham City)

MATCH OFFICIALS

Referee: Andre Daina (Switzerland).
Linesmen: Peter Scherz and Dennis Perrenoud (Switzerland).

TODAY'S BAND

Musical Recitals will be played before the match and at half-time by the Band of the 1st Staffordshire Regiment (The Prince of Wales's). The Band appears by kind permission of the Commanding Officer, Lieutenant Colonel J. R. Collins and is under the direction of Bandmaster M. Lee.

Cover Picture: "It's a goal!" cheer the Northern Ireland fans on the Spion Kop at Windsor Park as Victor Moreland hammers a penalty past England goalkeeper Peter Shilton for his team's solitary score in the European Championship last month.

Pictures: TREVOR DICKSON, News Letter

★ THE AGHALEE BAR ★ 27-29 GLENALPIN ST., BELFAST
Tel. 28010
When out and about call and enjoy the pleasant atmosphere which always exists in our Lounge and Public Bars

3

SPECIAL OCCASION

ny quits on Glory Day

lls after victory Republic

SOCCER: JIMMY DUBOIS
NORTHERN IRELAND 1, EIRE 0

Martin was not injured, it was just a case of manager Blanchflower considering he should bring him off, as he has not played a full game for some weeks for his club.

Cassidy has been playing well for Newcastle United, but somehow just could not get into the game yesterday on a day when there were no failures in either team, but Northern Ireland just deserving to win because of their second half display.

Eire goalkeeper Mick Kearns made several saves during the early part of the match from Spence and Armstrong, with Jennings excelling with fine stops from McGee, Tony Grealish and two headers from Stapleton.

Northern Ireland really piled on the pressure after a scoreless first half and Kearns saved from Spence, then watched helplessly as a shot from the Northern Ireland forward bounced wide off John Devine, followed by a Chris Nicholl effort, which just shaved an upright.

But the pressure finally brought its reward in the 54th minute, when Nelson swung the ball over from the left and as the Eire defence hesitated, Armstrong nipped in to nod the ball wide of Kearns.

The southern team really displayed urgency after this setback and central defender David O'Leary joined in two attacks, was deprived of a possible equaliser from a Mick Martin centre by the alert and well positioned Jennings and even watching a shot from the edge of the box flash just outside an upright.

Jimmy Nicholl had two shots charged down by the Eire defence in which Pierce O'Leary had an excellent game and David McCreery sent a powerful shot over the crossbar from a McIlroy cross.

Grealish had a last chance for Eire with a fine run across

Gerry Armstrong beats goalkeeper Mick Kearns to score the goal which gave Northern Ireland yesterday's memorable victory.
PICTURES BY EDDIE HARVEY

Tie hole exit for

SAD TO SEE DANNY GO

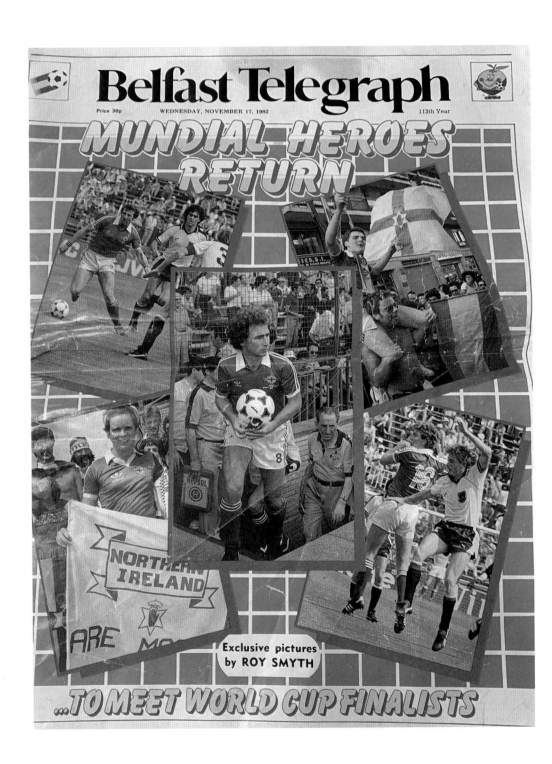

THE BAND OF BROTHERS RETURN

REV IAN PAISLEY AT RIADA STADIUM

WITH SNOW PATROL'S GARY LIGHTBODY

ASSISTANT MANAGER OF OUR WEE COUNTRY BACK IN THE '90s

CHARITY FOOTBALL MATCH AT WINDSOR PARK WITH THE GREAT GEORGE BEST IN ATTENDANCE

BAND OF BROTHERS REUNION

A STAR IS BORN NORMAN MAKES HIS DEBUT V YUGOSLAVIA ,
YOUNGEST PLAYER ON THE WORLD CUP STAGE!

THE HEAT IS ON

THE CALM BEFORE THE STORM IN VALENCIA

ARMSTRONG 1 ARCONADA 0

VICTORY IS OURS! MISSION ACCOMPLISHED!

WITH DAVID BECKHAM AFTER OUR HISTORIC VICTORY V ENGLAND SEPTEMBER 2005

DOUBLE NUTMEGS

JUMPING WITH RAFAEL GORDILLO

TEAM PHOTO AFTER BEATING ISRAEL 1-0 TO QUALIFY FOR THE 1982 WORLD CUP FINALS
LR BILLY BINGHAM, JIMMY NICHOLL, TREVOR ANDERSON, GERRY McELHINNEY, GERRY MULLEN,
NOEL BROTHERSTON, MYSELF, JOHN O'NEILL, CHRIS NICHOLL, SAMMY NELSON, PAT JENNINGS,
FRONT ROW, JIM PLATT, MARTIN O'NEIL, MAL DONAGHY, BILLY HAMILTON, TOMMY CASSIDY,
SAMMY McILROY, DAVID McCREERY

CONSOLATION GOAL V FRANCE, TIME TO GO HOME

THE CAPTAIN CALLED IT RIGHT, SMILES OF JOY

WATFORD IN THE HAPPY YEARS

WHAT A PLEASURE TO HAVE PLAYED FOR THE BOSS AND A GREAT MENTOR

OUR WEE MIRACLE

IF YOU PUT IN THE EFFORT YOU GET THE REWARDS

LIFETIME ACHIEVEMENT AWARD WITH JACKIE FULLERTON, MY BROTHERS KEVIN & EUGENE, DEBBY, MYSELF, DAD & BROTHER SEAN

of that I don't know, but she would take phone calls from everybody and thank them for their support. The amazing thing was it was coming from all parts of the community and I think it showed that underneath all that was going on, the vast majority of people just wanted an end to it, they wanted something good in their lives and they wanted to come together. Looking at those old papers, the Belfast Telegraph, on the front page, it was "Provisional IRA blow up army base" or whatever, and then on the back page is "Northern Ireland through to the finals of the World Cup". It was like day and night.

How did people actually live through that? I'd speak to my parents and family and friends on the phone, but I couldn't really get a grasp of it. I was in England, playing football every day, mostly oblivious to what was going on back in Northern Ireland where people were getting killed and injured, atrocities on a daily basis. We never thought we'd see the end of it. Thank God we have, but we have to make sure it stays that way. People are determined that they don't want it to happen again. A lot of the political groups in the past used to control the people but now people are voicing their opinions and saying, "We're not going to vote for you". Then they need to change their policy. I've seen that develop in the last three years since I've come home and long may that continue.

Back then, Northern Ireland was a hard place to live in at the time with the Troubles. But we did something that the politicians could not do. We brought the communities together. We had telegrams from every part of the community and it was it was brilliant to behold. Later that year, they gave us a big party in the November, there was a big celebration at the City Hall, which was great.

Of course, the job wasn't finished yet. We moved on to play in the second group stage which put us with France and Austria, having won our group – Spain ended up with England and West Germany, which pretty much finished their chances of winning the trophy at home.

Mal was suspended after the Spain game so Sammy Nelson came into the side and Pat Jennings picked up an injury from that Spanish game too, so Jim Platt replaced him for the game against Austria. He was a very good, very experienced goalkeeper, but if we'd had two or three injuries elsewhere, we would have been in a bit of trouble. Austria had lost 1-0 to France in the first game, so they absolutely had to beat us if they were going to have any chance of going through. About 25 minutes into the game, I went on a run down the right hand side and crossed to the far post, and Billy got a brilliant header on it, towering header, plenty of power and we were in the lead. We were very good in the opening 25 minutes but they had made quite a few changes from the France game and they were fresher than we were. I have to say, we were still on cloud nine from the Spain game, we were full of belief, and we played some really good football. We should have won the match but we couldn't get that second goal before half-time.

Then they had a bit of luck because the equalising goal was a shot that deflected off Pezzey's heel, their centre-half, and went into the back of the net, he knew nothing about it, right at the start of the second half. Then they got themselves in front. The wall disintegrated at a free-kick and there was no chance for Jim Platt. Hintermaier hit the ball straight in the far corner, so it was 2-1 with 25 minutes left.

We pulled it back to 2-2, Billy scored again, and we had chances to win that match. I remember being on the halfway line, taking the ball off Pezzey. He had taken a heavy touch and I picked his pocket, I just nicked the ball. I went from the halfway line and there was nobody that was going to catch me and so Pichler took my heels from behind, clipped me. He got booked for it, but I'd have fancied myself going through on a one on one after that with five minutes to go.

It wasn't to be, and that made the France game very tough for us, though Pat and Mal were back for that one. It meant it was winner take all. That still sticks in my throat because we played France a few months earlier in a friendly and lost 4-0 in Paris, but we were a different team by now and they were very wary of us. We played really well again in the first 15 or 20 minutes and there was one particular interchange of play between myself and Martin O'Neill. I controlled the ball back into the space for Martin, he played a one-two with me and I can still see him hitting it, it hit the back stanchion, it was a great goal, but the linesman put the flag up. When you looked at the replay, Martin was at least a yard, a yard and a half onside. If that goal had counted, we'd have done exactly the same as we did against Spain, got everybody behind the ball and made life hard for them, but the fact that we had to win meant we had to take a few risks.

They had several days more rest than us, because they played Austria first, so they were they were probably fresher and we got caught on the counter-attack. Once we went 1-0 down and then 2-0 right at the start of the second half, we were chasing it and, in the end, we lost 4-1 – I got a consolation goal 15 minutes from the end to make it three for me in the competition. But if Martin's goal had counted, who knows, we might have gone through and played the West Germans in the semi-final. It was a bit unlucky, but that's the way it works.

In fairness, the French were becoming an awesome side at that stage. They were better than the Germans in that semi-final and I don't know how West Germany got away with Schumacher taking out Battiston, that was a disgrace. There were a lot of good players in that side, Platini, Giresse, Didier Six, Rocheteau, Tigana, Tresor was a colossus at the back. Bossis, the left-back, I accidentally caught him with an elbow in our game and busted his nose. We were jumping for a ball and my elbow caught him right on the bridge of the nose, a lot of blood! They really did have a fantastic team. Michel Platini came over to me to swap shirts with me at the end, that was something else. I kept quite friendly with Michel when he became president of UEFA. He used to invite me to his golf days. He was a good guy.

That was an end to it all, but the fun we had out there was fantastic, to achieve what we achieved, that was incredible. It was a great tournament personally too. I was voted the best British player and I was the top British goalscorer as well. That was a big achievement for a wee boy from Belfast. I was very proud of that. About four or five months later, they had a big award ceremony at the Café Royal in London and I was allowed to go to the awards to pick up my Golden Boot from adidas. Kevin Keegan was there, he got the Golden Boot as top goalscorer in the league that year. Elton John was my guest, it was great fun. I didn't have so much luck with the premiere of "G'Olé", the official FIFA film of the World Cup. I was invited to attend but Graham Taylor wouldn't let me go because it was too close to a game. I was a bit upset by that because Sean Connery, who narrated the film, was going to be there and I was big fan of his!

When we'd started out on that adventure against Israel a couple of years earlier, there weren't many people who felt that we had any real chance of even making it through to the World Cup finals – Northern Ireland didn't do that any longer. Two years later, we'd not only gone there, we'd made the world sit up and take notice of our football. More than that, we'd made the people in Northern Ireland – all over the island of Ireland – start to think about one another in a different way, start to understand that we had a lot more that united us than divided us. We'd shown that if we came together and worked together, there was nothing that we couldn't achieve. That was the spirit of '82.

CHAPTER TWELVE

....

ROCKETMAN

Our World Cup ended on July 4th 1982 and the next season in England started eight weeks later, so there was only a very short break before I was back hard at work again with Watford in pre-season, but that was fine with me. I loved the training anyway and we had something special to prepare for – a first ever season in the First Division.

When I got back in, nothing much had changed just because it was the top division we were facing. Graham was still confident in his beliefs about how we were going to play the game and he was confident that it would work in the top division too. But he was a shrewd man too. In my first couple of seasons, everything was kicked long but when we got promoted to the First Division, we also got the ball out to the full-backs, and then the next one would be kicked long. We alternated, we mixed it up and so teams didn't know what to expect. Then on top of that, we worked really hard to get as fit as we possibly could and we worked on our strengths – organisation, set plays, discipline, shape. It was a tough shift that we put in to get ready, but it was good fun too.

Graham was brilliant at playing people off against each other. Of all the managers that I played for, he pushed me the hardest to go out and play to my strengths, to do what I could do best and to maximise myself. We were in pre-season at Cassiobury Park in Watford and we would have a break after working really hard in the morning. We were having our lunch on the pitches, five or ten minutes for a sandwich or a bit of salad, and then you'd got another half an hour or 40 minutes to yourself before the next session. Players started playing a bit of cricket, just to keep themselves occupied, and then Graham would give the nod to Pat Rice. Pat would say, "Who wants to take the Paddy on? He's too quick for you." And so he'd have us all sprinting in our lunch break!

A little bit like Northern Ireland I suppose, nobody expected very much from us. A lot of people just dismissed us because we're coming up from the Second Division for the first time, but we had a real belief in ourselves and we wanted to show people what we could do. Graham had a formula that worked and one that we believed in completely. A lot of people said we were lucky to get up, which was nonsense because we were ten points clear of the team in fourth place. There were some big teams in that league then too, the likes of Chelsea, Palace, Norwich, Newcastle, Derby, Leicester. Luton had won the Second Division, played some really good football and scored more goals that season than us, which was saying something. They were a good team under David Pleat, they played attractive football and they had some cracking players, but we were every bit as good as they were. We had quite a lot of young players, but everybody knew what Luther Blissett could do and what big Ross Jenkins could do. Pat Rice was the experienced player along with myself. Steve Sherwood was the goalkeeper, then you had Wilf Rostron, who was originally a left winger as a youngster at Arsenal, he was playing left-back. Ian Bolton and Steve Sims were two big centre-halves who did really well and complemented each other. In the middle of the park was Les Taylor, who was different class, along with Kenny Jackett. We had Nigel Callaghan on one wing, John Barnes on the other, both kids like Kenny, straight out of the youth team. There was a lot of young blood in there and none of them were frightened by what was coming. They were relishing it.

There was a big debate in August '82 over whether I was going to start the first game of the season against Everton after all that had gone on in the World Cup. There was a big question mark in a lot of peoples' minds over that for some reason. Graham told me on the Thursday before the game that I was definitely playing, but I didn't know where he was going to play me after I'd played on the right of midfield in the World Cup. It was strange what he did in the end because he played me up front with Ross Jenkins, who was six foot four. Ross became the target man whereas I was usually the target man for Luther Blissett. He dropped Luther into midfield and that was fine because Luther could play anywhere. Again, that had that element of surprise to it.

Graham always had his own ideas. He said after the game, "I was always playing Gerry. He's had such a run, he's in such good form, there's no way I wasn't playing him." Confidence is so important. When you're scoring goals, you're looking forward to each game coming along. You can't wait for the next one. You just want to get out there and when you get a half a chance, you hit the target or you score a goal. That's the difference. I remember starting off at Bangor, then starting off with Tottenham. In new situations, when you're uncertain of your strengths and your ability, then you don't always do the right thing. If you've got two or three choices, you inevitably make the wrong one! But as your confidence grows and your ability grows, you start making more right choices, you score more goals and you go from strength to strength. You always have lulls when things aren't going your way, but when they happen, it's easier to be positive because you know you've had success before and that it will come round again.

That Everton game was exactly what we needed at the start of the season. We had this belief in ourselves and we just tore into them and things took off from there. We won 2-0 at Vicarage Road and I went into the history books by scoring Watford's first goal in top flight football. Pat scored as well, a shot-cum-cross and the goalkeeper stepped back over the line with it and they gave the goal. Then we went away and played down at Southampton. Peter Shilton, Alan Ball, Chris Nicholl, Mark Wright, Justin Fashanu, David Armstrong, they were a strong side, but we beat them 4-1, they really didn't know what had hit them. The next home game was Swansea City. John Toshack was in charge, they were a good team who had beat top of the First Division in the March of the previous season, so they were a danger, but we beat them 2-1, then we turned over West Brom, 3-0 at home. We'd won four out of the first five, we'd only lost at Manchester City, we were top of the league and people couldn't believe it.

The following week, we played up at Nottingham Forest. I felt that we were the better team, we had about eight or nine shots, we hit the target two or three times but we didn't score. They had two shots and scored twice, so we got beat 2-0. It felt like it was just one of those days where things weren't going to go your way no matter what, but Graham read the riot act to us at the train station, heading back to Watford Junction. He told us, "See you all tomorrow morning, 10 o'clock at the ground." We did the cross-country run on the Sunday. Monday, we were in training again. We finished at half 12 and he said, "Right. You've got an hour. Get your lunch. I'll see you back on the training ground again at two o'clock." So we were out again in the afternoon. Then it was, "Right lads, see you in the morning." Tuesday, training again. At a quarter to one, "Lads, that's enough, have some lunch, I'll see you out on the pitch at two." It was the same on the Wednesday, yet another double session, and by the end of it, we were absolutely wrecked.

After training on Wednesday, he told us to meet up at Vicarage Road on the Thursday morning. There's nearly always a buzz in the dressing room when you get in in a morning, but that Thursday morning, there were no stories, no buzz. Everybody was shattered, all of us still half asleep, tired, aches and pains, everybody feeling a bit sorry for themselves. Graham came bouncing in. "Alright, lads. I don't know what all the long faces are for. I was talking to my wife last night and she said to me, "The lads haven't done badly Graham, they actually played really well at Forest." And I thought, "You're right Rita. They did." So we're not going to train today. Get your tracksuits on, we're going over to the hotel, we'll have a big breakfast and I'm paying for it, not the club. It's all on me." Everybody started smiling and laughing, then the jokes started coming out again, it was happy days, "I could never have done another run", all that sort of stuff. It was just building the spirits up, good psychology.

We went over to the hotel and we sat down in one of the big rooms, bacon, egg, sausage, everybody was helping themselves. Martin Patching said to me, "Ask the boss, can we have a wee drink, a pint of lager to wash it down?" So a couple of jugs of lager came out, and we sat there until half past two in the afternoon, talking about the games, talking about tactics and it was brilliant. It was like a coming together of mates, like a party atmosphere. In the finish he said, "I have to say I'm sorry about this week lads, but I'll see you all at training tomorrow." We went in on the Friday and everything was back to normal. We did free-kicks, crosses, corners. It was an easy morning. We only did about 35, 40 minutes and then we went in, got changed and went home.

The next day, we met at the hotel before the game against Sunderland, and we were really buzzing, we couldn't wait to get out on that pitch. I remember Jimmy Nicholl was playing for Sunderland at the time and I saw

Jimmy when he came in with their team. I said, "Jim, you better be careful today, we're buzzing!" "Oh, we're a good wee team Gerry," he says. It was 8-0. We destroyed them. We ran them into the ground. It was men against boys. They were in the dressing room afterwards for an hour, getting a rollocking from their manager! That was a side of it that Graham was very good at, motivating the players and getting the most out of every last one of us. If you can do that, you get on a roll and then you have belief and faith, and you just keep getting results.

We continued doing well, but then in late October, I got a really nasty injury that put me on the sidelines for about ten weeks. It was a real blow to me because I'd never really suffered with injuries before that. I'd had the odd hamstring and pulled muscle and stuff, but I could play with knocks - most games I played, I had an injury of some sort. I just played anyway, because I was rough and ready. But hamstrings, you can't run, you have to rest for those. I'd had two or three hamstring injuries, but never really anything too serious until I broke the ankle, fibula and tibia at the same time – that was a nightmare.

In the midweek, the players were all off up to Birmingham for the day because the Motor Show was on at the NEC. I wasn't really interested and didn't want to go, so I said to the boss, "Can I just stay here and train instead?" He said, "There's a reserve game that you can play in, that'll be okay, just play the first half." So I get ready for that, but five minutes into the game, I went up to win the ball and as I headed it, the centre-half came and hit my legs. I spun in the air, I went 180 degrees, and I tried to land on my right leg. But as I came down, I landed on the ankle and I just went over on it. At the time, I thought I'd sprained my ankle ligaments, no more than that. I didn't know I'd broken it. I tried to get up and walk but I couldn't put my weight on it and so I came off.

I came home and I remember going to bed and thinking, "Let's see how it is in the morning." Billy Hails was our physio and I had arranged it so that I was going to Vicarage Road to see him at ten the following day. But by two o'clock in the morning, I was in absolute agony. I couldn't even bear the bedsheets to touch my feet. I had to get up. I had a set of crutches and it seemed to be better when I was up and the blood was running properly. At about 6.30, I couldn't stand it any longer, so I had to phone Billy and I told him, "I'm in a lot of pain here". He came and picked me up, took me straight to the Watford General Hospital, and we got there about seven o'clock. I went in and they did the X-ray and told me I'd broken my leg and ankle. I couldn't believe it. I had the surgery done that afternoon, the surgeon put it all back in place and put me in plaster. I was in plaster for six weeks but I still trained every day. Billy would pick me up, he'd bring me in, and I did my weights. Then after I was out of plaster, I had to get fit again.

It's funny looking back, but Graham Taylor never spoke to me for about four or five weeks after I got injured. He'd come into the treatment room and he just ignored me. After five or six weeks he said, "Gerry, I'm not being funny, but until you're fit, you're no use to me. Get fit and then I'll have a chat with you again. You've got the right mentality, I know you'll be fine." I think it was two or three weeks after I came out of plaster that I played against Luton in the reserves, and I scored. I got a kick in the second half on the ankle and it was really sore and I started to get worried about hurting it again. You do have a hesitancy after a nasty injury like that and in training the next week, I would normally have been straight through people in tackles, but I wasn't. I was tentative and you just can't play like that. I got annoyed with myself and thought, "If it's gonna break, it's gonna break," and I just went in again. Once you do one tackle, you know you're fine and away you go.

The team kept going well and I got back in the side around the February. We were so consistent that season, we kept on picking up points wherever we went, whoever we played, it was a great season. We beat Tottenham home and away and I knew exactly why we beat them. We were better prepared than they were, and of course we had that surprise factor that a new team can exploit as well. When you're watching these players play week in, week out on "Match of the Day", we all knew what Glenn Hoddle could do, we knew what their players were about. We knew that if we put them under pressure, and played at a really intense pace, they couldn't stick that pace with us, because there wasn't any team in the league that could. There wasn't anybody who had that stamina, that determination and the strength and power, just because we were a young, hungry side. And at that point, nobody knew who John Barnes was, who Kenny Jackett was. He was a central midfield player, naturally left footed, and he knew that you don't take any chances. He just hooked the ball on, and him and Les Taylor screened the two centre-halves. When we had the ball, it was 4-2-4, if we didn't, it was 4-4-2, Barnesy and Nigel Callaghan would shuttle back.

Everybody had to work. If you didn't work, you wouldn't be in the team, you wouldn't get selected. Those were things that I started learning much more under Graham. Football was a lot more committed, with a lot more contact involved then, and it certainly suited the Watford style because we put ourselves about. The tactics worked. Teams didn't like it, they couldn't handle the pressure. And once again, just like Northern Ireland, it was all about the group, not the individual. You don't get success if you don't have team spirit. It's as simple as that. You have to be 100% behind each other, you have to believe in each other. You have to know their strengths and their weaknesses. You have to realise when your team-mate is in trouble and you've got to go and help him. Those are all things that come through bonding, and it's a bonding that happens over time. When we arrived in Division One, we would do anything for one another, we would go through brick walls for each other.

We had a really good finale to the season, but we were a fitter team than anybody else so that didn't surprise me. We beat Liverpool 2-1 at Vicarage Road in the last game of the season to finish runners up to them. They were 11 points clear in the end, but we had to get something from that game to finish above Manchester United. That win was evidence of how much we'd come on across the season, because we'd played at Anfield in December and we were 3-0 down at half-time. I was watching the game and the players were a bit shell shocked. Then Graham gave them a rocket in the dressing room and in the second half, they blew Liverpool away and scored after about 15 minutes. The last 25 minutes, Hansen and Lawrenson were kicking the ball over the stand just to get it away because we were all over them like a rash. That's the way we played, with that momentum, keeping the pressure on them.

Who would have imagined we could be runners-up to that great Liverpool side in our first crack at the First Division? Second place in the First Division is the highest position Watford has ever achieved, probably ever will achieve given the way the game has changed, and it took us into Europe, the UEFA Cup, for the following season. Once the steamroller got going, it became very hard to stop us. It was crazy how many games there were where it was a real battle for 70 minutes, really nothing in it, and then in the last 15 or 20 minutes, the opposition would start to flag only to find that we were still flying. We would just run over the top of them and win lots of games in that period because physically and mentally, we were so much stronger. It was a phenomenal season.

Every year, Watford had a players' do at the end of the season at a place called Bailey's in the town. It was a big nightclub, it must have held at least 800, maybe 900 people in it, loads of famous bands played there over the years. The players had to go and perform at this night, they had to do different things like comedy routines, dancing, singing, but John Ward and Steve Harrison wrote the script for everything. They had Nigel Gibbs as Orville the Duck. Steve Terry was a big centre-half, six foot three, and he was the ventriloquist and Nigel was the duck and they had him sat on his knee with a big duck's head on. The script was brilliant. Pat Rice was the subject of "This Is Your Life" and John Ward was Eamonn Andrews. He said, "Now Pat, your two sons are here today to celebrate with you" and out comes Charlie Palmer and John Barnes!

The rumour went around that Elton John was going to perform at the end, as a special surprise for the fans. I even got Pat Jennings to come down and watch it as a guest, because he's an ex-Watford player anyway. He was on the floor laughing at some of the stuff. At the finale, there was a piano on the stage. Some Elton John music starts playing and out comes this guy and initially, I thought it was Elton, in all the gear. But it turned out it was Steve Harrison dressed as him. He started playing the piano and miming the song. He had his foot on the piano, playing it. Then he was leaning over the top of it, playing from above. One part of it, he actually jumped off the piano and they had a trampoline at an angle. He hit the trampoline and somersaulted back onto the piano again, holy shit! The fans loved it.

At the end of that season, the club were going off on a trip to China, which was a big deal at that time. I was playing in the British Championships first, so were Luther Blissett, John Barnes, Kenny Jackett. We missed the first two or three days of the trip and the first game. After we'd finished our international games on the Saturday, we met at Heathrow Airport, got a British Airways flight to Hong Kong, stayed over and then we flew into Shanghai.

We turned up at Heathrow, and we had been told that to travel, we had to wear the full Watford suit, tie the whole lot, so we were fully kitted out. Lo and behold, who's on the same flight as us but the Liverpool team, off on their end of season trip, a bit more relaxed than we were. The Liverpool staff went to the back of the plane and left the players in the middle to get on with it during the flight – and they were a riot. Kenny Dalglish and Graeme Souness were the two main men. They all just sat and drank the whole way, which we would never have been allowed to, that was Graham Taylor's level of discipline, you were representing the football club. Graeme had this little gadget, he had a fiver attached to a very thin line. He threw the fiver in the aisle and people were coming up, they'd see the fiver and as they bent to pick it up, it would shoot straight back into his hand! They had a rule that you had to stay sober, but if you got drunk, you could get abused. One of the younger players got pissed. Bruce Grobbelaar, Mark Lawrenson, the whole lot, they undid his trousers, got his jeans round his ankles, got some shaving cream and spread it all around his balls. Then they pressed the buzzer for the hostess to come! Those were the pranks that went on. We certainly got our eyes opened, Luther, Kenny, Barnesy and me. We arrived in Hong Kong and had a drink with them. They were going out for the night, but we couldn't go with them because of an early flight the next day. We were only up with them for an hour.

The next day, we arrived in Shanghai at about half two in the afternoon and the lads were all sitting at tables in the foyer of the hotel. Graham and some of the directors were on one of the big round tables, and Elton John, who came with us, was sitting with one or two of the lads and there was another table with some more players. They were all looking really low. I said, "What's wrong?" "We're not allowed a drink. The boss said we're representing Watford Football Club, he says he doesn't want any problems." That's a bummer at the end of the season, so we were telling them what the Liverpool lads were getting up to.

I said to Elton, "You're the boss, you own the club, tell Graham we can have a drink."

"No, no, he's the boss, not me! I'm not telling him anything!"

So I said, "Right, then we'll have some coffees."

"I don't want a coffee".

"Yeah, you do. You do. Trust me." So the coffees come up and I took over. I put my hand down in my bag and I had a bottle of Drambuie from the duty free. I brought the cups underneath and poured a slug into each. We were like big kids. Elton thought this was hilarious. And, of course, I ordered another round of coffees, so suddenly, the bottle of Drambuie was done. Elton said, "Don't worry". John Reid, his manager, was with him, and he called him over.

"John, discreetly go and get a bottle of Drambuie from behind the bar and come over and slip it under the table, by Gerry." They hadn't got any, so Elton said, "Get a bottle of brandy instead." John comes back – bear in mind this is 1983 – and says, "It's 50 quid a bottle!" So Elton says, "Well, get fucking two then!" We were in tears by then.

Elton was always, "You go and pay for it John". We went on a trip, out to the people's store and we were in the garden part of it. They had these massive stone statues of the Chinese lion, six or seven feet high and about four or five feet wide. That must have been about seven or eight feet long, they weighed tonnes. Elton said, "They are gorgeous. I'd love two of them in my garden. John, find out how much they are." I think they were five grand each, so he had two! It cost a hell of a lot more than that to ship them back to England. Then we went inside and we saw all the jewellery, cashmere jumpers and stuff like that, it was dirt cheap. It really was for nothing. The boys walked around, picking presents up and Elton sees this peacock. It must have been a foot tall, all different colours and it had gemstones in the eyes and the plumage. It was amazing. There were 30 or 40 different diamonds in it. Elton said, "I fancy that." He sent John to find out how much and it was tens of thousands, but he had it – that really was a different league! You could tell where he got it from though because the one year, we went to Jamaica. Elton couldn't go on the trip for some reason, so he sent Sheila, his mother, instead. She was hilarious!

Watford was a fantastic place to be and through the years I've always kept an eye out for it. My old skipper from Spurs, Steve Perryman he went in to manage the club in the '90s. Glenn Roeder was in the team, coming towards the end of his career, but a good influence on the dressing room, so Steve offered him another year. Glenn was very gracious about it, but he turned him down and he said, "I'm going out to Lazio with Gazza." Glenn knew Gazza from his Newcastle days and he was going as a bit of a minder really.

About a month later, Steve got a call from Glenn. "Hi Steve, sorry to have messed you about, but that offer of an extra year you made me? I'll take it now if that's ok?"

"Sorry Glenn, I've got somebody else in now, I've used the budget we've got.

Why aren't you going to Italy?"

"About a week ago, Gazza was getting ready to go and he came and stayed with me. We went to bed and the next morning, my wife woke up and at about half past eight, she took him a cup of tea in. She went in, dropped the cup and screamed. I jumped out of bed and ran in to see what the problem was. In the middle of the night, Gazza had gone down to our garage and got some paint, and he painted the ceiling bright red. My wife said, "There's no way we're going to Italy with that lunatic!""

After coming back from China, there was a little break and time to have a think and reflect on an amazing season and an amazing three years at Watford. I had already learnt so much, Graham Taylor taught me so many things. I had never trained so hard in my life as at Watford. We worked hard at Spurs and we were fit, but nobody really pushed you to get that extra 5% out, though in my case maybe that was because I was always in the top group, I didn't have to push myself that hard. But at Watford, when I went there, there were ten players who were faster, stronger, more athletic than me because they'd been doing this with Graham for a long time - and they would be training twice a day. Graham really upped the ante for me and got me to an unbelievable level of fitness. Looking back, if I'd known that earlier, I probably could have done more at Tottenham, but I just thought I was doing the right thing, doing what was asked of me. Graham asked for a lot more!

Years later, he did an interview with me on the pitch for BBC at Old Trafford when I was assistant manager at Northern Ireland. I said then that without him, I wouldn't have been the player I was at that World Cup in '82, because he got me to a level of fitness I'd never had before, mentally too. A lot of what I achieved there was down to him. I was someone who could lose my concentration. I'd have two or three great games and then I would turn up and not think about it too much. That meant that I wasn't doing what I had done in the previous two or three games, so I'd end up getting the hook, getting taken off the pitch. Graham wouldn't stand for a drop in performance. So then Ross Jenkins would be in and Ross had played along with Luther Blissett for years, they had a real good understanding. Ross was a giant, he won everything in the air and Luther just gambled on knock downs and flick-ons, he knew where they'd be going. I would be sitting on the bench and trying to get back in again, kicking my heels, but when you got your chance, you had to take it, because if you didn't, you wouldn't get another chance for another month. That was good competition.

I was looking forward to another season of it and the chance of taking on a fresh challenge by playing in Europe. I did end up playing in Europe the following season too, but not in the way I would ever have imagined.

CHAPTER THIRTEEN

VIVA ESPANA!

The only nagging doubt I had in my mind as I went back for the 1983/84 season at Watford was whether or not I would get enough football, whether I would be a regular starter. Everything had gone fine for me there until I broke my ankle, fib and tib, but after that, it was hard to get back in the side and although I got a lot of substitute appearances, I only made one start once I was fit again. Fair enough, the boys in the team were doing so well that they deserved to play, but it was very frustrating.

You have to remember it was a very different game back in those days. We didn't have any squad rotation when I played. If you had a winning team, you never changed it. You'd keep the same formation, you'd keep the same players in there and it was all to do with maintaining confidence and belief. If you got injured and were out for a long spell like I was, it could be hard to get back in again once you got fit. Somebody had to have a bad game, and not very many people had bad games at Watford, because we were on a really good run. I was nicknamed The Judge for a while when I was fit, because I was sat on the bench so much! You only had the one sub as well of course, so that made it even more difficult.

Because I was on the fringes and not starting games, a lot of clubs did come in and showed interest in me, but as far as I knew, none of them had actually made a big bid. It seemed to me that it was just a lot of paper talk and I wasn't that worried by it, I was looking forward to a fresh start and getting my place back over the course of pre-season. Then in the summer of 1983, I remember getting a phone call from Graham Taylor saying, "Gerry, it's true that we've had quite a few clubs come in to ask about you, but this club has made an offer. It's Real Mallorca. They want to come and speak to you." Once I knew the club were happy to let me talk, I thought there was nothing to lose by speaking to them.

The agent came over and we had a girl who was acting as an interpreter. I remember going to the hotel in Watford and trying to find out as much as I could about the club because I was really in the dark about it all. We didn't get Spanish TV on football in those days, so I knew nothing much about it. The agent said, "It's in the top flight, they have just got promoted. The Estadio Lluis Sitjar stadium is for 35,000 people."

So I said, "What's your average crowd?"

"It is 35,000."

"Full houses every game?"

"Yes, we do".

Interesting! So I asked about the players. They'd just signed Andrés Sabido, and I remembered him playing in the European Cup final against Liverpool for Real Madrid. They had Paco Martinez, he'd been playing for Barcelona, a left footed midfield player. So they'd signed a Barcelona player, a Real Madrid player, they had others coming in from Racing Santander, another one came in from the Canary Islands. There were loads of players being signed, and I thought, "You know what, nothing ventured, nothing gained." They asked me what kind of salary I would require. I was earning £500 a week at Watford, and that was a decent wage to be earning in 1982. I didn't know what to ask for, but I thought if I was going to go over there, for all the upheaval for the family and everything else, I'd got to be asking for at least double that.

The more I talked to him, and the more questions they asked, the more doubts I had in my mind. I wasn't entirely convinced, but in the end I said, "Look, if you want me to go over there, you're going have to pay me a lot more money than I'm earning here." He said, "The President wants you," so I asked for a contract worth £60,000 a year and he agreed it straight away! I couldn't refuse that because I couldn't earn anything like that sort of money in England. It was an interesting opportunity, but I didn't begin to realise how it would change my life in the years ahead, the opportunities it was going to present to me long-term with that Spanish football connection, because I had years commentating on La Liga as a result of that. It was an adventure, but I felt it was a risk worth taking, particularly for that kind of money.

It was obviously a big gamble going there. Very few players went from here to Spain, I was one of the first, it was more typical to go to Serie A. The likes of Ray Wilkins and Liam Brady went the same time kind of time as me, but out to Italy. It was a leap of faith from my point of view, to take a chance and go to Real Mallorca. It was an opportunity to try out football in another country and find out what it was like. As I discovered, it was totally different. I learnt a lot by doing that. Not many players had ever taken that sort of a gamble, and with my record against Spain in 1982, it was an even bigger risk! But I felt it was worthwhile doing it at the time, that was my gut feeling. I was excited to go to Spain and with the fact that I'd had such a good tournament in '82, I felt good about it. I'd lived in Spain for three or four weeks during the World Cup and had enjoyed it, it was a good time, so all the omens were there. I was pleased to do the deal and join Real Mallorca. A few other clubs were interested, like Seville and there were West German clubs too, but I made the right choice. Mallorca was probably a nicer place to live than Dusseldorf!

It was an adventure, but there were periods of frustration early on, with the language especially. I was living in a hotel in Can Pastilla with a player called Juan Carlos Veron, an Argentinean lad, lovely fella, but he couldn't speak English and I couldn't speak Spanish. We would be in the room together and he would be talking away in Spanish and I wouldn't have a clue what he'd said, so I got my phrase book and started trying to learn words. You think you're making progress, but I couldn't string them together! That's the hard part. I'd go down to the pool after we'd finished training. He put his fingers towards his mouth and go, "Comer, comer?"

"What, eat?"

"Si. Comida?"

"Si".

We'd go to the restaurant, and all the staff there could speak German, French, Spanish, English, Dutch, they were all multilingual, so the waiters were my interpreters for many, many weeks. It was part of the process, but I knew I had to learn Spanish. It took me probably about five or six months to learn enough to be able to do interviews properly. Even a year later, I was still learning, two years later, there's words even now that I still don't know. But it was very frustrating early on and the language barrier did create a few issues between me and some of the players.

I remember the first game of the season was against Zaragoza. We drew 1-1 and I thought that as a team, we played pretty well, though Zaragoza wasn't one of the biggest clubs in Spain. Our goalkeeper was a guy called Tirapu, he was always making jokes and taking the piss out of me. He would say, "Something, something Gerry" and they'd piss themselves laughing. This went on for weeks. Veron was my mate and he never laughed. He always put a scowl on his face. But Tirapu crossed me one time too many after this Zaragoza game. I had a diving header near the end and their keeper saved it - that would have been the winning goal, which would have been a perfect start. I was a bit pissed off and went in the shower after the game and Tirapu was in there with several other players. He said something, I don't even know what he said, but I know it wasn't nice. I got him with a right hook and he went down and the players all ran out of the shower.

The manager - they call them Mister in Spain - came in and he didn't speak English either. He started shouting at me and then Veron started in saying, "Listen, Mister, he's been taking the piss out of Gerry for three, four weeks now. He's out of order." So the manager held his hands up said "Okay, no problem." That was the end of it. I had made my mark and made a point, but then I became even more determined that I was going to learn the language and be able to communicate. The rest of the players respected that and responded. I remember trying to learn words like spoon and cup and saucer and knives and forks. And if I said it slightly wrong one of the players would put me right, they would help. Because they knew I was trying, they would help me and that was good, and that created a bond, a team spirit.

Our results weren't great, the first four or five games, we weren't winning enough matches. There were seven new players who'd come into the club, myself included, and it was taking time for things to gel. Then we played Barcelona at home. I remember scoring my first goal against Barcelona. It was a shot from Barrera from the left hand side and the keeper had made a save but I came in with a diving header at the far post and headed it down into the bottom corner. We were 1-0 up, and that was after Maradona had looked sensational in the first 10 minutes. Then after we scored, he really turned it on. He did stuff I've only seen George Best do, he was unbelievable. They beat us 4-1, he scored, Schuster scored, Carrasco scored.

Playing against Maradona, I just went, "Wow!". His acceleration, his touch was unbelievable. He just was amazing. Maradona would control the ball and then he was away and nobody would catch him, he was special. You know when you're in the presence of somebody who's especially gifted. The last 10 years, I've watched Lionel Messi and Cristiano Ronaldo a lot while I've been covering Spanish football. When Real Madrid finished training, Ronaldo would go off with a bag of balls and start practicing free-kicks. If you work hard at the game, then you're going to get the rewards. Even if you're naturally gifted like Messi, he still has to work hard at the game. Gary Player used to say, "the harder I work, the luckier I get!" That's a great point. But playing against guys like Maradona was something else. He was amazing at Barcelona, just different class.

We were in trouble early on in the season, we weren't getting results. The thing that annoyed me was when the games were over, the players used to just take a shower, go out of the dressing room and walk about 100 yards to their apartments, go and see their family and spend the rest of the day there. There was no players' lounge, none of that. You played, you went home. That was it. I like team spirit, I like the bonding I'd known at Watford and with Northern Ireland. To me, that's so important. I was trying to explain this when one of the directors was talking to me. He spoke good English, he'd gone to college in Dublin. I was saying that the team wasn't functioning as a team. He wanted to know how to fix it. I said, "Look, when I play for the international team, we're all best mates. Same at Watford. We're all friends, everybody helps each other. Why don't we get everybody down to where my apartment is on the beach in Portals?" We had a big swimming pool for all the apartments, right on the beach. We had a private pier for diving and swimming. I said, "What about getting the players down here and have a bonding session, have a barbecue?"

We got the players to come down about six weeks after the season had started. I said the players would pay for all the meat for the barbecue and the President said, "I'll get the wine. I'll get the dessert." So it was a big effort, everybody came down, all the families were there, the kids, the wives and we had a big barbecue and everybody got to know each other. The seven new players got to mix with everyone and we had a ball, a lot of fun.

The following week, we went away and we won 3-0 at Sporting Gijon – we only won three games all season, drew 15, lost 16, we drew way too many games. With a draw, you think it's fine because you haven't been beaten, but we did that too often. But after winning that first game, I said, "Right, next week we'll have the barbecue again!" Then the third week, Paco Martinez said, "We can't keep doing it at your place Gerry, next week we'll go to mine." He was just outside Palma, he had a bit of space in his garden, so we started sharing it around. The bonding and the closeness of the players was better, we got better as a unit.

As things came together in that way, it was just a breath of fresh air to play in Spain. I loved it. It was a great thing to be living in Mallorca. I learned when I went to Spain that they really did admire the British style of football. They didn't have that type of battering ram up front. That's why I ended up going there, but there was an interesting variety of teams over there. The Basque teams, they were strong and physical, more like the British game. There were technical teams like Atletico Madrid. They had Hugo Sanchez, wow, what a player he was. Left footed Mexican, small, but he could do it all and he was top goalscorer for five seasons out of six in La Liga at Atletico and then Real Madrid.

I learnt a lot about tactics because we were very defence minded, we played five at the back quite a bit. We would put four in midfield and I would be up front on my own, I was a lone ranger. I had to try and make the ball stick for them to come and support me. Rafael Guillardo was our sweeper, and he was a tall lad but technically, he was brilliant. He could dribble, he could nutmeg people, he could do it all. But he couldn't tackle. I like my defenders to be able to tackle! It was swings and roundabouts. I found out an awful lot about the Spanish game over a short period of time.

In the September, Northern Ireland played Austria in the European Championship qualifiers and I'd only been at Mallorca a couple of months or so. I got a calf injury in the game and my knee was swelling. I went back to Mallorca and that weekend, I couldn't play. That didn't go down too well with the president, and then I missed the following game as well. The big problem was we had people who could play wide positions, but there was no other centre-forward, nobody to make the ball stick. I had a meeting with the president and one of the other directors. The insurance policy the Irish FA had only covered half my wages when I was injured, so that was a problem for the club if I got an injury and was out for a while. There were some big qualifying games looming and the club weren't going to let me go – and they had all the players' passports in the safe! In the end, I had to get my own policy to cover the international games. You'd get £200 to play in an international, and the policy cost more than that. But I got the policy, showed it to the president and they allowed me to join the squad.

In Mallorca, in training, everything was done with the ball. There wasn't the same level of hard, physical running. I felt my fitness level drop as a result after three, four, five weeks there, because I needed that running we'd had at Watford. I still couldn't speak Spanish at that point, so I was floundering a bit. The warm up was just five minutes jogging, sometimes you were jogging on the spot, you weren't even making any movements going forward, and when we were running, you had to keep up the pace of the coach. He went at a really slow pace and you couldn't go past him, you had to stay behind him. We jogged round the pitch, and it could take four or five minutes for one lap, whereas if I was doing that at Watford or Tottenham, we'd be doing that in 70 seconds, jogging at a steady pace. I had to embrace it and understand that it was a different country, they had their own ways.

The stretches before training were a lot longer, I actually liked that, they made sure you weren't going to pull a muscle, and then it was all ball work, one touch, two touch football, they loved head tennis too. When I was at Watford there was definitely a lot more structure to it, but I could see the benefits of both approaches. The problem for me was that I needed to stay at that level of fitness where I knew I had the pace and had the strength to go past people. I wanted to do more physical training. After one session, about six or seven weeks in, I thought I hadn't done enough. We'd been training for about an hour, maybe an hour and a half and I'd not even broken sweat. The coach called an end to it but I thought, "I'm going to do some running, I need it." So I started running. I did from the goal line to the six yard box and back, then to the penalty area and back, then to the halfway line and back, then to the far penalty area and back, to the far six yard line and back and then the goal line and back.

Some of the players actually stood and watched me doing it. Then I took a breather for 20 seconds and they were shouting at me in Spanish – I couldn't understand what they were saying! Then I did the same run again. Four of them had watched and it turned out they were the Argentinean players. They had a similar ethos in terms of keeping fit and doing a wee bit extra. Then I started doing my abdominals, 200 sit-ups. I used to do 200 nearly every day when I was at Watford, and you hit them in sets of 40. A few of the boys came over and joined in with me. I finished them and we went in, and by now I had a good sweat on, I'd done my running, I felt a bit better in myself, the endorphins were going. When we got back to the hotel, my friend Veron asked me why it was I'd been doing extra training, and I explained I didn't think we were training hard enough physically, that I was used to a different thing in England, and that I didn't want to lose my fitness level. He agreed with me and asked if he could join in with me, along with two or three of the other boys. That started another bit of bonding amongst us.

I was really getting into it as my time at Mallorca went on, and the fans really took to me because I gave 120%. They loved the fact that I had time for them as well. But whenever I went on the Spanish mainland, especially the trip to Valencia, that was a different story! It was October, November time and my Spanish still wasn't great. There was a really bad atmosphere there, but I didn't notice it, I just got off the coach like you normally would. As I got off, there was shouting and screaming - and it was me they were shouting and screaming at! I got hit with everything. They threw apples, oranges, bananas, eggs, you name it, the whole heap was chucked at me. I had to duck and run through to get to the dressing room. The players were all looking through the window laughing because they knew what was coming. It had been in the press that morning, "the guy that knocked us out of the World Cup is coming back and don't forget to give him a good reception". This was the norm apparently in Valencia, so they gave me that sort of reception. Certain parts of Spain would treat you differently, like Seville. The further south we went, the worse it was!

Nothing much happened against Real Madrid at the Bernabéu, but I had to play centre-half because we had a big injury problem. I had to mark Santillana, which was something else because he was a bit special. He was a very good target man, he scored a lot of goals. My job was to stop him scoring and I did do that, but they still beat us 1-0 with a fabulous goal from outside the box, a 25 yard volley.

I remember the Barcelona match in Camp Nou. We desperately needed points and the president tried to give us a bit of incentive. I think our standard bonus was £200 or £300 for a point, so he doubled it. Some of the lads weren't on the big money, so that geed them up. About 15 minutes before we walked out for the game, the president came in and he said, "treble bonus". I tell you what! Damian Amer was our hard little midfield player, a real character, a Mallorcan lad, and he kicked lumps out of Maradona that day, he kicked him all over the place! Maradona's face, he was not happy! But we played really well and we took the lead in the second half. We had a substitute come on, and about five minutes after he came on, he pulled a hamstring and couldn't run, and we couldn't replace him, we were down to ten men. It was backs to the wall for the last 10 minutes, but they equalized. If somebody had offered us a draw beforehand, we probably would have taken it, but we needed more than one point. We needed a lot more victories and we didn't get them.

The day before that game, we were in the hotel, and the four Argentinean lads in our squad were all big friends with Maradona. They phoned him up and said, "We're in the hotel. Do you want to meet up for a beer?" That was about half nine on the Saturday night, and we went across to a wee coffee and beer place across the road from hotel. I was in with the boys and listening to Maradona, it was so funny. Just great stories, great company. I got chatting to him, because my Spanish was coming on, I'd been there over six months so I was able to communicate better. Listening to someone like Maradona talking - those were the days!

Coming towards the end of the season, we had a big game against Valladolid and we were on a really good run at the time. They were fourth from bottom, and we were third from bottom, but we were closing the gap on them. If we won, we would go above them. I scored after about half an hour, I went on a run and hit one from 20 yards and the crowd went crazy - the stadium was always full. We had this dry moat round the pitch, and the fans all surged forward and the wall broke. Fans started spilling and falling and it was an eight feet drop onto the concrete below. There were about 20 or 30 bodies slammed down and I thought, "Shit, this isn't good." It wasn't. Thankfully, the stewards got in and started pulling people off each other. The worst injury was for somebody who landed badly and broke his wrist but thankfully there was nobody seriously hurt because it could have been much, much worse.

145

The game was stopped for a while and then we carried on. We had one player, Juan José Estella, who came from Barcelona, technically a very good player, but he wasn't one that made lots of tough challenges. But he went in for a tackle and the referee blew the whistle, gave the free-kick and booked him, for nothing much really. I was shocked that he got booked and then about 15 minutes later, he went in for a 50/50, and the other player over-reacted. They all did in Spain, they all over-reacted. Their guy goes down, our boy gets booked again and off he goes. I thought it was ridiculous. We were down to 10 men. Then we had another player sent off, Zuviria, so we were down to nine, and I ended up playing centre-half.

They had a Uruguayan centre-forward, Jorge Da Silva, he was decent, he wasn't a bad player. The ball was played over the top and I turned to go with him. I can still see him put his two arms out as if he's going to catch the ball. He controlled it with both his hands, and then he hit it on the volley into the back of the net. It was a hand ball all day long. But the referee gave the goal and the crowd went crazy. And I mean, crazy. The match ended up a draw and as we came off the pitch, the ref had to get a police escort, the fans chased him all the way to the airport.

With my broken Spanish, I heard the arguments going on in the corridor, because the referee's room faced the two dressing rooms. It wasn't like a normal, narrow corridor, it was quite wide. There was the president of Valladolid, there was the president of Mallorca, there was the referee, the players were standing there and Paco Martinez is trying to explain to me, as best he could, that they were saying money had changed hands on the result. There were accusations being made everywhere. The big show there on a Saturday night was "Estudio Estadio", like "Match Of The Day", it showed all the goals in the top flight, and our manager and our president were interviewed on the pitch about the incident where the fans fell, and then about the argument in the dressing room corridor area. There were a few accusations made on TV and then we were barred from playing at home. We had six or seven games left in the league, and we still had a chance to stay up, but it meant we could have no more home games, all our games were away from home. We were relegated as a result. It wasn't nice, but it's part of a learning curve, you see things that happen in different countries. It was an introduction to what life was like in Spain and how things are done differently to the UK.

I finished their top goalscorer that first season, I was in double figures, so

I can honestly say my finishing must have improved, because I never had that many chances. Whatever half chances I got, I must have been taking them! It was a big change from Watford with lots of crosses coming into the box, lots of opportunities to get shots away and I had really thrived on that. But with Mallorca, it was more tactical, and you wouldn't get that many opportunities, plus we were struggling at the bottom end of the table. My finishing ratio was pretty high, but I did feel the pressure of being expected to score every week.

I think the way I played the game, that typical British centre-forward style, impressed them over there, it offered a different dimension. A couple of years later, I met Michael Robinson and he said he'd had an offer from Osasuna, up in the north of Spain, Pamplona. He was asking what it was like and I told him, "Spanish football is right up your street because they don't have enough hustle bustle centre-forwards like you and me, you'll be perfect for them." He took a gamble on that and he had an incredible career there, on the pitch and then off it. He was huge. He was interviewing the presidents of Barcelona, Real Madrid, he used to go and interview golfers like Seve Ballesteros, he was a huge name there.

Both Michael and myself had good careers in the media in Spain after we'd finished playing, the people took to us, maybe because we had the bravery to go there before anyone else did from this country. I think because we were from outside, that helped, because we weren't associated with Barcelona or Real Madrid, which is always a big thing in Spain. People have always said to me, "Are you a Barcelona supporter? Are you a Real Madrid supporter?" Neither, I'm a football supporter. I appreciate the likes of Ronaldo and what he did at Real Madrid and the goals he scored and Raul and the goals he scored and all the different star players over the years but then I equally enjoyed watching the likes of Maradona and all the superstars that played for Barcelona. I loved watching Messi, I loved watching Xavi. Not being pinned down as a supporter or a player for one of those sides is an advantage for a broadcaster over there I think.

Over the season, the reality was that ours was a team that wasn't really ready soon enough, we needed months to gel, which was too long. We got better as the season went on, but we were drawing too many games. That was the reason why we got relegated. But personally, it was a learning curve and it was a life lesson, that's part of the journey. Obviously getting relegated was all doom and gloom because the players had signed contracts for two or three years, the club were hoping to stay up. I had another year on my contract and I was just looking for us to bounce back. I wasn't frightened by going down. Just like in England, there were some great teams playing in their second division, Celta Vigo for one. You have to look for the positive sides and for me, it was playing football, getting paid good money, and living in a lovely part of the world. I felt we were in with a shout of going back up, and like I had at Tottenham, I wanted a chance to put things right.

That following season, we were a bit inconsistent, and personally, I had a couple of injuries. I got a couple of bad ones and maybe because I'd turned 30 then, I started to feel them more and it took longer to recover. One came when we were playing Barcelona's B team. We were at home and a cross came into the far post. I was coming onto it, so I threw myself at it, diving in to get the header and the goalkeeper was coming out at the same time. It was a 50/50. He knew I was coming in with my head, but he came out feet first, and he caught me. Luckily, he didn't catch me in the head, but he caught me on my side and he ended up breaking three of my ribs. That put me out for about six weeks. Injuries are the worst thing for any footballer. It's great when you're able to train every day and you can play. But when you stop, start, stop, start, it's horrendous. We all know the horror stories about somebody who's been out for two months, they come back, they play two games and in the third game, get injured again. That is a total nightmare, a disaster. Every player will tell you, certainly those from my era, that most of the games we played, we were carrying some sort of an injury, a knock of some sort, but you got on with it, you played through it. Sometimes though, you just can't and that was the case with my rib injury. But eventually I got over that that and got back in the side.

We were going pretty well, still in the promotion hunt. We were in the top four or five, but only two teams went up. I pulled my hamstring for the second time that season, about six or seven weeks from the end. I knew it would take at least a couple of weeks to get right, but the big game that was coming up was Celta Vigo away. They were pushing for promotion as well, so we had to get a result. Ahead of that game, they sent me and another player to see a bruja, which is like a witch doctor, and he put hot herb poultices on my hamstring. I wasn't allowed to run, I was just doing a little bit of walking. The team were going to arrive four or five days after us and the hope was that I was going to be fit to start the game. I didn't do any training, I just got the treatment, then two days before the team arrived, he got me to start doing a bit of jogging and stretching, and that felt really good. I only had about six or seven days of treatment, but we were hoping it would be ok.

On the Sunday, the morning of the game, I did a bit of light jogging, no sprinting, just took it easy, but it felt good. I told the manager that and he put me in the starting XI. I felt ok, but I was playing within myself. I never tried to sprint in the first half. I was a bit wary of going flat out. The game went ok, we played pretty well, and we got to half-time at 0-0.

I was waiting on an opportunity where I could get one on one with the centre-half, because I fancied that I could outpace him if I get the right service. There was about 25 minutes to go, it was still 0-0, and Pepe Delgado stuck a pass through in between the centre-half and me. I knew this was the time that I just had to go for it. I hit the turbo and I remember sprinting past the centre-half, I was flying, and the ball was about seven yards in front of me. As I was getting towards it, I just felt the hamstring go, it went straight in the same spot again. I grabbed the back of my leg and that was me off with the pulled hamstring. We never got another chance and they scored three or four minutes from the end. That was our campaign over. It was so disappointing because the club needed to bounce straight back. Had we done that, I probably would have stayed on.

Of course, there were other considerations apart from football to weigh up. At the end of that second season, Ciaran was coming up to being eight, Brendan was six and a half. The boys started their schooling when we were back in St Albans and then when we moved to Spain, both went to the American College there. The first thing they did was learn Spanish and even though we were only there for two years, that was enough for them to pick up the Spanish language. It was a great experience for them, going to live in Mallorca and experience life abroad and learn another language. I didn't really want to move back from Spain to be honest. I liked the life there and Mallorca were trying to keep me on, even in the Second Division, which I was considering, but Ann didn't really want to stay, she wanted to go back.

The big issue was the boys were getting a bit older and was it better for them to go back and get their education in England? I do think learning languages was a big plus for them from living in Spain, but anyway, we came back. There was a possibility of going to France at that time too, because my manager at Mallorca was a French guy called Marcel Domingo. When we didn't get up, he left at the end of the season, that's how they are over there, they change their managers every year sometimes. He went back to France, to Nimes, and he wanted me to go with him because he knew I could do a job for him. I had another offer to go and play for Sporting Lisbon at that point too, but I didn't fancy going through that settling in process all over again. It seemed the time had come to go back to England.

Coming back to England in the summer of 1985, I hadn't got a club fixed up, and so when pre-season started up, I trained at QPR along with Ray Houghton. Jim Smith was the manager there and he wanted to sign both of us. That would have been handy because we had moved back to St. Albans and it was just a 15 minute drive to the training ground. Then Jim told us he couldn't sign us because the Chairman, Jim Gregory, wouldn't give him the money until he sold some players first, but we could still train there until we got fixed up. That was a blow, but I got a phone call the next day, from John Giles and he needed a centre-forward at West Bromwich Albion. I loved John because he was a Leeds player and I had been a big fan of his as a kid, so I was really excited by it and we sorted an agreement out.

Albion had a good squad at the time. Derek Statham was playing at left-back and Derek was so unlucky to be playing at the same time as Kenny Sansom or he would have had loads of England caps. Big Ally Robertson was playing centre-half, Jimmy Nicholl was there, which was great for me, Garth Crooks too, who I knew from Tottenham. Mickey Thomas was on the left, he was a great little footballer. Imre Varadi was there, Gary Owen, we had some cracking players. They had a really decent side and they had some good youngsters coming through like Steve Bull, Carlton Palmer and Gary Robson, Bryan's brother. It was a lovely club, good bunch of lads, Nobby Stiles was taking the reserves and the kids, Tony Brown was there as a coach as well. I was happy to sign anyway, but then I got a call from Crooksy. "Big man, we can travel up to training together!" He was in London, I was in St Albans, so he'd drive up to me and then one day we'd go up to West Bromwich in my car, the next we'd go in his, sharing the driving. It sounded good to me.

We started off the season and we had a terrible time. We drew the first game at home to Oxford and then lost nine in a row! John didn't like the fact that we weren't playing the way he wanted, he was very particular about what he wanted from us. We lost 3-0 at Coventry at the end of September and then he walked into training on the Monday and said, "I've got better things to do than watch that rubbish!" He gave us all some real stick, told us what he thought of us, and away he went. Nobby Stiles was in charge for a while as caretaker and then Ron Saunders took over. Nobby was a lovely character but I don't think he was strong enough to be a manager, and he didn't fancy it anyway.

When Mr. Saunders took over, the first thing he said was, "Anybody who doesn't live within a 25 mile radius will not be selected." Jimmy Nicholl and Steve Mackenzie were travelling from Manchester, Mickey Thomas was travelling down from Wales, Imre Varadi was coming from Sheffield, myself and Garth Crooks were driving up from London, so half the team were travelling. That was the end for us! I enjoyed that trip with Garth every day. We had our conversations on the motorway on the way up the road and put the world to rights, we'd pass an hour and a half chatting on the way up. But it did get hard going. When you've trained that day, and then you jump in the car and travelled back down again, it was difficult to get your hamstrings straightened out and you were tight as anything.

When Ron came in, I was injured, I'd got an intercostal muscle problem in between my ribs. George Wright was the physio, he was brilliant, and he took me for acupuncture on it. That started to help, but it kept me out for about 10 or 12 days, and that's when Ron Saunders was appointed. I still couldn't train so I was out of the picture, but I remember him reading the riot act to the players. He slaughtered Jimmy Nicholl, Mickey Thomas, Steve MacKenzie, Crooksy, everybody. Everything was negative about him. He was giving a load of stick out to the players and I was sitting there thinking that I was glad I wasn't fit!

I was able to train about a week later and I got my fitness level up pretty quickly so that I was ready to play in the reserves. Ron said to me, "I need a centre-half. I remember you playing centre-half at Spurs so you're playing tonight for the reserves against Leicester." I was alongside Ally Robertson, Steve Bull was up front, Gary Robson in midfield, it was a half decent side. We kept a clean sheet, won the game and I did well, I marked Mark Bright. I always found playing centre-half dead easy. Win the ball in the air, don't commit yourself, and I had enough pace and experience that I knew where the players were going to go. It was an easy game to play for me. We came in afterwards and Ally said, "Big man, you did well today. He'll have you in the first team at the weekend. Obviously he doesn't know where you live!"

Ron walks in. "Well done lads. That's a great result. You're all off tomorrow except you Gerry, I want you in with the first team. I've got my centre-half for the weekend." I drove home, phoned Crooksy to let him know I was training the next day and we went up together. He couldn't believe it. "You're in the squad? You're kidding me?" We were in the car laughing all the way up talking about it.

We got to training and as soon as I walked into the dressing room, somebody said, "Gerry, the boss wants to see you in his office." So I go into the office.

"You never told me you lived in London!"

"You never asked!" One of those conversations - I was dropped from the team before I even played! The writing was on the wall, but I had the World Cup coming up in Mexico in '86, and I needed to be playing games.

The next day, I got a phone call from John Duncan, because the story about me and Ron was already on the grapevine – news travels fast in football. John was manager at Chesterfield at the time, and of course, we'd played at Spurs together. I explained what was going on, how Saunders wouldn't pick me or any of the other lads from outside the area. John said, "Look, we're second bottom of the Third Division, I am absolutely desperate for a striker. You could come and do me a big favour. Come here on loan to the end of the season."

There were about a dozen games left, so I thought about it for a bit and I decided it was the best way to get games, because I wasn't going to get any with West Brom. We worked it all out. I signed for Chesterfield for the season and John allowed me to train at Tottenham. I organized that with Peter Shreeves, who was manager, he'd taken over from Keith Burkinshaw. Pat Jennings was training there as well, which was brilliant. We went and trained and we did what everybody else did.

Peter played me at centre-half in training matches because he remembered me from first time around and he said, "Gerry, I've tried to sign you for Spurs again to play centre-half, but the club won't do it because you're coming up to 32." It probably didn't help that I caught Chris Waddle in a tackle in one of the games and put him out for a week! I'd travel up to Chesterfield on a Friday for games. It got me seven or eight games,

Chesterfield stayed up, so everyone was happy.

I was fit again, sharp from those games and now, I had a second World Cup to look forward to that summer.

CHAPTER FOURTEEN

BRITISH CHAMPIONS – AGAIN!

Coming back from the 1982 World Cup was an incredible experience because we began to really have our eyes opened as to just what an impact we'd made back home. We'd seen the telegrams and the messages in the hotel out there but when we went back to see friends and families after the competition, we started to hear a bit more about it at first hand. The tales about the celebrations, the street parties and all that had gone, they were incredible, as was the fact it cut across all the divides in the community. Whatever your denomination, whichever side of the Irish border you were, everybody was genuinely thrilled by what we had done.

The shame of it was that our first game after the World Cup was away from home, a European Championship qualifier out in Austria, because it would have been nice to play in Belfast straight after that. I don't think our mentality was quite right for that game, we were probably still on a high from the World Cup and we weren't as focused as we normally were in that sense. We didn't play particularly well, we conceded after three minutes, we were 2-0 down at half-time and that was how it finished. In the end, that proved costly to our chances of qualifying.

The next game was the homecoming, West Germany at Windsor Park in November '82. By then, I'd broken my leg and ankle at Watford and ordinarily I would probably have stayed at home, but the day before the game, we were having the welcome home party from the World Cup. We went on an open top bus through the streets of Belfast, there was a reception at City Hall, all of that, and I was stuck on crutches! It was a memorable day though and something very special for the country.

It's an amazing wee country is Northern Ireland, it punches way above its weight as a sporting nation. Our population is probably about 1.9million, something like that. When I was playing back in the '80s, it was a lot smaller than that, probably 1.5million, so for us to qualify for two World Cups and win two British Championships in the 1980s was incredible. But then go back to 1972 and Mary Peters winning a gold medal at the Olympics, that was absolutely amazing. Joey Dunlop, the top motorcycle racer in the world, he won event after event. We've got the boy Jonathan Rea at the moment who's the Superbike world champion, won six world titles in a row. Then you look at golf, Graeme McDowell, Darren Clarke, Rory McIlroy, all of them have won majors. All from this wee island. We've got great boxers like Carl Frampton, snooker players like Alex Higgins and Dennis Taylor, both world champions. Great rugby players. George Best, maybe the greatest footballer who ever lived. How is this possible?

I don't know if it's because of the circumstances in our history, the partition and then the fact that Northern Ireland became an entity in itself, yet still wanted to be part of the United Kingdom. Then we've had the Troubles, the civil rights issues, the bombings and everything else, so the people have been through an awful lot and maybe it's been a reaction to that, some kind of an escape? Through it all, there's a determination and a fantastic attitude here, I've always found that. They really do give you 120% and they always find a way to be different from the herd as well.

Look at Dennis Taylor and Alex Higgins, they are chalk and cheese. Dennis was just as good with his right hand as the left, being ambidextrous was a big advantage. Dennis was very, very professional, that was his key, he worked hard at his game, considered every shot. Alex was the complete opposite, a one off, an artist. He wouldn't spend half a second setting up, then, bang, he'd hit the red straight in the top corner, the cue ball goes around two or three cushions and drops in front of the black. That's just pure talent, all completely natural and he played off his instinct. Northern Ireland has produced so many naturally talented stars, athletes, actors, singers. It's just ridiculous. I have a lot of pride in what this country has achieved.

I took a lot of pride from that West Germany game in 1982 too, even though I wasn't playing. A day after all the celebrations in Belfast, up against the World Cup finalists, it wasn't the most promising set up for the game, because again, the players' minds could have been elsewhere, but the boys were brilliant. Ian Stewart scored after 20 minutes and from there, we did exactly what we'd done against Spain, only with 11 men this time. We won the game 1-0 and we were back in the picture for qualifying. That was a fantastic effort, but it underlined exactly what that squad was about. There was a really solid mentality about that group and I have to say that team was pretty special.

We had a 0-0 draw in Albania that I also missed and then I was back fit again for the home game with Turkey, which we won 2-1, then we won the home game against Albania. At the end of the 1982/83 season, that qualifying group was pretty tight. Austria were top with nine points from five games, we had seven from the same number and West Germany were two points behind us with a game in hand. When we came back the next season, we really opened everything up by beating Austria 3-1 in Belfast in a game we absolutely had to win. We were just so confident every time we went out onto Windsor Park, we never thought we were going to lose there, and we always felt we could beat anybody. We'd lost 1-0 to Wales in the British Championship in May that year, but before that you had to go all the way back to October 1979 to find the last time we'd lost at home. Football clubs talk about making their home a fortress, but it's no different in international football. In fact, its probably even more important because there are so few games in qualifying groups and you have to make them all count.

Austria lost again in their next game in West Germany and that pretty much ruined their chances. Our game in hand was in Turkey. They were well out of the running, so it was a big opportunity for us. We should have won the game, we had some good chances. I had a diving header where the goalkeeper made a great save, Jimmy Quinn had another chance, but we ended up losing the game 1-0. Ourselves and Austria had nine points with one left to play, and our last game was in West Germany, who also had nine points, but with two games left.

The fixtures were pretty strange because whereas now, you would try to have everybody playing their last game together to make sure there was no fixing of results or anything like that, back then Austria played – and lost - in Turkey and we went to Hamburg, but then West Germany finished off the group against Albania four days later, which was obviously a big advantage to them.

For us, it was the Spain scenario all over again, we had to win in their country, only this time, it still didn't guarantee us getting through. It played out in very much the same way as the Spain game had. Billy had us set up really well, we were organised and we still had real consistency in the team. Eight of the players who started against Spain also started in this one nearly two years later, with Gerry McElhinney, Paul Ramsey and Ian Stewart coming in for Chris Nichol, David McCreery and Sammy McIlroy.

The real plus though was that Norman Whiteside had got two years of regular football inside him. He'd barely played a senior game when we went out to Spain in '82. He was already a man then, at 17, but now, two years later, he was scoring goals for Manchester United for fun. He had a great left foot. He was physical, he was so good in the air, he had it all, he was world class. Had he not had his injuries that finished his career far too early, Norman would have been something really special. He took on the responsibility that night in Hamburg and he scored five minutes into the second half. From there we all did our jobs, we worked so hard, and we saw the game out. We'd won in Hamburg and we became the only team to beat West Germany home and away in any qualifiers for a major competition, and that is still the case with Germany to this day. But would it be enough?

Nowadays it would, because it meant we had a two point lead over West Germany and, even if they had won their final game to level things up, we would have gone through on the head to head results. That wasn't the way they were doing it then though unfortunately, because everything was decided on goal difference. They had a much better goal difference than us, so all they had to do was beat Albania at home in that last game. It was much closer than we'd expected and they didn't get the winner until the last ten minutes of the game, but we were out and that was a tough one after getting such great results against West Germany. But it happened for a reason, because it was a reminder that in a group format, every single game counts and you have to be at your best in every one of them. Those points dropped against Austria, Turkey and Albania were costly and we were determined we weren't going to let that happen again in the World Cup qualifiers that were coming up.

Before that, we were straight into the British Championship, which was being played across the season rather than in a single week at the end of it. We already knew it was going to be the last one because England and Scotland had announced they were pulling out of it after that 1983/84 tournament, which was a pity. We got off to the best possible start by beating Scotland 2-0 at Windsor Park. We played really well that night and they were never in the game after the first few minutes. We played England at Wembley in the April and we had plenty of chances but we didn't take them and ended up losing the game 1-0 which was disappointing because we really did deserve more out of it than that.

Our last game was against Wales in Swansea. Pat Jennings got hurt late in the first half, diving at the feet of Ian Rush, and he had to go off and then Mark Hughes put them ahead early in the second half. I scored to put us level and the game finished 1-1. It turned out that that was one of the most important goals I scored for my country because England drew with Scotland a few days later which meant that all four countries finished on three points. This time though, goal difference was our friend and we came out on top. We had won the competition outright for the second time in four years and, as we've never played the competition again, we're still the holders!

I must say, I didn't want the British Championships to finish. We learnt so much playing England, Scotland and Wales every summer, it was fiercely competitive and that's where you learn. When you're away as a squad for three games over a 10 day period, there's a real bond that draws you together. It's not like where you meet up for three, four days, then you go away again. That was the key, seeing your mates and having that bond. That's where the strength really develops. We all loved each other's company, we loved meeting up, we loved the banter and the craic that came with it. We all knew every strength and weakness of every member of the team. I look at some of the friendly matches that are played now and I wonder what they get from those games. The games in the British Championships meant something. For me, it was playing in those that created that team spirit and the understanding on and off the pitch that carried us to Spain in 1982.

After the disappointment of just missing out on the European Championships, now we needed that spirit to take us to Mexico in '86.

CHAPTER FIFTEEN

....

END OF AN ERA

Going into qualifying for the 1986 World Cup, things were a bit different to four years earlier. We were probably even more confident in our ability as a group now. We'd got the monkey off our back in '82 by qualifying for the first time in 24 years, so we knew it could be done. We'd beaten West Germany home and away, we were British Champions, we were that bit more experienced at the top end of international football and in Norman Whiteside, we had a lad who was now fully matured and was approaching world class, at the age of what, 19?

The draw wasn't the easiest. We were in with England, who were obviously the big favourites to win the group. We had Turkey again, and we remembered how we'd dropped points against them in the Euros, then the group was rounded out by Romania, who had Hagi in their side, and Finland. After coming so close in the Euros, we knew that every game, every point, every goal would count. We didn't get off to the greatest start, losing 1-0 in Finland, but then Windsor Park came to our rescue again. We beat Romania 3-2 in a really good game and then we came from behind to beat Finland 2-1. I scored the winner, a penalty, and that was my 12th goal for Northern Ireland, which put me joint top of the country's goalscorers with Joe Bambrick and Billy Gillespie, though years later, they discovered Billy had actually scored 13! I'm still joint fifth on the all-time list and that's an achievement that means a lot.

We slipped up at home to England, Mark Hateley got the only goal of the game late on, then we beat Turkey 2-0 in Belfast, Norman scored twice. Billy Bingham had been quite cute with arranging the fixtures because after that opener in Finland, we then had four straight home games and we got some good points on the board with three wins. It meant we then had a better idea of what we were going to need to do away from home in the latter stage of the group. The disappointment was that we started that run off by drawing 0-0 in Turkey. We should have won that game and won it well. We had chance after chance but we couldn't score. Me and Jimmy Quinn had opportunities, the keeper made a couple of good saves, we missed some good openings, but it was a big blow not to win. The same night, Romania got a draw at Wembley, so again, we came to the crunch game – we had to go away and win in someone else's country, this time Romania. We heard that they hadn't lost at home in a World Cup qualifier for over 20 years, but those were the kind of situations we always relished. Jimmy Quinn scored after half an hour and, yet again, we stood firm through the rest of the game, we didn't concede and we got ourselves back in the driving seat in the group.

The last qualifier was at Wembley. England were already through with 11 points, we had nine and Romania, who were away in Turkey, had seven. A point would see us go through to the World Cup and the game ended 0-0. People said it was fixed, but Pat Jennings made seven or eight saves in that game and some of them were unbelievable. We defended for our lives, Jimmy Nicholl headed two off the line, you can't plan any of that. Alan McDonald got really annoyed about it when people were saying England were helping us get over the line and finish second. He said afterwards, "We had to work hard for that, England played well. Anybody thinks that was fixed, tell him to come and see me!" which was a great quote. He was right as well though. That was how we played, organised, hard to break down. Just like when we'd qualified four years earlier, we were a difficult side to score against. We only conceded five goals in eight games and two of those came against Romania when we still won 3-2.

We were absolutely thrilled to get through to the finals again, especially because a number of us knew this was going to be our last hurrah. Although we had experience, it also meant that the problem we had in Mexico was that as a group, we were all getting too old. We were not the same squad as in Spain, four years is a long time, a lot of things change, players had got older. Pat was 40, I was 32, Sammy McIlroy was 31, Jimmy

Nicholl was 29, Martin O'Neill had finished, John McClelland was 30, and ended up not getting a game, which I thought was crazy. We had some younger players like Stephen Penney and Ian Stewart who were talented boys, but you need a bit of experience to play at a World Cup and they hadn't had that. We didn't have the same nice balance that we'd had in Spain. But all the same, we were really looking forward to having another go at the World Cup.

The big question mark was over Norman Whiteside, who had had a bad year with injuries. He was going to play the World Cup and was booked to go for an operation straight after it on his knee. He'd already had one before that, but it hadn't worked completely. The draw wasn't much help either - we had Brazil and Spain in our group, as well as Algeria. We weren't frightened about Algeria but we knew Spain were going to be difficult, they owed us from '82! Brazil in Mexico were going to be very difficult too, but we were ready to have a go.

In preparation, Billy took us off to New Mexico so that we could do some training at altitude. It was fun, but it was hard work. The players had a great craic, the spirit was good, and those boys that were having their first World Cup, David Campbell, Jimmy Quinn, Alan McDonald, Steve Penney, Bernard McNally, Nigel Worthington, they were all really excited. Nigel was the fittest player we had out there, he could run all day. He'd been playing under Howard Wilkinson at Sheffield Wednesday, so he was really prepared for it.

The conditions in New Mexico were something else. It was the same heat as Spain but the altitude is something you can't acclimatize to, because your body needs months to get used to playing at 8, 9 or 10,000 feet above sea level. We couldn't get that kind of time obviously, and we knew we were snookered after a day or two of training. Billy Bingham got us a great hotel, the Hilton in Albuquerque, about 6,000 feet above sea level, near the Sandia mountains. He had us run up this mountain and the top of it was about 10,600 feet above sea level. It was ridiculous. The boys were breathing out of their arses, it was hilarious. That was where it really hit us. Wee David McCreery was having a nosebleed halfway up the mountain with the altitude.

Once we were up at the top, Billy had us doing 400 metre and 600 metre runs. In groups of four, we'd run the one lap on the top of the peninsula.

163

It was 80 odd degrees, so we had the humidity and the heat and the altitude to deal with. All the players were finding it difficult - even the warm up was difficult! Billy called out the first group. "David Campbell. John McClelland. Gerry Armstrong." The boys were looking at each other and saying, "Don't want to be in this group!" And the fourth one was Alan McDonald, and he put him in on purpose because Alan wasn't as fit as he should have been, and Billy wanted to make a point. Alan went, "Oh Jesus, I'm finished now, I can't run with you boys!"

I said we'd keep it steady, nobody would go crazy and John was fine with that, he was happy to help Alan out. David said nothing, he was 20, trying to impress, so next thing, David sprints away! John says, "Sorry lads, I'm going to have to go now," and he sprints after him. Big Alan says to me, "Don't leave me Gerry!" But I had to go, "Sorry Big Man, you're on your own, all the best!" So I chased after them. John caught David, then I did, then I caught John and came in first, then John, then David and Alan was 20, 30 yards behind. Billy laid into him and Alan told me that he'd said that if he didn't get fit, he wouldn't be playing in the World Cup.

Sammy McIlroy was captain, but he used to tell me to talk to Billy, "He'll listen to you, he won't listen to me!" So I had a chat with him. "We had a really hard session today, the boys put it in."

"You're right, I was impressed, especially up on the plateau. They can have the morning off tomorrow."

Sammy came over and said, "So what's going on?" I decided I'd have a bit of fun and I told everybody we were going up on the plateau again, doing the same run up there. Alan looked at me and said, "That's it. I want my bed. I'm not even having dinner. I've got to lose some weight." So off he goes and we had to go and get him back down and tell him I was only joking. You had to make your own entertainment in those days!

Billy wanted to get us fit, the way he had ahead of the World Cup in '82, he had us running up the mountain and trying to handle the altitude after we'd all finished long, hard seasons, where before, we were doing cross country runs over the Downs. It was a bit different! We were running up the slopes and it wasn't a proper walkway, it was like a dirt track and so the gravel was slipping under your feet. Jimmy Quinn damaged the underside of his foot as a result. He bruised it and though we didn't realise it then, it was that bad that he was never going to play in the World Cup. But we did the best we could with the 10 days that we had.

The one time we were running, a helicopter came over and it was Jackie Fullerton, the main television guy from UTV and BBC. He came and watched us run up this mountain and got the helicopter to come down lower to get better shots. Of course, that just churned up more dirt. We were all shouting, "Fuck off Jackie!" He was up there saying, "Oh, look, the lads are waving to me!"

While we were there, we played a friendly match against Scotland. Jock Stein had died not long before the competition, and Alex Ferguson had taken over the Scottish team on a temporary basis. They were hardly training, just going for walks and stuff like that because Alex said there was no point trying to get used to the altitude, there was nothing you could do, your body would just do it in its own time. We would run hard in the morning, do some real physical training, then in the afternoon, we'd do ball work, crossing, set plays, shape. When we played the friendly, there was an agreement between us that the game was going to finish a draw, but because we were training harder than them, we were much better prepared and we went 3-0 up in the first half hour. Second half, we were taking it easier and Billy was telling us to let them score. They got one, then another and we wanted the ref to blow the whistle and get us all off because it was getting hotter and hotter. Billy was telling John McClelland to give away a penalty, foul somebody, anything. So the ball comes into the box and John just punches it away! "Not like that John!"

We still had such great team spirit, and we had great craic, but dealing with the boredom in those training camps is a big thing. Every day we tried to do something different to break things up. We played golf, we went to the New Mexico racetrack and watched four or five horse races, the boys all had a bet on - that's the sort of thing you have to do to break the monotony, to keep the squad happy and all together and on the same wavelength. I had a few words with Billy about giving the players a drink, because we weren't supposed to because of the altitude and the impact the alcohol had on you. But the players needed a chance to relax, we were training hard, the boys needed to let their hair down. Eventually he agreed that though we couldn't go out, he'd let us have a few drinks at the bar. We sat and had a few until about 11 at night, but once a few lads had had a couple of beers, they didn't want to pack it up! A few of the players were already sneaking out every night to a wee bar across the road, Charlie's. Martin Harvey, one of Billy's coaching staff, used to come over to me and say, "Billy thinks some of the players are sneaking out to the bars." Pat Jennings and I looked at each other, "No? Really? Is that right?" He said, "I've been told I've got to go over to Charlie's bar across the road and check it out. I will be going in five minutes. If you want to go and just check it first before I go over, that would be good!" So we'd go and tell the lads, they'd leave and then Martin could go in and then say to Billy, "I went to the bar, and there was nobody there boss!"

About four or five days before our first game, we headed into Mexico and set off for Guadalajara. We checked into El Tapatio, the hotel, which was on top of a mountain in the middle of nowhere. It was even worse than the hotel in Albuquerque because we couldn't get out, there was nowhere to go, and FIFA had taken all the alcohol out of the hotel. There was also police all around the place because they were afraid in case somebody tried to kidnap a player. Fortunately, I could speak good Spanish now, so I was communicating with the police guys and organising stuff with Billy. He utilised my skills to talk to the chefs every day and tell them what we wanted and how we wanted it cooked, if we wanted chicken or pasta or fish or whatever. It was much more relaxed, but there was nothing to do. We were all in chalets and all you could do was walk around the grounds to try and stretch your legs. You have to keep players occupied on those trips. It can't be all just football, football, they need time where they can unwind. The lads couldn't watch TV because they didn't understand the language, so they needed a snooker table, or table tennis, darts or whatever. We were bored out of our minds. That's when it got really stupid!

One day, Billy Hamilton said to me, "Gerry, have you seen the size of these rats? Wait 'til you see them." I'd seen all these big holes in the garden and the next thing, one sticks his head out and comes out of the hole. It must have been the size of a badger! It wasn't a rat, so I asked one of the policemen, "What's this thing?" He said, "It's a tiacuache, they only come out at night. Really good meat!" It was like a possum, and I couldn't believe they'd eat them, but he said the people had nothing to live on and they looked on these things as a delicacy. He said they weren't dangerous, so I said, "Come on, we'll catch one!" The lads were playing cards, so I thought we'd catch one and throw it in the room where they were playing. The policeman was killing himself laughing.

I remember trying to corner it, I got round one side of it and the policeman got around the other side. As soon as I put my hands down to grab it, he said, "Behind his neck!" I went to grab it and you want to see the teeth this thing had! I held it down and he had a bit of string and tied it round its snout so it couldn't bite. It must have weighed seven or eight pounds, and we took it in to the chalet where they all were. Billy Hamilton said, "Jimmy Nicholl is my room-mate, let me get him out first." Norman Whiteside was sitting at the end of the table, there was Paul Ramsey, Jimmy and Colin Clark, I could see quite a few of them. I stepped in, pulled back the curtain and threw this animal onto the table. It landed on its claws and slid along the table and landed on Norman's lap. He absolutely lost it, but before that, I'd already heard this scream, because Colin Clark's wife was in the room as well. Paul jumped up and as she was running for the bathroom, he knocked her out of the way, got into the bathroom in front of her and slammed the door! We got the tiacuache back, I took it out, cut the chord off it and let it on its way, back to its hole. That was the sort of thing we did to keep ourselves amused!

What did become obvious in those preparations was that we were confronting a different scenario to Spain, totally. The circumstances meant we were never ever going to be able to run and chase and be in the opposition's faces for 90 minutes, which is what we did four years before. You just can't do it there because of the altitude on top of the heat and humidity. We'd play great for the first 20 minutes and then we were busted! We just ran out of energy.

Looking ahead to the group, Spain and Brazil were two of the best teams in the competition, not the Brazil of 1970 or 1982 maybe, but still a really good side, and obviously, the climate suited all the South Americans. Technically, they were very good, they could keep the ball better than we could. It meant there was a lot of pressure on our first match, Algeria. We needed to win that one and we should have, we had chances. Norman scored very early but we couldn't get the second goal and then in the second half, they equalised. It was pretty disappointing for us and for me, it was a frustrating game because I was on the sidelines, just watching on. It was great to be there, but like any player, I just wanted to be on the pitch. But age catches up with you, especially in those conditions. Steve Penney played where I had in Spain, on the right of midfield, with Norman and Billy Hamilton up front.

I was still looking on for the Spain game, though Colin Clarke, a bustling centre-forward, came in for Billy Hamilton in that one. Spain had lost to Brazil in their first game, so they had to win and looking at the fact that we still had Brazil to come, so did we. If we won, Spain were out, and so they came at us like a train from the start. Butragueno scored in the first minute and Julio Salinas made it 2-0 after about 20 minutes, he was a good target man. Colin played really well up front and he got one back right at the start of the second half, he got to a header before Zubizaretta and nodded it past him, but we couldn't get an equalizer. Spain were the better side on the day and they probably deserved to win.

I didn't get a chance to play in that game either and I was a bit disappointed in that. I felt Billy could have put me on against Spain or even started me, because I'd played out there, I knew their players and how they would play. I felt I was better prepared to play against Spain than anybody else we had in the squad given my experience. I knew they'd be wary of me, not just after '82 but having played out there for Real Mallorca, and I felt I could have contributed something in that game especially. I'd trained really hard, I was really fit, so I can't say it wasn't frustrating, because it was. John McClelland was in the same situation, which surprised me because he looked in good shape, but in the end, Billy went for Alan McDonald and John O'Neill at the back. I think Billy felt that in the heat and the altitude, those of us who were 30 and over were going to struggle.

We went into the Brazil game with just one point and honestly, we couldn't see ourselves progressing. We would have to win to have a chance of getting into the top two and even then it might not be enough. There was a chance of finishing as one of the best third placed teams, but we would need at least a draw for that against a great side. Deep down, I think we all knew that it was going to be a last hurrah, all on Pat Jennings' 41st birthday, on the 12th of June, at the Jalisco Stadium.

We lost 3-0, Careca scored twice and Josimar scored that incredible goal that is still getting shown on TV and on social media today. It moved everywhere. It did everything except loop the loop! I was watching it from behind and if you'd have had three goalkeepers, they still wouldn't have saved it. It looked like it was going two yards wide of the left hand post and two yards too high. And then it just started moving and it flew in. Even though we lost 3-0, Pat was absolutely brilliant that day, he made three or four saves from one-on-ones, just to keep the score down. If Pat hadn't been in goal, it would have been six or seven. He was the best goalkeeper I've ever seen, but he just kept on going. I phoned him not long ago, in the summer of 2021, and Pat was still coaching at Tottenham at the age of 76. He was complaining to me that his right knee was killing him! "I'm half-volleying the ball from 30 yards at the young goalkeepers, and it's starting to give me a bit of gip!" If I'm half-volleying the ball from 30 yards at 76, I'll not be complaining!

I was on the bench for the Brazil game, Billy Hamilton as well, and second half when we were 2-0 down, we needed a goal to give us a lift. Billy Bingham said to us, "Get warmed up boys, you're going on." We went for a warm up and as we started running down the side of the track, the crowd just erupted and started screaming. Billy looked at me and he says, "What's that all about?"

"Come on Billy, they know all about Armstrong and Hamilton over here. The Mexicans know who we are!"

He was doing some stretching and he couldn't see what I could see behind him - Zico was warming up at the same time as we were! Zico then comes jogging past us and Billy says to me, "You big bastard!" Both of us came on for the last 20 minutes of the game. We saw the end of it, which was a fitting way to bow out, because that was my last game for Northern Ireland. It was the end of an era because Jimmy Nicholl finished then, so did Pat Jennings, Billy Hamilton, Sammy McIlroy too.

We had organised a party for afterwards and Billy Bingham was fine with that, but as I said, there was no alcohol in the hotel, FIFA had made it a dry hotel. I spoke to the lads and I got $1,000 out of the players' kitty. The security around us was always very intense. Every time we went to training, we had a couple of jeeps with soldiers in them with rifles and machine guns, and then there was a big truck behind that with another 10 or 12 soldiers, and we had outrider motorcycle police too. Then at the very back was an ambulance, in case of any injuries or whatever. When we went to the first game against Algeria, the ambulance came with us to the stadium. The second game, when we played Spain, the ambulance came again, and I got chatting to the driver. I said, "How long have you been an ambulance driver?"

"Six or seven years. There aren't many jobs you can get in Mexico."

"What does it pay?"

"$25 a week.

"$25 a week? If I give you $1,000 and you keep $100 for yourself, and then the other $900, you go and buy beer and load it in the back of your ambulance when we're playing our last game against Brazil, is that ok?"

So he loaded $900 worth of beer into the back of the ambulance. We got on the bus after the game and I told Pat that we had a wee party set up for him, and we'd sorted the alcohol out. We pulled up at the hotel and once we were there, the jeeps and the motorcycles drove off. Then the ambulance pulls up and I said, "There you go lads!" We opened the back of the ambulance and started taking crates and crates of beer out and put them in the fridges in the rooms. We started opening them up and the party started. It was good fun, but it was a little bit sad too, because a lot of us knew this was the last time we were going to be together like that. Billy Bingham said to me, "Look, I've got to bring some new players through, I've got to develop a new team." We understood that, fair enough. But I wanted some answers before it was over, like why didn't he take Derek Spence in '82, why did you pick this one and not that one. And we had a great talk, going through what he thought at the time. I learnt a lot from that.

A year later, Billy gave me a call because he wanted me to go with him to Saudi Arabia. He'd got a coaching job there with Al-Nassr that he was combining with the Northern Ireland job, and he wanted me as his assistant. But I wanted to keep playing. I was 33 then and that's one thing I do say to a lot of players, keep playing as long as you possibly can and enjoy it while you can. One thing I've noticed in the last ten years or so is players can keep going longer. If you look at Northern Ireland, boys like Gareth McAuley, Aaron Hughes, they kept going at a great level through to 37, 38. If you look after yourself, the sports science and all of that is so good now that you can go on longer. The ways of keeping fit are better, nutrition is better, the surfaces are better, the footwear they use is better, the ball is better, physiotherapy treatment is better. The opportunity is there for players who want to take it and who have a bit of luck with injuries.

As we got back on the plane to come home from the World Cup, I had to accept my career with Northern Ireland was over. Now I had to find myself a new club if I was going to carry on playing at all.

MY STORY, MY JOURNEY

CHAPTER SIXTEEN

··

CROWD TROUBLE...

Unlike the previous year when I returned to England from Real Mallorca, coming back from the World Cup in 1986, I was pretty confident that I already had a club to go to for the new season. I'd had a phone call while I was in Mexico from Alan Mullery and he said, "I'm managing Brighton. When you get back, come and have a chat. I'd love you to come and join me here." I went in to see him and pretty quickly, we had everything sorted out. They were in the Second Division, they'd been there for three years after getting relegated, but Alan was ambitious and was looking to push for promotion.

I was feeling a little bit unsettled because I was definitely at a crossroads in my professional life and I didn't really know where I was going. I was 32, my international career was over, and playing for Northern Ireland and being part of that group had been such a big part of my life, so that was a really big wrench. Psychologically, I think I started to feel, "Well, is that it? Is my career over at 32?" But I was fit, I carried on working hard and I felt I could still play for two or three years more.

The chance to move to Brighton looked good on the surface, but it meant we had to move, because it was too much travelling from St Albans. We got an apartment next door to Dean Wilkins and then, later on, next door to him was Alan Curbishley. It was a nice place to be and it was a good

171

setup under Alan Mullery. I played up front with Terry Connor and Dean Saunders. We had Stephen Penney and Danny Wilson in the middle of the park, Steve Gatting played at the back with Chris Hutchings, Perry Digweed was our goalkeeper. We had the basis of a good team, but it wasn't really coming together. We were a bit inconsistent and we weren't threatening to get promoted. Gradually, the situation inside the club started to change. We played away at Grimsby in January 1987 and we won 2-1, but we were without one of the centre-halves, Gary O'Reilly, who had been at Tottenham with me. We all thought he was injured, but on the coach on the way back, Alan said, "Right lads, I need to have a chat. I told you Gary wasn't able to travel, but he wasn't injured, we're selling him to Crystal Palace."

Clearly, by then, there was real pressure from the board to sell players and balance the books. A lot of the players had been on bigger wages when they were in the First Division and some were still on those contracts with big bonuses too. Selling Gary was the start of moving some of those boys on and Alan was on his way pretty much that week too. That sums up how precarious life as a footballer can be. I'd joined Brighton to play for Alan Mullery, I'd moved down there to live, and then within a few months, the manager was gone – it was a kick in the teeth. Everything was up in the air and it only added to what was already a really difficult period.

Barry Lloyd, who was a coach at the club, took over from Alan and he made it clear that he didn't want to use me in the side, he was going to rely on some of the younger players that he'd signed from non-league. Kieran O'Regan was a player at Brighton and he seemed to have information that nobody else had, that this had all been pre-planned months before. I raised a lot of questions and, as a result of that, I got frozen out. Barry had been manager of Worthing and he had done well there, so he deserved his chance. He had some good ideas, he was a good coach, but all of the changes were happening much too quickly, as the results proved – they went 12 matches without a win after that Grimsby game and dropped from 15th to 22nd, bottom of the table.

As Barry took over, I got a phone call from John Docherty and Frank McLintock over at Millwall. They asked me if I fancied going on loan there and I said, "I've just moved to Brighton and you want me in London again!" They signed me initially on a one month deal, then it was extended to two months. It went well, I enjoyed it because they were a great family club, a real team. There was a real bond there, they all worked hard for each other. I was playing up front with a young lad called Teddy Sheringham, we had Terry Hurlock in the middle of the park, Keith Stevens, Les Briley, Alan McCleary was the centre-half, David Byrne was a right winger. It was a good squad. I made the ball stick up front, I won it in the air, Teddy played off me, we played one-twos and he loved it because he was getting plenty of chances. At the end of the two months, it had all gone pretty well and I had started talking to John and Frank about maybe doing some coaching. They wanted me me to join the club permanently as a player and to do a bit of coaching as well. I went back to Brighton at the end of the loan and went in to see Barry Lloyd. I told him that I had this opportunity to sign permanently there and do a bit of coaching, which was a good opportunity for me at the age I was, coming to the end of my playing days. He said, "I don't want you to go, we're not selling you. We need your experience to help us out of trouble. We need somebody who's going to make the ball stick. I'll let you do some coaching here as well."

I went back to the apartment and that afternoon, I got a call from Peter Sotherby, who ran the reserves then. "What are you doing tonight? There's a reserve game up at Ipswich. I could do with you, I've only got kids, 17 and 18." I got my boots and I got on the bus. We were 3-0 down at half-time. The kids were petrified of the occasion and of the opposition. I remember Peter and me having a real go at them at half-time and saying, "You've got to be better than this." I really got the bit between my teeth from there and second half, we won every tackle, every loose ball, every header and we won the game 4-3. It's the only time a referee has come over to me at the end of the match to say, "What a credit you are. You were unbelievable, everything you did there." I suppose at 32, 33 people think you're done, but my mentality was different. I always had a really good mental attitude. I still hated losing.

From there, I played in the first team for the last eight games of the season, we won a couple and drew a couple, but the damage had already been done and unfortunately, we got relegated. Part of me wonders if they wanted to go down, because that was the only way they were going to get a lot of the players off the contracts. Certainly, a lot of players left the club that summer. Barry Lloyd had his own ideas about what he wanted to do and the direction he wanted to take the team in, and that's when he started recruiting new players. He had a big Chelsea connection, so he took a lot of players from there like Doug Rougvie, Kevin Bremner, which was a great real stroke of genius, and of course, Gary Nelson, who scored lots of goals. He was a brilliant player who really did do well for Brighton, he transformed the team. Barry got a really good team together actually, they played good football, passed the ball well, and Brighton got promotion the following season.

I was on the bench for quite a few games in that 1987/88 promotion season. I added a bit of experience to things but beyond that, I was running the reserve team and expanding my coaching experience, which was something I was getting more and more interested in as the years were passing. I was fortunate that I was able to play as long as I did, and I kept playing amateur football up towards 50 in a very competitive league, but as you get older, it does hit you. "Hold on a minute, I'm not getting any younger!" It does plant the seed of doubt in your mind, "How many more years can I play?" You don't want to admit it to yourself, but you do get slower, you can't quite reach that pass you would have got a couple of seasons before, you can't get away from the defender the way you did. I knew I'd reached that point at Brighton, at least as far as playing at a high level in the Football League went. That impacts on your personal life as well as your professional one, as I was to discover.

I actually did my first coaching badge at Tottenham when I was 24. As you get older, you think about getting the full badge, but it wasn't until I was at Brighton that I finally did it up at Lilleshall. Peter Reid was there, Tony Currie, a lot of the ex-pros. It was great talking about the games we'd played against each other. "Did you really mean to hit that ball in the back of the net!?" All the stories came out. I thought it was a really good exercise over 10 days up there, I got a lot out of it. As players, we had the knowledge, but it's being able to put that knowledge across to others. That's what they teach you, how to put on a training session, how to make it interesting for the players and what the end product is going to be. Then you add your own ideas to that. There's no one true way. You look at how Spanish clubs dominated with possession football and in later years, I loved commentating on that. But then I'd worked for Graham Taylor and his theory was, the more shots and crosses you had, the more chance you had of scoring goals and he could then quantify all of that with statistics. That made every bit as much sense. However you do play though, it's only one part of the equation – in the finish you've got to hit the target, you've got to score goals. You can have 75% possession and still lose 1-0 if you can't finish!

All the guys I'd played with and against seemed to want to go into coaching and I regularly came across them at games. Around that time, Pat Rice was running the reserve team at Arsenal while I was running the Brighton reserves. We were doing really well, we had all kids in our team, 17, 18, 19, all hungry to learn. I had them fit, I ran them, and I had them physically and mentally prepared for it all. We went to play Arsenal up at Highbury and they had Charlie Nicholas, Niall Quinn, Paul Merson, Kevin Campbell, Perry Groves in their side at the time. Cracking players, players who had all been in the first team. The experience for my young lads to play against them was unbelievable and we drew that match 2-2. The kids learnt so much from that 90 minutes, from playing against those players who knew the game. You can't buy that kind of education. It's such a shame that reserve football has changed since then, to the point where it's an Under 23s game now. I don't think it's helping them develop in the same way.

I'd been coaching Brighton reserves for about a year and we were doing really well. I was pleased with the progress, but I was under a lot of pressure from a personal point of view. It was a difficult time because I didn't know what I wanted to do next professionally, having done nothing but play football and sport nearly all my working life. Was coaching the direction I really wanted to go in for the next 30 years? I was stuck between a rock and a hard place and it was unsettling. On top of that, Ann wanted to start a business, running a care home, and one became available in the Brighton area. We sold our place in Spain and we used the money to buy that. By then though, we weren't really so close any longer, we were more like brother and sister rather than husband and wife, and that's when we started drifting apart. Ultimately, I ended up getting involved in another relationship a bit further down the line.

Looking back, I was struggling a bit at that stage and I hadn't a clue what I wanted to do. I was just getting up to go to training and go through the motions, so it was a difficult period for me. We had a Sussex Senior Cup match against Southwick, a local amateur team, a decent side, but very physical. I had a lot of young kids who were technically very good. The game was at the Goldstone Ground and we played really well, but they worked very hard and got a draw out of it. We had an opportunity late on where the ball was crossed from the right. There was a bit of a scramble, and then one of our lads headed the ball towards goal and a player on the line saved it with his hands - he dived across and pushed it round the post. The referee was looking between people, he couldn't see properly, but the lineswoman pointed for the corner kick. We couldn't believe it. We were all appealing for a penalty because the goalkeeper was already on the ground and it was the full-back who had saved it, but we didn't get the penalty. That was to prove a life changing decision for me, because the game finished in a draw and the replay was set for Southwick the following week.

Southwick were stronger than us, they knew they had to mix it up because we were better footballers, so it became a kicking match. To be fair, I was playing centre-half and I don't mind a tackle! The game took on an edge as it went on, and the crowd rose to the occasion. It just got out of control and there was lots of nasty stuff going on. I was getting a lot of stick from the fans in one area, asking whether I had a father, what my mother did for a trade and all that stuff. I took a lot of it on the chin, but then I went in for one tackle, and then jumped up from that to go into another one. There was a lashing out of feet and the referee singled me out and sent me off.

I was absolutely fuming and I totally lost the plot. Ted, my assistant, who looked after the youth team, he was sitting in the dugout with about four or five of the kids. He was trying to get me to just sit down, but I was getting a lot of abuse from these people who were hanging over the fence, who'd been giving me a load of abuse the whole time. I'd had enough of it by then and I just saw red. I jumped the fence and one of the guys who had been mouthing off, I headbutted him. The next guy to his left, I hit him with my right hook and the whole of the area that was packed - there must have been 100 people in there - it just opened up like the Red Sea, everything just fell apart.

The next thing, one of the directors from Brighton was trying to get me off the terraces, so I went down the tunnel and into the dressing room to get out of the way, because I was only going to get more angry. I was still boiling over, just sitting in there, steaming. After five or 10 minutes, there was a banging on the door – there were two doors, one that went out onto the pitch and another at the other end, out into the boardroom and the lounge area. Jock, our kitman, opened the door and in off the pitch came Geoff Cooper, our midfielder. He'd been sent off as well and he was the only other experienced player we had. We were down to nine men and so we ended up losing the game, but before it was over, there was a bang on the other door, from the boardroom side. I opened the door and it was Beau Reynolds who was the chairman of Southwick, their doctor was with him, and there was Wayne Marmont too, with stitches in his head - he was the guy I had headbutted. He said, "I supported you in the World Cup!" I said, "You were slagging me off, you said my mother was this and my dad was that and all the rest of it!" Then he said something else, and I lost it again and had another row with them. Jock closed the door on them and it was never resolved.

The players started coming in at the final whistle and I was just so wound up it was untrue. I got myself out of the dressing room and into my car and away. Then the police arrived at the ground, looking for me. When I heard that, I knew then that it was all over. I had to retire, there was no other way out. It was a really low moment, when you look at the circumstances like that. After all the things I'd done in football, it was going to be ended by getting sent off and jumping into the crowd. I spoke to Barry Lloyd and I spoke to Billy Bingham, who was very good. He helped me and said, "Right, you need to do your letter, apologise and resign." That's what I did, and I thought that was that, but then somebody started proceedings to prosecute me.

It went to court and I got the barrister from Worthing FC, who was also something to do with the England rugby setup. He was very good. I listened to the prosecution, and even I thought I was Jack the Ripper, the way he made it sound so bad! All this stuff about kids saying they didn't want to go to football anymore because of what I'd done. Whereas when they were calling me a "fucking Irish wanker" and all the expletives about my family, I didn't see too many kids saying they didn't want to listen to that anymore! But it was what it was. I was given a conditional discharge, and fined £200 in compensation. It all finished on a very low note, which was really disappointing after the career I'd had.

It was funny though because straight afterwards, I had a lot of people trying to get me to come and play for their club, so it hadn't done that much damage to my reputation! It was shortly after that that I ended up joining Crawley as a player-coach. I got back into it, I started focusing again. I had a job working for Nynex too, the New York New England telephone exchange, and that was something totally different. They were breaking up the BT monopoly in the UK and Nynex were an American company who came in to offer competition. Basically I was selling telephones lines and I was selling Sky too, trying to get them off the satellite dishes and to go to cable because it was cheaper and it was better reception. Then I started doing a little bit of work with Sky and that coincided with meeting up with

George Best again and him getting me involved with Spanish football, which I'll come onto later – basically, I went from selling Sky Sports to actually working on Sky!

Crawley was okay for a while, but the manager, John Mags, was also the chairman. Things are done very differently at non-league level and John had his own ideas. He had plans for the club and how it was going to be developed and, to be fair to John, it did eventually happen, but not within the two or three years that he said it would. I was there for a year and then I had a couple of months back in the Irish League with Glenavon, which was good fun.

At the end with Crawley, it was getting harder to play and when the moment came that I realised I was going to have to stop, it was one of the worst points in my life. Something that I had done and loved from being a child, but I couldn't play professionally anymore. It was like somebody had cut off one of my arms, I just felt totally lost. It plays tricks with your mind, "What am I gonna do? Nobody wants me as a professional footballer anymore". Then you just try to cling on, and that's why I probably went to Glenavon and played there for a bit.

I got a call from a guy called Gordon Hanna, who was a newspaper reporter from Northern Ireland who I'd known for years. He said, "Glenavon are pushing to try and win the title and if you're free, they'd love you to come and play for them." This was March 1990, I was coming up to 36 at the time, but I was still reasonably fit, so I went and played in the Irish League again, completing the circle. One of the games was against Lisburne Distillery and Billy Hamilton, my World Cup striking partner, was their manager and he was younger than me! I remember playing really well, I scored a goal or two and it was great craic. I enjoyed going back home to play and we never lost a game, but unfortunately, we missed out on the title by one point. We finished runners up but at least that qualified Glenavon for the Europa League. That was a nice note to go out on.

But now what?

CHAPTER SEVENTEEN

....

POACHER TURNED GAMEKEEPER

Things were still a bit confused for me professionally after coming back from Glenavon, but on the personal front they had already started changing too, and not for the best. Mentally, I probably wasn't in the best shape at that time, and I ended up doing some things that I really came to regret.

I was still married to Ann when I began seeing a girl called Caron, which would lead to the end of our marriage. That was entirely down to me, I have to hold my hands up about that. When I was at Brighton, after games the players used to go to a pub called The Cricketers in Hove, near the Sussex county cricket ground, and I would still join them all through my time at the club, even when I was coaching more than playing. That was where I met Caron one night and the relationship then developed over a long period. As things turned out, getting involved with Caron wasn't one of the best decisions I ever made, in all kinds of ways. I wasn't thinking properly, it was a difficult period in my life when all kinds of things were happening and when I wasn't really sure what I was doing or where I was going. I was around 33 then, Caron was ten years younger, and I was flattered that she was interested in me. It all played into the way I was feeling about finishing football, about getting older and losing my way in life. It was an ego boost, I must be honest.

We started a relationship but I was never planning on getting married to her, it didn't feel right in my gut. I think she was very attracted by the idea of being with a footballer or somebody famous. A lot of my friends from the area who knew us both had told me to be careful and warned me about what I was getting myself into, but sometimes you don't listen to advice. I didn't then and it was a bad situation that was created as a result.

I split up with Ann as a part of the way that relationship with Caron developed, and it was very unfair on her. It was basically my fault and that's something in my life that I'm really not proud of. I didn't really want to leave Ann, but I wasn't happy. We'd grown apart, probably because we'd got married so young and we had both grown up and changed since then. But from there, I found myself in a situation where I wasn't happy with Caron either. I didn't know what I wanted, I was at a crossroads in my life, finishing my playing career after playing sport for 20 years. I thought my career was over and that my life was basically over too, when at that age, my mid-thirties, it was really only beginning. In that sense, I was really confused, and I know I'm not the only one who has been through that. A lot of players never come to terms with the fact that they're not footballers any longer, and it's something that needs to be looked at. The PFA really should see how they can help players to get over that and to help with their mental health once the game is over for them. In saying that, it's not just a problem for football but for other sports as well.

If I knew then what I know now, things would have been different, and I would have taken things in another direction, but that's the story of life isn't it!? As it was, Caron got pregnant and on August 13th 1991, we had our first child, a daughter, Aishleen, and we moved in together. That was obviously the end of things with Ann and we got divorced.

On a professional level, I was looking to get back into football after coming back from Glenavon. I did a bit of coaching in the summer when I went over to America and worked for a company called World Class Soccer with Danny McGrain, David McCreery and George Best of course. Some fantastic names. We flew over to Massachusetts and coached for four weeks through the summer. It was just brilliant and we had a lot of fun teaching the kids some soccer skills. At one point, George's son Calum came up to see his dad. He was living in Los Angeles with his mum, so he came up and we put him on the coaching course. We put him in my group and I looked after him – he was 11 or 12 at the time. He was really athletic, but the American kids were all good athletes. That's one thing I picked up on. The majority of the kids we were coaching were girls, probably two-thirds, and they were so enthusiastic and really athletic. It was no surprise that women's football became such a big sport over there.

We got involved in a game on the fourth of July, Independence day. It got a wee bit nasty because the Americans were very enthusiastic and they were a lot younger than us. They started taking the mickey, so I resorted to putting the boot in as they say! George said to me afterwards, "Thank God you're on my side big man!" It was a real battle, for us to get a draw was a good result because they were so young and so much fitter. I hadn't lost that competitive instinct!

Back in England, a good opportunity came along in November 1991 when I got the call to be manager at Worthing. They were in the bottom two or three in the league, the Isthmian Division Two. Going there worked out really well, because the three years I was there were very successful for the club. I developed the players, the team, and I was really enjoying coaching. I used my connections in the game and I got the likes of Mark Falco and Gary Brooke and Tony Galvin to come down to play for me. John Robson was my coach, Ivan Cocker was my assistant, and we built a really good team, one of the best teams in the south of England at the time.

I signed two or three PTI players from Portsmouth, boys in the Navy. Steve Reilly was a fantastic athlete in the middle of the park. Darren Robson was a brilliant midfield player. I also signed Jimmy Quinn, who was the anchor man. He was solid, the enforcer, then Darren was skilful. He could run with the ball and create. I signed a boy called Darren Freeman who was 17, and he was a flying machine. His dad had brought him along for trials and after ten minutes, I knew I could make something out of him. He was so quick and he just wanted to learn the game. I took him under my wing and developed him and he scored goals for us. There were some local lads too like Richard Knight, a six feet four, left-footed centre-half and he formed a good partnership with Graham Waller, a couple of local lads. Steve Reilly was there in the centre of defence for us as well. Micky Montague and Spencer Mintram played together down the left hand side, Spencer was so quick from left-back and Micky played in front of him. I got Richard Tiltman to come down from Brighton as well, he was a really good player, he'd had a great football education and he had a big impact on the side.

We had a lot of pace in the team, we played entertaining football, we scored goals, we were unbeatable at home and in 1992/93 we ran away with the league. At the start of the season, the chairman, Beau Reynolds, was saying, "I haven't got a lot of money to pay bonuses", so I told him to give us £1,000, and we put that money on ourselves to win the league – that paid the bonuses! In 1994/95, the club got promoted to the Premier Division, so they were good times down at Worthing. We had a great spirit there, we got into the proper rounds of the FA Cup, we were on "Match of the Day", all of that, and the lads loved it. There weren't many teams that wanted to play us, I can tell you that. Things were going great, and we were looking set to work our way up to the Conference, which was our goal. Unfortunately, the chairman sat down and worked it all out and said, "Look, we can't afford to do that. It'll cost me too much money. I can't afford to pay the wages that we'll need to do that, to pay players to take days off to travel the length and breadth of the country."

I was really fed up with all of that because I had been for an interview a few months earlier for the job as manager of Northern Ireland, when Bryan Hamilton got the job in early 1994. Although I didn't get it, there was an opportunity there for me to go in as a potential future coach of the national team, to learn the ropes by being Bryan's assistant. I didn't think I could do it if Worthing got in the Conference, because that would be a full-time job, so I turned it down at that stage. But when the chairman then did a U-turn and decided that we weren't going to spend the money, that we were not going to push into the Conference, I just couldn't stay on. I told him I was leaving because there'd been no point in me spending three years to develop the club if there was going to be a limit on what he wanted to do and where we were heading. Fortunately, I was still able to take the offer from Northern Ireland and I went off to work with Bryan Hamilton.

Bryan was very professional and he was very meticulous. He wanted everything to be right, training had to be spot on, every session. But players being players, they were always looking for angles. Could they get a sneaky pint somewhere here and there? Being an ex-player myself, I knew the circumstances and all the tricks because I'd been there – I was a poacher turned gamekeeper! Since those days, I've talked to Jim Magilton and Iain Dowie from that group, lads who've become managers since, and they both say, "How did you put up with all the crap from us!?" What you have to do is make sure from day one that the players know who is in control. Because if the players are in charge, you get nothing done and that's when you've lost the dressing room.

A squad of footballers is an interesting dynamic because you've got all kinds of personalities in there, boys who like to prepare in different ways, who need different things to help them perform at their best. Some players didn't even want to go out, they just wanted to train and then rest, they would drink tea rather than go looking for a pint of beer. Aaron Hughes was like that, one of the best professionals I've ever seen. Nigel Worthington was another fantastic pro, one who I knew from the '86 World Cup squad. Those were boys who just wanted to work hard. Then we had other players like Keith Gillespie, Jim Magilton, Neil Lennon, very good footballers, but they wanted to work hard and then they wanted to have a bit of fun afterwards. You had the two sides of the coin and, as assistant manager, it was down to me to try and pull it together.

I wanted to make the training fun, keep it enjoyable for them so that they would buy into it. I didn't want the players being bored – as I knew full well, players do get bored very easily, so you have to keep them occupied. You have to find the happy medium. They're adults, so you treat them like adults, but when they behave like kids, then you have to step in. We had situations where players were suspended and sent home for breaking curfews. That happened on two or three occasions in my time as assistant manager. Some of the players who were sent home weren't even guilty, but they were in a situation where they wouldn't squeal on their mates. Players have their own code and they abide by it! But one thing I will say for all of the Northern Ireland teams I played for or coached, they were never short of commitment and determination. The desire to represent the country was unbelievable and they all did put 100% in, even the ones that were ducking and diving.

For me and Bryan, it was important to keep the players together as a unit, a family, keep them occupied, keep them happy, make it enjoyable. Then when they're not training, they could relax and wind down a wee bit. A big part of that is that you have to pick the right location to stay in and to train at. We generally stayed at the Hilton in Templepatrick, just outside Belfast, not far from the airport. It had a golf course and a putting green, it had a swimming pool, it had a gymnasium, players could get into the pool after training, or if they wanted to soak their legs in a hot bath or whatever, all the facilities were there. You had to make sure that you were ticking all the boxes, and that side of it was quite demanding. Then the food has to be the right food. You vary it, but you have to make sure it's the right thing at the right time. We would always eat in a private room, players only, just the squad and the staff, so that nobody was bothered. Of course, there were always demands from fans who wanted autographs, and you want to accommodate that, and so we organised it all properly. Maybe as the players went in to eat, there'd be a table just inside the door with half a dozen footballs on it and some shirts to sign. It would be a ritual, they'd come in, sign everything, then go and sit down. That's them giving back to the fans and doing their part, which is very important.

The biggest difference is that an international team is not like a football club where you're playing and training every day together. These lads would have played for their clubs on a Saturday and met up with you on a Sunday. In those circumstances, you would never really want to do too much on a Sunday when they'd played the day before, so you'd take them for a walk, maybe some were getting treatment. On the Monday, you had to determine what type of a session you could run, but it was never too strenuous. I always took warm ups for at least 10 or 15 minutes, where they could jog and just gently make sure they stretched every part of the body, very much as we had done at Real Mallorca. You didn't want anybody pulling a muscle on a Monday in the training session, so all of that was meticulous.

We would have staff meetings in the mornings, maybe around 7.30, just to discuss with the physio who was injured and who wasn't able to train. You go through all of that, then you look at who you have to work with, so maybe you would do a session in the morning, have lunch, then have a team meeting, get the video out on the opposition, look at all the players that we needed to talk about, who were the danger men? At that level, you can't leave anything to chance.

I learnt a lot from Bryan Hamilton. He was a very good manager who had managed before at various different levels. We had a good little team going, helping the young players to develop. It was good to learn about the up and coming players at that stage, lads like Tommy Wright, Iain Dowie, Jim Magilton, Keith Gillespie. Back then, we needed to find out what the players could do but also recruit new players, find players who maybe had a Northern Irish grandparent so they could qualify to play for us. We were trying to build a squad, keep them strong, make sure we'd got some quality in there, develop them and keep the conveyor belt going. Not easy!

We needed games too and they weren't always easy to fix up outside of the qualifiers for the major tournaments. At one stage, I got a phone call from friends of mine and they were looking to get a game on in Thailand. They were paying decent money, the Irish FA wanted money, we needed the game, so it was perfect. It came at the end of the season. We played the game on the second night we arrived - Roy Carroll made his debut in that game. The next day, we flew to Phuket and spent three or four days there and then came back. We got a chance to look at some of our players against different opposition and that's what you have to look for as an international manager, you're looking to get experience. Thailand weren't the best team in the world, we weren't worried about playing them, but the trip as a whole was an experience for the players. It built the camaraderie, it got that group feeling going. That was something that we concentrated really hard on.

The first task we had was trying to qualify for the Euros in 1996. Obviously that was something we were really keen to do with the finals being held in England, which would have been great for the fans too. It was a fierce group that we were in with Portugal, Austria and the Republic of Ireland, the top team going through and second going into the play-offs. The big blow for us was in our fourth game when we played the Republic at Windsor Park. We'd started the group reasonably well. We beat Liechtenstein at home, then got a great result by winning in Austria when Keith Gillespie scored a screamer, but in between, we'd lost late on to Portugal in Belfast.

That made the Republic game even bigger than it was anyway, but they were too much for us in the first half and they were 3-0 up at the break, eventually winning 4-0. We made amends to a degree with a 1-1 draw in Dublin but ironically, that cost us dear. Where in 1984, we hadn't gone through against West Germany because teams on level points were separated by goal difference, this time, it was the head to head record that counted, so as we went into the final game, we knew we couldn't go through. Portugal were top on 20 points, the Republic of Ireland had 17, Austria had 16 and we had 14, so even if we beat Austria in Belfast, we couldn't go above the Republic because of the head to head. In their last game, they were away in Portugal, so they needed a favour from us. If they lost in Portugal – which they eventually did – then if Austria got a point in Belfast, because they'd beaten the Republic home and away, they'd be in the play-offs instead. Big Jack Charlton was in charge of the Republic then, so he was soon into Bryan and myself, telling us we needed to get him a result!

Relations between us and Austria weren't great anyway because in the first game, they'd been very, very physical in the first half. A fight broke out in the tunnel at half-time, one of their guys shouted at Iain Dowie and spat in his face so Iain unleashed his left hook! It all kicked off from there! The referee was a Spaniard and I was in his face, telling him it was all his fault because he'd let the Austrians kick lumps out of us in the first half and that's why it had spilled over, so the second half, he gave us everything!

There was no love lost between us and Austria coming into that last match and it turned into a terrific game for the crowd to enjoy. We won 5-3 in the end. We really went to town in that one. We had a lot of big lads in the side. Barry Hunter and Gerry Taggart were at centre-half, very good at set plays, Gerry in particular scored a few goals for us. Looking back on that group, we were a wee bit unlucky not to get into the play-offs, but we had quite a young group and that tends to bring inconsistency with it. We lost at home to Latvia having won out there, and that was costly for us in the end, but we had a fabulous result when we got a draw in Portugal. It was a lot of boys learning their way, gaining experience. You are a bit up and down in that situation, but I felt we were moving in a positive direction.

I really enjoyed being back in the thick of things with Northern Ireland but another opportunity was about to open up for me – and all thanks to the greatest footballer that my country has ever produced.

CHAPTER EIGHTEEN

....

TALKING TELEVISION

The direction that the second half of my professional life would take came about pretty much by chance. It happened when I was still assistant to Bryan Hamilton with Northern Ireland, but it was a great opportunity that would change the way my career would go over the next 25 years – the chance to work in television.

It was the great George Best that started the ball rolling for me. In the summer of 1996, he called me up and said, "What are you doing this Sunday? Would you play in a five-a-side for me? Chrysalis are making a documentary for Channel 4 about small sided games and how they are better for youngsters. They get more touches on the ball, they get more involved, and it improves their skill and technique."

Any chance to play football with George Best was ok with me! It was all very familiar to me too, because all they do in Spain is play Fútbol Sala. You play with a smaller ball, your touch gets better, it's good fun. They were filming the programme over at Battersea Park in London, so I was up for that. Just to be sure, I called George on the Friday before, just to check it was all still on and he said that he couldn't make it and could I find another four players! I called Kenny Sansom, my son Ciaran played in goal, we managed to get a team together and we did the documentary. I did an interview after we'd played, the usual kind of thing, I didn't think much about it, but then I got talking to the guy from Chrysalis who was running things. He wanted to know what it had been like playing in Spain. We talked about that for a while, how the ball skills are different, the way they look at football from a different angle. I told him I learnt an awful lot when I was out there. Then he said, "I've been asked to do a show for Sky, it starts in a couple of weeks, all about Spanish football. We know absolutely nothing about it. Would you be interested in coming along as a guest to talk about it?" That was how it all started.

I love the fact that it was George who put me in contact with these guys at Chrysalis. They were doing the Spanish football on behalf of Sky Sports at a time when putting Spanish football on TV was seen as a big gamble in the UK - I think they spent £100,000 for a one year contract. We quickly created a cult following, there was millions who used to just watch the Spanish football because it was technically brilliant. It was Ronaldinho, Ronaldo and Raul, all the superstars.

We got down to work on it and the whole thing just took off, audiences grew every week and it was so successful that Sky decided that the following year, they were going to take it on board themselves and use their own producers, their own directors. Dave Lawrence was a producer there and he was going to be in charge of it, so he called me and asked me out for lunch. We met up and he said, "We've got a two hour show, how are we going to do it?"

"Why are you asking me, you're the producer!"

It turned out he'd never done any football before - he did the greyhounds and the horse racing! I helped Dave out for the first couple of months, showed him the ropes. I said, "Look, normally you've got 90 minutes of a game in a two hour show, so you've got to fill in a bit at the start for the 15 minutes before kick-off, then you've got the half-time analysis and then you've got 5 or 10 minutes at the end."

"What do we do at the start?"

"People will want to know about Spanish football, what it's all about, and what's the difference between it and the Premier League? For me, it's a technically better league, so we want to portray that to the public. If we take a player from one of the teams that's playing, one who's particularly skilful and tactically aware, then we can show footage of him and his techniques. We've got the footage from last season, so we can show him scoring a goal, taking a free-kick, dribbling past somebody. That's the sort of stuff people want to see and that will quickly give anybody who's new to it the idea of what Spanish football is all about."

One of the first games we did was Celta Vigo against Deportivo La Coruña. I suggested that we do a feature on one of the star players, Aleksandr Mostovoi at Celta Vigo, because I knew they had footage from the previous year, and we also did a feature on Rivaldo, the Brazilian international, who was at Deportivo then. That idea became a regular in the show, a feature on a player from each side and so that show really introduced La Liga, its players, the tactics, the techniques, to the people in the UK and Ireland.

At that time, my job was to be the analyst, sitting in a studio with the presenter to talk about the teams and the game, but pretty soon, I had to start multi-tasking. In those days, they didn't have a co-commentator but after a few weeks, they decided it would be worth trying me out at the job. Nobody taught me how to co-commentate. It was one of those where they just threw me in the deep end and I just played off the commentator, Rob Palmer. There was a rapport built up over weeks and months, and we ended up working together for over 20 years. I'd be in the studio as an analyst before the game, talking through the players and how the game was going to go, and then just before kick-off, I'd dash up the stairs to the voiceover booth with Rob and do co-commentary during the game. Then at half-time, I would go downstairs, back into the studio, do my analysis stuff, then be back to the voiceover booth. After the final whistle, I'd be back down to the studio to analyse the game – I was working double time!

All of that went great until one day, I'd done the analysis and got upstairs, gone into the booth, got my headphones on and was ready to talk. The game started but about five minutes in, the satellite feed went down. I got a shout in my ear, "Gerry, quick. We need you back in the studio." So I chased down two flights of stairs, got hooked back up with the microphone and sat down, by which time, the satellite feed had come back on again and I had to chase back upstairs. I swear it happened three times in the first half. I was running out of breath but the rest of the boys couldn't breathe from laughing!

All of that was part of us building a team and having a group of people who worked so hard for each other. They were so dedicated, they just did a brilliant job, putting in seven, eight, nine even ten hours every day just to get prepared, cutting videos and putting the footage together for a feature on a player. There's lots of research goes into that, so the backroom staff are so important in all of those kinds of shows. It was a real family. I loved that everybody really worked hard. We really did work long hours. People don't realise the preparation that went on beforehand, for days. If you had a feature on one player, somebody was working on that for two or three days to get that 60 second piece done. Sky set a lot of standards during that period. They were the forerunner of how football is covered by everyone now.

It was a sign of how well things were going that I never talked to any of the bosses at Sky for about a year and a half, but eventually I went to see Andy Melvin, who was in overall charge of things. I wasn't quite sure why I'd been summoned after so long, but he said, "It's a great show, the numbers are going up all the time. If it's not broke, don't fix it, just carry on doing what you're doing." From there, I only saw the bosses about once a year or so!

Once I'd started working for Sky, I got the chance to do some work for the BBC on a Saturday, doing a programme on News 24 with Chris Hollins. We'd get in about half past 11 and run through the day's sport – we'd have rugby, we'd be looking at the big fight that night, previewing the motor racing or whatever and doing all the football stuff. I started checking out all kinds of sports so I had at least a few things to say about them. The show would start at midday and we would do a sports piece every quarter of an hour. One day, it was the start of the skiing season and there was a guy who was training up in Scotland. We had a three minute interview set up with him.

"So you're training up in Scotland?"

"Yes."

"Is it difficult to get prepared there, because the snow quality must be different?"

"Yes."

About 30 seconds into the interview, Chris has asked him all his questions, so he turns to me. "Gerry, do you ski?" I couldn't believe he was going to go there, but he was desperate! I started laughing, but I could see we needed to fill the airtime. "No, I've never skied before. It's a sport I'd like to try but I've never had the opportunity. It looks quite difficult to me." We just made stupid conversation for a couple of minutes before the director cut it and took us to another topic. But that's the nightmare for an interviewer, somebody with one word answers!

Because I was now seen as an authority on Spanish football in the media, from there I got an invitation from Eurosport to do Champions League and Europa League coverage on a Tuesday, Wednesday and Thursday, in Paris. My boss out there was Simon Reed, Oliver's brother, and he was great fun to work with. It meant I was working on the Saturday for the BBC, on Sunday for Sky, Monday I'd be off, then I'd have Tuesday to Thursday in Paris with Eurosport and I'd maybe use Friday to do some preparation for the next week ahead. I was also still involved with Northern Ireland, so during the international breaks, I'd be away with the team. I think the TV work actually improved my coaching because I was able to look at the techniques of players in different countries and try to put that into a framework where I could use some of those ideas with our players. It also gave me ideas for set plays, free-kicks, tactics, that kind of thing. All of that work was right up my street, it was a very exciting period.

Living in Brighton, it's not far from Eastbourne, which is where they hold the women's tennis tournament a couple of weeks before Wimbledon. The one year I decided I'd go down there and watch a bit of tennis, maybe sample the strawberries and cream. Eurosport always covered the French Open and lots of other tennis tournaments, so they were well connected within the game. I asked someone in the office if they could sort me out with tickets for semi-finals day, and that was fine. I thought I'd get a couple of decent seats but nothing special, nothing OTT. I got there and I was in the Royal Box! I thought they'd really pushed the boat out for me, but it turns out there's two Gerry Armstrongs. The other Gerry Armstrong is the famous umpire who did all the Wimbledon finals. They thought I was that Gerry Armstrong…

The variety of the work I was doing was great, there was always something new and interesting happening. As far as Northern Ireland were concerned, we were looking towards the 1998 World Cup now. Our qualifying group for '98 was very, very tough. Germany won the group, Ukraine went through to the play-offs in second place, Portugal didn't even qualify, that's how strong that group was! Again, it was ups and downs for us, we were a bit erratic. We got another great result in Germany, we drew 1-1, Tommy Wright made eight or nine brilliant saves in that one, and then in the return game in Belfast, we were 1-0 up against them with about 20 minutes to go before Bierhoff went berserk and scored a six minute hat-trick.

Our last game in that group was in the Stadium of Light in Lisbon, and we lost 1-0 to Portugal. They had Luis Figo, Conceição, Paulo Sousa, Fernando Couto, they were a tasty side. I spoke to some of their players afterwards and they couldn't understand why we still gave our all, even though we were nowhere near qualifying, but that was just our attitude, we always gave 100%. Jim Boyce was the president of the Irish FA at the time and he came down to the dressing room afterwards to congratulate everyone on the performance. We were building a side and losing 1-0 to that Portugal team was no disgrace at all, Jim understood that. There was a board meeting coming up soon after that game and Bryan had spoken to Jim about a new contract for us. That all seemed to be coming together, Jim was happy with us. When the meeting happened though, it didn't go that way. There were people on the board thinking we should be beating teams like Portugal in Lisbon! That's what you're often up against in football.

I was doing a bit of coaching with some young lads down in Omagh. I finished the session and I popped in to see my mum and dad on my way home from there. While I was there, the news came on and the headlines were "Bryan Hamilton and Gerry Armstrong have been sacked by Northern Ireland." The mobile signal down there was pretty terrible back then, but eventually I managed to get in touch with Bryan. He said, "So you've heard the news?" I told him I'd seen it on TV. "What? Nobody got in touch with you?!" To be fair to Jim Boyce, the next day he called me and said he'd been trying to get hold of me but he couldn't get through. He told me that other people on the board wanted a change and he was outvoted on it. That was us finished.

I did get to the World Cup in the end though – I covered it for Eurosport, travelling all round France. I was working with Steve Cram, the Olympic runner. He was one of the presenters and we would go to different stadiums, it was a brilliant experience. He was a big football fan, a Sunderland supporter, his uncle had been a player in the '60s, Bobby Cram, at West Brom and Colchester. The one day, we'd finished covering our game, the afternoon match between Romania and Croatia in Bordeaux, and we wanted to go and watch England, who were playing that night, against Argentina. We ran into this bar, and it was just full of England fans, it was packed – if England had won their group instead of finishing second to Romania, they'd have been the game in Bordeaux that day, so a lot of fans had gambled on being there and ended up going to the wrong game.

We ordered a drink and started watching the game. Michael Owen's goal was sensational, then David Beckham got sent off and the place went crazy! We got to the penalty shootout and as the players were going up to take them, Steve was asking me, would they score or not. I was getting it right. "Simeone – very clinical, he'll score." Then David Batty comes up to take a penalty and I said to Steve, "I've never seen him take a penalty, he doesn't do it for Leeds!"

"Oh no, don't tell me that!"

And of course, he missed it, so I got that one right too unfortunately!

Working with Eurosport was good fun and it got me well acquainted with Paris in particular, because I spent a lot of time there covering the Champions and Europa Leagues. It was a real United Nations set up they had there. All the voiceover booths were in one big hall, partitioned off from each other, but the partition didn't go up to the ceiling, it was only about five or six feet high. We would be sitting on one side, then you'd have the Germans, then the Spaniards, the Italians, whatever. We all did our research in the office together, we'd be talking about players, and it gave me an even bigger insight and knowledge into the players, guys coming in from Africa, especially into France. I saw all these young players coming through before they made a bigger name for themselves.

Around that time, I did the African Nations Cup with Angus Loughran, Statto from the "Fantasy Football" show. I was his co-commentator. Nigeria against Ghana was the first game we covered, and we didn't have any team information coming through to us, nothing. We're all in this hall, the Italians, the Germans, the Spanish commentators, all asking where the team information was, when were we getting it? We had no squads, no numbers, we had no teamsheets, nothing, and we went on air like that. Angus was trying to blag his way through it, "Welcome to the stadium, the first game of the competition," just trying to fill the air.

"So Gerry, what can you tell me about Nigeria?"

"Not an awful lot Angus!"

We were just desperately filling time, but then once the game kicked off, we could only refer to players by their number because apart from a couple of exceptions, we didn't know who they were. "The number seven looks dangerous, got a lot of pace, good balance, he's gone past the full-back really easily and put in a decent cross." This went on for about ten minutes - it seemed like hours - and finally, somebody came running in and threw the teamsheets at us all and we could get on and do the job properly. If you can deal with that, you can deal with anything on live TV. Anything that went wrong after that, I just thought how easy it was compared with that!

Eurosport also covered the Toulon youth tournament, which was great for spotting young players. During the tournament, somebody had a brainwave – why not put a microphone in the goal. Portugal were playing the Republic of Ireland. There was a free-kick after five minutes and the goalkeeper called, "Four in the wall! Right, right. I said fucking right! For fuck's sake!" You could hear everything. They took the kick, the 'keeper's diving and you can hear him scream, "Fuck!!!!" as the ball went past him and in. He was screaming and swearing at his defenders and we were just crying laughing, me and the commentator, we could hardly speak. If you're doing a live show, it's a live show, there's nothing you can do about it!

Working with Eurosport in particular was brilliant for me because it broadened my outlook and career in terms of learning about all the players who played in other countries, not just the UK or Spain, but in France and Germany and Turkey and Holland. I got to learn about all of the top stars, and then because we did the youth tournaments too, we saw the young talent coming in from South America. That was very beneficial for me, I built up a good reputation and a good bank of knowledge. I had lots of coaches or managers phone me up and ask me for advice on players. I realised that some players who looked fantastic in Spain, Portugal or France, they weren't going to be as sensational in England because it was a very different type of game, you needed to have certain qualities and the right mental attitude. I did find that very interesting. When anybody wanted information on a player at Sky, it was me that they came to - maybe I'd seen him play in the Belgian league or in the French League, or whatever, but I would give whatever information I had. But Sky and

Eurosport did start a real trend of people who wanted to know more about football and to look outside the box, to study what other countries were doing.

A bit later on, I remember having a meeting with Arsene Wenger at London Colney, their training ground. He was looking ahead to the next season – Pat Rice was his assistant at the time. Pat met me there. "Did you bring your boots? We've got a practice game before lunch, half an hour each way, staff against the youth team." Arsene was playing and he said, "Gerry, you play with me!" Every time I got the ball, he was asking me for it. I'd give him the ball and he was being closed down and he gave it straight back again! Pat was refereeing the game and I was amazed at the challenges, there were some unbelievable tackles going in there, it was really competitive. I ended up as a target man, making the ball stick and playing passes off to everybody. David Dein was on the sidelines watching it, it was a lot of fun, especially because the staff beat the kids.

Afterwards, we went in for lunch and Arsene said, "I just want to pick your brains. I need a centre-forward and I need a goalkeeper." Fernando Morientes was on the bench quite a bit for Real Madrid, but he was six feet two, good in the air and he scored goals. He was getting 15 a season, and he was only starting maybe 20 games, so I recommended him as a target man who would do really well in the British game. While we were having lunch, we were making contact to see who the agent was, who they could speak to, all that kind of thing. I got the details of his contract - if they wanted to buy him, that's what it would cost. It wasn't the fee that stopped Arsenal, it was because he was earning around £32,000 a week and that was above their threshold. Arsene wasn't going to bring somebody in and pay them more money than the players that he already had, which I thought that was quite commendable.

I said 15 years ago that they should have capped wages to try and keep it under control, because it has spiralled out of control. Families can't go to watch football anymore because it's too expensive. It's like a once a year trip for some now, whereas a lot of the families had season tickets in the past. But now, if you go to watch a club in London, with your son and daughter and your wife, it's over £200 just for the seats. Then there's transport and then you've got your food and everything else, it's a fortune. It's putting it out of the reach of the normal punter, which I don't like. I think everybody should enjoy football, it's the world game and it should continue to be that way. Football was the working class game, but now, half the working class can't afford to go to a football match because they have to cover the wages that they're paying players. I'm hoping that the pandemic has taught people a lesson, that it's not all about money. It's about people and people's lives.

I look at Burnley and what they've done and that impresses me. They keep their wage structure. Every year they stay up, they stay in the league, they finish sixth or seventh from the bottom, but they stay up and they produce players. There's a system there that works. But under the current system, Burnley can never win the league. They remind me a lot of Watford in 1982/83 when we just took the league by storm. Who could ever have envisaged Watford finishing second? Seven or eight years before that, they were in the Fourth Division. That's a great story. That's what you need. You need to have something to aspire to, something the fans and the players can dream about. But Burnley can't do what Watford did because of the way the finances are now.

Going back to that meeting with Arsene Wenger, wages were the issue with the goalkeeper too. I recommended Santiago Canizares at Valencia, he was really consistent, but again, he was on over £30,000 a week, so they backed off both him and Morientes. We got taking about other players, one of them the little left winger at Seville, José Antonio Reyes. He was 20, 21 at the time, so I got a lot of background detail about him. I didn't think he would travel especially well out of Seville. He was a gitano, a Romani. I didn't think a big city like London would suit him, a different climate, he didn't speak the language, I thought they should be careful on him. They still signed him, but it didn't really work out for him and he went back to Spain after a couple of years.

I was working flat out by the late '90s, even after finishing with Northern Ireland and while I was so busy, Caron used to organise all my booking. She had my diary sorted out and believe me, I was booked to go everywhere. She was still desperate to get married and she had even changed her name to Caron Armstrong by deed poll. The alarm bells were going off then, but I was stuck in a no win situation because we'd already had Aishleen together. My gut was telling me not to get married, but over the years, I must admit that I felt a bit more comfortable with her and I thought maybe she was changing. Eventually I gave in, and we ended up getting married. That's when the real trouble started. I was still working around the clock, earning good money, but I didn't know half of what was going on back home. Let's just say she was enjoying herself while I was away, and I later found that out to my cost.

We had another daughter, Caitlin, who was born on March 2nd 2000, but even then, the marriage never really worked out. Reflecting on it all later, I think there was a bit of the hairshirt about it all for me, some old fashioned Catholic guilt. I felt like I deserved what was happening to me with Caron, it was my comeuppance if you like, because of what I had done with Ann and the boys. You've made your bed, now you've got to lie in it, that type of thing.

When I split up with Ann, obviously I continued to see my two sons who were still at school then. I was still living in Brighton, so I saw the boys every day and went to their football training and I was involved with them at the school. But it was still difficult for them, growing up with the fact that their father wasn't living in the same house with them and again, that's something that I do regret. Thankfully, we were able to keep a good relationship going. Ciaran and Brendan were both quite sporty, Ciaran loves golf, both of them played football. I actually played Sunday morning football with Ciaran when he was about 18 or 19. He's a big lad, six feet two, a decent centre-forward with a good touch. But he was a nice lad, he wouldn't have been nasty or rough or anything like that, not like his father! He was doing really well in the Sunday morning team and I was playing at the back, I was probably 48, 49 then. Ciaran was doing really well in a game up on the Brighton University pitches one Sunday morning and giving the opposition a hard time, so one time when he went up to win a ball, the centre-half who he was playing against threw his elbow and smashed Ciaran in the face. There was a bit of blood and he had to come off, he couldn't carry on playing.

I was having a go at the referee and said, "Hey, do you not want to send him off?" He said, "It was an accident Gerry." I told him I didn't think so, but he wasn't having it. Danny Bloor was our manager, and he played in the team at right-back. He was going to bring the sub on and stick him up front. "No you're not," I said. "I'll go up front." The first ball that came in, there was no way I wasn't going to do him! I threw my elbow straight in his face, and he went down like a sack of potatoes. The referee didn't know what to do. The guy looked up at me and I said, "It's good when you dish it out isn't it, but it's terrible when you have to take it!" The guy never said anything, he just got up and walked straight off the pitch. The referee looked at me

197

and I said, "Don't say anything!" That's when I knew I was going to have to hang the boots up. Once it starts affecting you like that, you can't play in the same team as your son!

Even through all the break up with Ann, myself and the boys stayed close, which is great credit to both of them and to Ann. But things were much more difficult with Caron. She would put me in really awkward situations all the time. She put me on the spot, and she was very demanding. We would go to places and she'd say, "Do you know who I am? I'm Gerry Armstrong's wife!" Stuff like that was really embarrassing for me because I'm not that type of person. She always wanted to be the centre of attention though, and that was true whether I was at home or away working. As I said, I started getting vibes from different friends about what Caron was doing while I was away and that marriage came to an abrupt conclusion. Going off with Caron had been a big mistake, she was bad news from my point of view. It did not end well and we split up. When we came to divorce, she just basically wanted money, and I gave her the money and the house just to get away from it all, because things were never going to work out between us.

When I split with Caron, in 2001, I ended up moving in with Frankie Fraser Junior and his wife Maria. I'd played football with Frankie, he was a friend of mine and I was there with them for a few months. Frankie's dad used to come down to Brighton every three or four weeks to see him, and I'd get talking to him and the stories he could tell about his life, about the Krays and all of that, they were unbelievable! But Frank and Maria took me in and then gave me a wee break there for about three or four months and they were really good to me as I was trying to get things sorted out and get myself back together again. I had to readjust my life and refocus everything and get back on track. It knocked me for six, I have to say. It took me a while to get myself sorted but I got there in the end. For a time, I didn't know where I was going. I was drifting, I had no clue what I was doing. I was working but I didn't have an idea of what I wanted.

The one thing that I definitely did know was that I'd had enough of marriage and relationships. I didn't want any of that again, it was all too complicated. I'd had it up to there with women. Which shows you how much I know...

CHAPTER NINETEEN

THE BANGKOK ORANGE MEN

Like a lot of people, men especially, my answer to going through a bad time was to throw myself into my work. The television work kept coming in, I was heavily involved in all of that and then in early 2004, I became part of Lawrie Sanchez's management team when he took over as manager of Northern Ireland. I'll come back to the job side of it later, but it was taking that job that indirectly led to me meeting Deborah, which was the best thing that ever happened to me.

I was coming up to 50, I had no plans to get married again. I wasn't looking for a relationship after all the grief I'd had with Caron. Once that was over, that was it for me, but a chance encounter changed all of that. I went out with Stephen Watson from the BBC and a couple of other guys after a Northern Ireland game against Serbia & Montenegro in Belfast at the end of April 2004. I was staying overnight then flying back to England early the next day. We went to a place called The Apartment which is near the back of the city hall. It was a club upstairs, with a bar, music. We were having a chat about the game and in comes a girl called Alison Campbell – she's married to Darren Clarke now. Alison was Miss Northern Ireland in 1982 and I knew her from back in those days. She was running her own modelling agency by then and she had four or five girls with her, all models. She knew Steven and she recognised me from back in the '80s and we got chatting. She'd just been doing a gig with the girls and she introduced me to them.

One of them was Deborah, and that's how we first met. I found out later that she'd been an air hostess and had taken me on loads of flights from Belfast City to Gatwick over the years with Jersey European. She had also worked for Air France and remembered flying me to Paris when I was working for Eurosport. In fact, we'd crossed paths so many times. I've got photographs that she took of me when I was playing football for Northern Ireland, when we were staying at the Culloden hotel. She went there with a friend when she was 13 or 14 and they got some photographs of myself, Pat Jennings and Alan McDonald. I didn't even see these photographs until we'd been together maybe two years. I was looking at a scrapbook one night and saw photographs of me in it! It was a crazy set of coincidences. Nothing happened when we first met that night, because she was in a relationship at the time, although she wasn't happy in that situation. I didn't know anything about all of that at that stage.

About three or four months later, in the summer, I was back in Belfast to cover the Milk Cup, a massive youth tournament up the coast. I was working for adidas, doing some coaching up in Coleraine, Portstewart, Portrush. Again, I didn't know it, but Deborah had been a Milk Cup girl over the years too, another time when our paths had crossed. I was going to go home the day after the competition finished, but I got a phone call from Norman Whiteside who was staying at a hotel in Templepatrick. He was with Viv Anderson for a charity golf event. He had asked me to go the year before, but I couldn't because I was working. He said, "Big man, I hear you're over here? Our golf day and dinner's tomorrow. Can you not stay another day and come down and see us?" I rearranged a few things and stayed the extra day and went down. It was a brilliant day, they had a great sponsor with Bombay Sapphire, but because of that, I don't think we got round the 18 holes. I think we only played nine, Norman and I, because we went and had a wee drink every other hole! It was great catching up with him and the boys and we went to the dinner that night.

Every player or celebrity was at a different table and Alison Campbell's agency also had a girl at every table. I came down to get a drink before going into the dinner and there was a girl in front of me. She turns round and it was Deborah. She said, "Hi Gerry, you probably don't remember me."

"I do, I met you with Alison a few months ago."

"I'm just at the bar here. Do you want me to get you a drink?"

"No, I buy the girl a drink, you don't buy me a drink."

"This girl does!"

And so Deborah bought me a drink. That was our first real communication. I went over to sit at my table and she was on the table next to me. The girl on our table was Zoe Salmon, who went on to be on "Blue Peter" on the BBC. She's now a good friend of ours and we had good craic. But I kept looking at Deborah. She had her back turned to me and she was wearing a low cut dress, right down the back, and all I could see was this gorgeous girl sitting in front of me with her dark hair. I said hello to her again afterwards and we got chatting for an hour, we got on really well, we were having a bit of a sing song. It all went on until about three or four in the morning. She was telling me how she was in a relationship but she wasn't really sure where it was going. I found out afterwards that it was over as far as she was concerned, but I didn't know that at the time, so I didn't even know if I would see her again. But I was intrigued with her, I thought she was a really lovely girl. The next day, I asked Norman to get hold of Alison and get Deborah's number off her, I said I'd love to speak to her again. He got me the number after a couple of days and I gave her a call out of the blue. We talked on the phone over the next couple of weeks, chatting every other day.

Not long after, I was working for the BBC and doing a show called "Bits of Belfast". It was a documentary on the Falls Road and it was something different for me. I was always being interviewed on the football shows, but I was never an interviewer. This was me talking to people who were going back to World War Two, talking about when Belfast was bombed. We were talking about the Falls Baths, which is where I learned to swim, and how, because there were so many people killed, and they hadn't got enough room for the bodies in the mortuary, they took them to the Falls Baths and put them in the bottom of the pool, because they had more room there. I was talking to different people about their war stories, talking about Harland and Wolff, and about Gallagher's the cigarette factory, which were two big employers in the city back then. They were the names that had built Belfast really. One of the interviews was with Gerry Adams. He wasn't going to take part in the documentary with the BBC, but when he found out I was going to be the interviewer, because I knew his family and they knew me, he said, "If Gerry's doing it, no problem, I'll be happy to do that."

While I was there, I caught up with Deborah and she told me that she had finished her relationship. We got chatting about various things and she told me that her sister, Dawn, had lost her husband three or four months earlier, he had died. She had two young kids and was finding it a bit difficult. I had a flat in Brighton at the time and told her that if they all wanted to come over for a wee break, I'd get it all arranged. So over they came, we did a trip down to the Palace Pier and took the kids, Sophie and Jade, on the rides and all the rest of it. While they were staying with me, my mum phoned the one night and she said, "I heard you were over in Belfast, what was that for?" I told her about the show and I mentioned one of the places we'd been was the city cemetery, where a lot of the Belfast power brokers were buried. I went to the different gravestones and talked about them and there was a guy with me who was a historian. He could tell you all about the families and everything else. This one grave had a big stone, with a big cross on it, and it was for a guy called William Harbison. As soon as I saw the name, I knew I recognised it, but I couldn't remember what that the link was so I was asking my mum about him. While I was talking about William Harbison, Deborah and her sister were both looking at me strangely. I was on the phone for about half an hour and then when I'd finished, Deborah asked me why I was talking about William Harbison. My mum had told me that his sister, Jane, was my great-great-grandmother. And Deborah said, "Well, William Harbison is our great-great-grandfather." So her great-great-grandfather and my great-great-grandmother were brother and sister! What made that even more incredible is that I'm Catholic and Deborah's a Protestant. It got even more spooky later on because I had a great-aunt, Annie. She was a midwife, and she delivered my mum. Deborah and my mum were talking one time and it turned out that Annie also delivered Deborah's mum, which again is so strange because they're from totally different backgrounds, protestant and catholic.

Deborah was like a breath of fresh air. I was just out of a bad relationship and had been single for probably a year and a half. I was not a fan of being with women anymore, I didn't want anything to do with them. After Caron, that had been such a bad experience that I wasn't interested any longer, but Deborah restored my faith in women. That's being totally honest. My mum was the first person to see the difference in me, and things began to take off from there. She's had a big impact on my life without a shadow of a doubt. She was brought up by her mum, because her parents had broken up when she was a toddler. She only saw her dad in some of the various school holidays and in the summer because he lived in England. She's very self-sufficient, she'd help anybody, she really puts heart and soul into everything. And all those coincidences, the way we were getting on so well so quickly, it just made us think, "This was meant to be". We just embarked on an adventure together.

That adventure included leaving England and heading back home. I hadn't any plans to go back to Belfast before I met Deborah. She was quite prepared to come and live with me in Brighton, but she didn't know anybody there and both of us had families back in Northern Ireland. There was a lot of bad history for me in Brighton with people like my ex-wife, so I didn't really have anything that made me want to live there because it was easy enough for me to go over and see the children. Ciaran and Brendan were grown up by then anyway, both into their mid 20s, so they were doing their own things, but I could still get back to see Aishleen and Caitlin.

Deborah and I decided that we would come back to Northern Ireland and we'd start afresh. It was lovely to come back home at that stage, but because of who I was, and who she was, a Miss Northern Ireland contestant, a Miss Belfast, known in the modelling industry and for doing commercials and stuff on TV, we were both well known faces. Then there was the age barrier. There's just over 21 years between us, so we inevitably attracted attention. Everywhere we went, there was press. One night, we were in the Europa hotel and it was about two o'clock in the morning. We were sitting on a settee, there was a big bar, I think there was a wedding going on. We're sitting there and chatting away and this guy ran across, he was obviously a professional photographer, starts going click, click, click and he runs straight down the stairs, like a paparazzi. We just looked at each other and laughed. It just seemed funny to us. We thought it was a bit of a joke, we took it all with a pinch of salt, but it could get annoying sometimes.

With all of that kind of thing though, we decided it would be best not to get married in Northern Ireland - Deborah definitely didn't want that. At the time, my brother was going away to Thailand, to a place called Hua Hin, so we decided to have a look at that and see what it was all about. I phoned the Hyatt Hotel and the manager there was from Liverpool, I told him my name and he immediately knew who I was, because he was a big football fan. I told him we were hoping to get married in July, because that's when everybody takes time off in Northern Ireland, and so people would be free to come over. That conversation went well, so next we had to go and plan everything. We went into a restaurant in Holywood, and we sat down and we planned our wedding there for July 2005.

Deborah said she didn't want an engagement ring, she just wanted to go off and get married. We hadn't announced it to anybody at that point. I told Deborah I had an idea how to announce it, but I hadn't said any more about it. About 10 or 12 days later, Northern Ireland had a summer international friendly against Germany at Windsor Park, 4th June, and it was actually my niece Jade's birthday. I'd told Deborah we could go on the pitch before the game as a treat for Jade, so she could tell her friends she'd been on Windsor Park. In the meantime, I had been in touch with a friend who had a jewellery shop in Brighton and another one in Covent Garden. He had a stone that was three and a half carats, he said, "You're going to love this!" I guessed her finger size and he got a ring made.

What I'd decided to do was propose to Deborah on the pitch and announce it to everyone there and then. Lawrie Sanchez told me it was fine, and to do it around two o'clock before the kick-off at three. There were probably 5,000 maybe 6,000 fans in the stadium at the time. I'd prompted the TV company, they were in on it, so when we went out on the pitch with Jade, Sophie and Deborah's sister Dawn, they came over as if they were doing an interview. I'd made my Northern Ireland debut against West Germany, so I just told Deborah they wanted to talk to me about that. The commentator came over and said, "I'm with Gerry Armstrong." And so, live on TV, I announced our engagement and pulled the ring out of my tracksuit pocket. Deborah swore, live on BBC TV, "Oh shit!" It was hilarious because her face was a picture. She had no idea what was going on. She was very, very shocked, but she was pleased. I had told her dad the day before to watch BBC tomorrow, so he saw it as well. Things like that make your relationship stronger, but we were always strong from the very start. We were singing off the same hymn sheet and I just wish I'd met her sooner.

In the end, that summer we went out to Thailand. We used a wedding planner out there, called Suphaphorn Dicks… We went to the registry office in Bangkok to get married and then after that, we had a reception at the Hyatt Hotel. They do it differently over there. They do small dishes, like tapas. We looked through the selection of all the different tapas and we had 16 different dishes come out over the two hours. It was a fantastic occasion, everybody had a great time, everyone loved it. The funny thing about it was that the ceremony over there is something completely different. It was a fantastic thing to be a part of because it meant we were married by nine

Buddhist monks. They were all dressed in orange robes and so it turned out that on the 12th of July, we got married by nine orange men!

When I met Deborah, it was as if I took on a new identity. She gave me the encouragement and the enthusiasm to want to be a father again. The doctor had said it was doubtful that she could get pregnant, and on top of that, I was 51 now and I had had the snip, which I had to have reversed. Things were not in our favour! Seven or eight months after we got married, we came back from a trip to Barbados - we went over there for Christmas and I found out about rum! We had a ball and met a lot of friends out there, lots of parties and sing songs. Just after we came back, we were going to a birthday party. She was running around the house and trying to choose a dress, "What about this dress, what about that one?" As she was trying them on, I said to her, "I have a funny feeling that we're pregnant".

"No, I'm not. I would know".

But I had a real feeling about it, an instinct. We went off to the party that night, and I stopped on the way to buy a couple of bottles of champagne to take with us. While I was in there, I saw a pregnancy test, so I picked one up and it had two in it – I don't suppose they sell pregnancy tests and champagne together that often, it's usually one after the other! I got back in the car and told Deborah, "Right, there's two bottles of champagne in there for the birthday party and a pregnancy test with two units."

"What did you get that for?"

"I want you to try it tomorrow morning, I've got this feeling."

So anyway, we had a great night and came back after the party and woke up the next day and she was going to the toilet. I told her to take the test in with her.

"Are you kidding me?"

"No, just use it and see."

She did the test and came back and it takes a minute or two for it to come through. She was sitting there and she said, "Will you look at it and see what it says?" I was watching it and it came up that she was pregnant. I said, "You won't believe this. You're pregnant!"

She didn't believe it, she thought it must be a mistake. We waited for another 20 minutes or something and she did the other test, and it came up that she was pregnant as well. She was all excited now and she called the gynaecologist to let him know and to arrange to see him and he said, "Well, stranger things have happened!" We called my mum and Deborah's sister Dawn and brother Ian, everybody was just thrilled. We started to make plans, what we would call the baby if it was a boy or a girl. We didn't want to know until the birth, but we thought it was going to be a boy, and we were going to call him Bradley. Jim Corr's girlfriend was pregnant at the same time, she thought she was having a boy too, and was going to call him Bradley as well, but then changed it to Brandon. Of course, our baby was a girl and we called her after Deborah's mom, which was Marian. We call her Marianna, born on September 21st 2006.

It wasn't plain sailing though. When I'd sorted out the divorce with Caron, we agreed we didn't want to be together any longer, the settlement was worked out, I thought that was a chapter of my life that had been long closed. Caron had the house, whatever money there was, she had the kids, it all seemed sorted out. She seemed happy enough, but she then sold the house and moved into rented accommodation. As soon as she knew I was happy with Deborah, that we were settled down and that we're having our own our own child, she decided that she didn't want our kids.

She sent me a message saying, "I'm done. I don't want the kids anymore." I found out one weekend, when she left them on their own from the Friday night right through to the Monday. When I found out, I called Aishleen, who was maybe 12 or 13 at the time, and asked her to call her grandparents over there, tell them the situation and tell them that they were going to have to come and look after her and Caitlin. They did that and they weren't happy about what had happened either. From there, myself and Deborah had to take the girls on board. We'd only been married around a year and were starting a new life and for Deborah to suddenly have two kids arrive in the picture as well as our own baby, I don't know any other woman that would have done it to be honest. That's what makes her so special, that she did all of that and took it in her stride.

Aishleen didn't want to come and live in Northern Ireland but Caitlin was happy to live anywhere, just to get away from it all. Even before she moved over, she was calling Deborah her mum, she just wanted somebody to look after her. We brought Caitlin over and then I had to make arrangements with friends in Brighton to look after Aishleen and help her growing up. It was very sad for the kids that it all went that way.

Even now, I still can't believe Deborah did what she did, to take on the two kids and all that responsibility, because she was only 29 when we got married. I have to say, Aishleen was a nightmare for a while! She was a real fiery personality, she just wanted to clash all the time because obviously she was going through a really tough time, trying to grow up and having a lot of difficulties with her real mother. Everything came right in the end though. Nowadays, she's become a senior nurse. She's got her own child, and the first person she called when she found out she was pregnant was Deborah. She stayed with us throughout the pregnancy, Deborah organised all the food for Theo's Christening, and she is Theo's Godmother as well as his grandmother! Aishleen looks on Deborah as being her mum for what she's done for her and they are so close. It's the same with Caitlin, Deborah brought her up from when she was four years of age, and that takes a special type of person to do that. Caitlin did well at school too, she's up at university in Glasgow now, so thankfully, things are great within our family.

The stuff we went through over the first year or two with Caron and with the children, it was very hard. But I tell you this now, if I had to go through all of that again, and worse, to end up with Deborah - I'd do it in a heartbeat.

CHAPTER TWENTY

....

SOMETHING'S GOT TO GIVE...

When I got the sack with Bryan Hamilton back in 1997, I assumed that was the end for me with Northern Ireland, but I should have remembered what a strange game football can be.

At the start of 2004, the manager's job came up again for Northern Ireland and I was in for the job. When I went to meet the appointment panel they were keen on me getting on board, but they were insistent that it was a full-time job. I was working at least three or four days a week doing Spanish football for Sky, I was working for Eurosport, I was doing European football and so I didn't really want to pass all of that up for a full-time job with Northern Ireland. I told them if that was the case, then fair enough, I was out of the running.

Lawrie Sanchez was in the frame for the job and he called me and said, "What about if you came with me as my assistant, with your background and your knowledge we'd be a good team." He'd managed at Wycombe and they'd recently done really well in the FA Cup. He wanted to bring in Terry Gibson and Dave Beasant because they were old team-mates and they were both very good. I agreed, as long as it was only a part-time thing, and so I dropped into that role when Lawrie got offered the job.

We were a good management team, we all had different attributes. Lawrie was the brains behind it all. Dave was a brilliant goalkeeping coach. Gibbo was just a great coach, full stop, and a really bubbly personality. I was the so called legend who had played at two World Cups and had that experience and had the coaching badges as well. We weren't always singing off the same hymn sheet but 90% of the time we were, we had an agreement on how we thought we should play. Northern Ireland were not scoring goals when we took over, they had been going through a lean time, and it was something like 20 hours of football since the team had last scored. They weren't creating chances because the space between the front one and the four or five in the middle of the park was too big.

Lawrie's first game in charge came when we played against Norway at Windsor Park in February 2004 and lost 4-1, but at least we scored. David Healy got a goal, and that was Northern Ireland's first goal in 14 games, so the fans went crazy! Then the following month, we played in Estonia and won 1-0, David Healy scored again, an absolute screamer. It was only a first step, but at least everyone could start to feel like something positive was happening, that we were beginning to get somewhere.

The Euros were being played that summer. We weren't a part of that, so it was tough to get decent games on in Europe because a lot of the nations were preoccupied with that. We were scratching around a little bit, and we ended up going on a Caribbean tour. We had only just taken over and it seemed like it would be a good chance to bond the squad together and get to know everyone over 10 or 12 days. It was a low key opportunity for us to work with the players without the focus of playing in big games against major nations. It gave us an extended period to explain to them what we were looking to do and to get a better idea of what the players were like, on and off the pitch.

It was a pretty strong squad that we took with us, only a couple of the boys missing with injuries, so it was a good set up. We flew out to Miami which was fine, but from there, we got on this 40 seater plane and we were island hopping, from one to the next, dropping people off and picking others up like at bus stops, before we got to Barbados. That didn't go down too well with the players after a long journey, but once we got to Barbados, the hotel was good, it was on the beach, the lads had a couple of drinks and something to eat, and they were happy again.

The first game was against Barbados. The pitch wasn't great, the officials were awful. Me and Dave Beasant got sent off twice! We were making a substitution at a throw-in, which was on the other side of the pitch. We were sending a defender on, so normally, the referee lets him run into the box and you set up before the throw gets taken. But as soon as we made the change, he let them take the throw, and so we were a man short effectively. They nearly scored so we went crazy and he sent us both off, but then we came back down to sit on the bench again and then got sent off again later on in the game.

We drew 1-1 in Barbados and then went to play St Kitts & Nevis. We got there, the hotel was a bit Mickey Mouse, the food wasn't great. We were getting ready to take the players training and I must admit, we were a bit nervous because some of the facilities in Barbados hadn't been great. When we got there, there was no grass in sight, there were a couple of goats tethered on the pitch, there were sheep wandering through. Lawrie had come separately in a car while we'd gone down in the bus with the players, so he got there a few minutes later and I said to him, "Look at the state of this training pitch."

"It's worse than that Gerry. This isn't the training ground. This is where we're playing tomorrow."

I had to go and tell the players that, and that did not go down well! It has got to be the worst pitch I have ever seen in my life, but in the end, we won the game 2-0. The last game was against Trinidad & Tobago. That was at the Dwight Yorke Stadium, which was a cracking stadium, a brilliant surface. We won 3-0, David Healy got a couple of goals, so that was a good ending to it. After the game, Dwight took us all back to his place for a party and that was a lot of fun.

That was the point of the whole tour really, it worked, because for all the troubles we had, it brought us all closer together, we started to get a bit of a bond going amongst the staff and the players and we started to really improve. You find out a lot about each other in those circumstances and it became clear to Lawrie, myself, Gibbo and Dave that we needed to play a more attacking team. We decided to be a little bit more adventurous without going gung ho, and we wanted to try and develop the team and build the confidence.

We were very fortunate at the time to have David Healy who really could score goals. If you put him in the right situation, alongside a target man who was going to win the ball in the air and knock it down in the space, he could finish. He became the talisman. From there, we got the rest of the team really well organized. Jim Magilton was very technical as a midfield player, we had Keith Gillespie who had pace, Gerry Taggart was a rock at the back, Damien Johnson was captain, Michael Hughes was in the team, great left foot, could go past people, good free-kick taker. We had a nucleus of good players and the team bonded over that tour. Danny Sonner was great because he was a real comedian as well as a good player. You always need that around you because the entertainment value was different class. We just grew as a group.

World Cup qualifying was always going to be extremely tough because we were in a pretty fierce group of six, the top two going through. England, Poland, Austria, Wales and Azerbaijan were our opponents, so we were really up against it, and all the more so after we lost our first game, 3-0 at home to Poland. When you are in a group like that, obviously the first thing is to try and pick up as many good results as you can, because even if you don't eventually qualify, at least that will improve your ranking and your seeding in the draw for future competitions. Aside from that though, you're looking to produce a couple of special performances and results that give you the encouragement that you are heading in the right direction. Confidence grows as you win games and that creates a team, the players look forward to meeting up and you start to get on a roll. We were all realistic enough to understand that we weren't going to be winning one game after another in that group, but we wanted to put down a marker for the future.

We nearly did that in a crazy game in Wales, the second of the group, a few days after we'd lost to Poland. After nine minutes, Michael Hughes and Robbie Savage were both sent off and then almost immediately, Jeff Whitley scored a cracker from the edge of the box. Ten minutes later, David Healy got through to score and he probably got a bit carried away with his celebration – he ran over to the corner flag and kicked it out of the ground in front of the Welsh fans. He got booked for that, which was maybe fair enough, but then he raised his fist to celebrate, which is something lots of goalscorers do. No big deal. Except to the Italian referee, who got the yellow card out again and sent him off. It was 10 versus 9 for the next 70 minutes and Wales managed to pull it back to 2-2 which was disappointing, but it was still a really strong performance.

There was a better one to come in September 2005, when we played England at Windsor Park. They were cruising in the group at that point, unbeaten, and we'd already lost 4-0 to them at Wembley. We'd had a chat as a management team and looked at their team, the likes of David Beckham, Michael Owen, Steven Gerrard, Frank Lampard, Wayne Rooney, we were really up against it. We decided that we were going to really press them, work on their first touch, play a Wimbledon type game where we put them under pressure and wouldn't let them settle on the ball, give them no time to play. That was the way we'd played at Watford as well. We had the players for three days before the game, we met up on the Sunday, and we did training exercises on that for a couple of days, groups of players in twos and threes, closing down and working on the first touch of the opponent.

I remember when the first whistle was blown, England kicked off, the ball went across, and then it was passed out and Keith Gillespie was the one chasing. He chased after one, chased after two and then chased after the third player, put them under pressure. They didn't like it because they wanted time on the ball. That set the pattern, and everybody followed suit, Steve Davis followed suit, David Healy, the whole side. We kept pressing and we played really well. As the game progressed, the longer it went, the more we started to think that we could get a result, that we might do something. Wayne Rooney lost his temper, and threw a hand out and caught Keith Gillespie, and got booked. Then he had a swear at David Beckham and all of that was working in our favour. At half-time, it was 0-0. I remember speaking to Sven-Goran Eriksson as we're walking off for the break, and Sven was a mate of mine at the time. He said, "Hey, Gerry, your boys are playing good." I said, "If you think we're good first half, wait until you see what we're like in the second!" Ever since, people always ask what we were talking about. I've never told them, but that's what we were saying.

The players knew that they had a chance, they actually believed they could go on and win it. The half-time team talk was easy, because the players were really fired up. We just gave them more encouragement. "Listen, you're doing everything right. You're starting to get more opportunities. We'll get one or two and we can win this match." Northern Ireland hadn't beaten England since 1972, so this was a chance to do something special. We got the chance in the second half. Steve Davis put a brilliant ball through the channel and David Healy hit an absolute screamer, there was no saving it. We had more chances after that. Warren Feeney was completely unmarked at the far post but David went for goal again, but if he had squared it into

213

the far post, Warren would have scored. Still, 1-0 was fine with us! In fact, 1-0 was the right score because the night before the game, Deborah had a dream that we won 1-0 and David got the goal, so obviously it was meant to be! It was a massive result for the confidence of the players and great reward for the fans. They were fantastic with us. They just love the Northern Ireland team and they got behind us.

It was interesting being involved in coaching at that level again, even just part-time. It was a reminder that players always think they know best. Even when I was playing, we had our own ideas, but you have to stick to the preparation that the manager gives you. For us, Billy Bingham was the boss. He said, "This is the way we're gonna play," and that's how we set up. But once they cross that line, as a manager or coach, there's not much you can do until half-time, so you need leadership out there. In '82, we didn't just have the captain that we looked to, we had a lot of leaders. Martin O'Neill was the captain, but Pat Jennings was a leader, Sammy McIlroy, David McCreery, Mal Donaghy, John McClelland. You can lead by example, that's the key. When you see your team-mates performing, it gives you confidence, and it helps you to believe in them. That's how you create the character of a team, where you have belief in each other, and you know that you can get a result, whoever you're playing. If you have the psychology right, that mentality where you trust and believe in each other, you're a long way towards doing well.

As a coach, sometimes you didn't know what was going on in the players' minds, even when we beat England. Before that game? I don't think they were 100% sure we could win. But if you train them right, if you work on closing down and pressing and you have a game plan, if it works in the first 5 or 10 minutes, the players start to think, "Hang on a minute, this is actually working!" They start to believe and they do it better. That's how things happen. I've seen that happen in so many games in the past, and I could see some of the teams we were playing against actually shrink in stature, because we've been so forceful. One determined challenge can change a game. Graham Taylor once said to me that the first couple of minutes of the game will more often than not determine what happens. If we show more enthusiasm, and more determination, and we've got more vigour, then that puts the opposition on the backfoot. You can take control of the game. I think that's a good point to make. It's to do with mental attitude, and the belief you have in yourselves. Organisation and preparation is so important and that's what won us that game against England.

Going into qualifying for the Euros in 2008, we had a bit more confidence in ourselves after results like that one, even though we were picked in the same group as Spain. I checked with Lawrie when the first games were and they were going to be the first week in September. He was off to organise the fixtures with the various associations and I said to him, "Get us Spain at home in that first week." He couldn't understand why, because they were such a good team, but I told him, "They only go back to training in early August, they won't be sharp by then, we'll have six weeks advantage over them. We'll be fitter and that will give us an edge." He managed to pull it off and we played them on September 6th 2006. It was a brilliant game, it could have finished 5-4 either way, but we beat them 3-2 and David Healy scored all three goals. They were all good goals, against Iker Casillas in goal. It was the full team – Ramos, Puyol, Xabi Alonso, Raul, Xavi, Torres, Villa – but we caught them at the right time. That was my last game with Northern Ireland, and it couldn't have been a better way to go out – beating Spain again.

It felt like it was time that I cut back on some of the travelling I did with my work. I had the luxury of being able to do that because I was still involved in television, but something had to give and it was Northern Ireland that went. The fact that Deborah was pregnant was something that brought all that into focus for me. The baby was originally due in early October and Deborah had been having a few problems during the pregnancy. She'd been in hospital a couple of times with kidney stone problems and I decided that once the baby was born, I wasn't going to be doing the same amount of travelling away and that I needed to be home more. Thankfully everything went well with the birth and Marianna was born happy and healthy.

I was determined to do things differently once Marianna was born because I do regret not having had time for the kids before then, especially my two sons Ciaran and Brendan. I was lucky I was still living in Brighton when they were growing up and I did spend quite a bit of time with them but after we moved back to Northern Ireland, it got harder to see them and I don't get to see my grandchildren as much as I'd like. I must admit, I was probably oblivious to the way having a famous father impacted on the boys especially. As we've got older, we've sat and had a couple of pints of Guinness and chatted about it.

They tell me stories and I do cringe, because they tell me things that I hadn't really taken into consideration. Ciaran was a good footballer, but he wasn't going to be an outstanding player and the same with Brendan. But both of them had pressure from kids at school about how good they were. "Your dad played in the World Cup, why aren't you that good?!" Kids are very straightforward, they see things in black and white. Ciaran was about 14 when I split from his mom, and Brendan was around 12. They must have had a difficult period, even though I used to see them on a regular basis, but it's not the same when you're not there. I know more about that now from Deborah, because her parents split when she was about five weeks old and her dad lived in England. That's probably why she gets on really well with my two sons, because she understands where they're coming from. But when you're in the middle of it yourself, it's really hard to see. I didn't know about what was going on in the background, I was oblivious to it because I could only see it from my own point of view, my own angle. As I've got older, I hope that I've understood better the problems that they had, but then it was the same with the girls, Aishleen and Caitlin, because they were separated from me and then from their mum. I was determined that I was going to be around a lot more for Marianna and do things right for her.

Being involved with television does mean a lot of travelling and unsociable hours at times, but equally, it has meant a lot of unusual opportunities have come our way as a family. We've done a lot of travelling with the football, the punditry, we've been to different places around the world, but there have been other things too. We were asked to do the TV show called "Wags" in Northern Ireland, where the camera crew followed us three times a year, for a day or two at a time. One of the trips, Northern Ireland were playing in Iceland and I was covering that game. They came with us and Marianna was still a baby, 11 months old. I was sitting in the seat with Marianna and Deborah and they were behind us with a camera crew, following us and then going into the hotel, putting a special cot together so that she was going to be able to sleep in it. Then we were out with the fans, the fans were singing and it was just a great trip.

We had different people in our lives and one of them was Jim Corr, because we knew The Corrs really well. Jim and the girls were great fun, fantastic musicians, massively successful too. Jim had his own helicopter and he would land in our back garden after coming up from Dublin. We never thought too much of it at the time but now, if I ever reflect back on it, it was something special. There was one time when Jim said he was thinking of going across to Galway, over on the west coast of Ireland, to where they had this zip line and he said it would be great to go across. He took his son Brandon, who was six or seven, and our Caitlin, who was a wee bit older, she wanted to go, so they headed off in the helicopter. It took about 35 minutes to get to the other side of Ireland and they spent the day down there on this zip line doing stuff with the kids, and then flying back again. What kids get that opportunity?

Then in the summer, I'd be asked to go out to the likes of Singapore, or different parts of the world, to be part of a team doing a World Cup or whatever. I was able to take the family with me, we would have four or five weeks out there and see all kinds of things that most people never get the chance to experience. Actually, I got a tattoo done one time when I was in Singapore. Deborah was pregnant with Marianna at the time, so it was summer 2006, when the World Cup was on in Germany. I'd never had a tattoo done, but I wanted to put "Debby" on my back with Japanese love symbols underneath. That's the impact she had on me. Then about a year after she'd had Marianna, she decided to have a tattoo as well. She had "Gerry te quiero para siempre", which is Spanish for "Gerry, I will love you forever". I've got it in writing!

CHAPTER TWENTY-ONE

HAVE MICROPHONE, WILL TRAVEL

I've done 25 years in television now, and I'm very proud of the things that I have been involved in, a lot of which have changed the way that people watch football on TV. One of the things we really managed to do with the La Liga coverage was broaden the access the supporters had, taking them behind the scenes at the games they were watching. Knowing the right people is often a big part of that!

Fairly early on, around 2000 or 2001, we went over to Barcelona to cover a game. They were playing Real Madrid, and Steve McManaman was playing for them at that time. I knew Steve really well because I'd been part of him moving to Spain. I'd met Steve at Wembley along with his management people and they were asking about Spanish football, what it was like and whether would it be good for him. I said he'd love it and put him in touch with the right people in Barcelona and at Real Madrid to have negotiations with before he signed for Madrid. Steve has always kept in touch ever since. When we turned up to the game, Rob Palmer, myself, Guillem Balagué and the cameraman, we found the press room was packed. There was probably room for about 60, 70 people, but there was nearer 170 people in there! That really wasn't working for us. I thought we should go out on the pitch instead and get some shots of that, but access was restricted there, we weren't allowed on. We'd just got passes to go up to our booth up in the Gods.

I said, "What about if we can get to the manager?" Lorenzo Serra Ferrer had just taken over and I knew him, he'd been the reserve team manager when I was at Real Mallorca. We used to chat about the difference between English and Spanish football all the time and we got on really well. We asked the press officer if we could see him, and we were in straight away. So he said, "How can I help you?"

"We're hoping to get on the pitch."

"No problem."

He got us the access all areas bibs to put on, "Go anywhere you like!" This is like an hour and a half before kick-off or something, so we took a tour. We went into the tunnel that took you onto the pitch and there's a wee chapel on the right, so we took the camera in there, then we went into the Barcelona dressing room with the shirts up ready for the players. As we were going down the steps, the players had arrived from Real Madrid, and they were out on the pitch. Steve McManaman was among them and so that made it easy for us to have a conversation with Fernando Hierro, with Raul and with Steve. This was all live on Sky Sports News with Jeff Stelling. We were ground breakers in terms of what we were doing, having this insight. Sky just loved it. It was fantastic, a real special thing. We got a lot of credit for that and we started moving up the ladder and La Liga became increasingly important for Sky. Then it became a real competition with Andy Gray and Richard Keyes about which was the best league in the world!

Guillem wanted to start a review show on Sky of the Spanish games, "Revista de la Liga", but we never had a regular slot, Sky used to just drop it in the schedule when there was a space for it. We talked about the players, the up and coming talent, who was going to win the league. It was great because Real Mallorca were doing well at the time we started. They reached the final of the Cup Winners' Cup in 1999, the last one ever, and they lost to Lazio at Villa Park. They won the Copa del Rey for the first time in 2003 and to be commentating when they won their first major trophy was amazing. We really developed the show, and we ended up interviewing some really big names, presidents of clubs like Barcelona and the top players. Then we started inviting players on the show, Michel Salgado, Thierry Henry, Gaizka Mendieta, and the show really took off and developed. I was very proud of what everybody achieved. Sky were a fantastic company to work for.

It was brilliant that I could use the knowledge that I got from Spanish football and then later on from European football in general when I did more work for Eurosport. It was a really interesting period. There was always something going on. Martin O'Neill was at Celtic and he phoned me up, they were playing Valencia and he wanted information on them. He said, "I need to speak to our scout in Spain."

"Who's that?"

"You! What can you tell me about them?"

I'd start to get managers like Harry Redknapp and David Platt calling me up to pick my brains, trying to find who the future stars might be. Liam Brady was even talking to Arsenal about me going in there as a scout. For that period, it was wall to wall football, and I was in my element. I used to have Monday and Friday free, then Eurosport asked me to do the goals show on a Monday night as well, which was a review of all the goals that had been scored at the weekend. We covered seven or eight different leagues and then the leagues we hadn't got the rights to, we'd just talk about the top of the table as a bit of the review. One of the more difficult things was getting the names right in some of the leagues, but Turkey was fine because the top three were always Fenerbache, Galatasaray and Besiktas. Easy. But the start of this one season, a couple of weeks in, the producer says to me, "Have you seen the top of the Turkish league?" I had a look and it was this team with 14 letters in their name - Gençlerbirligi! How were we supposed to pronounce that? I put a call in to the Turkish embassy, "Can you help us out?" I spelt the team out and the guy was laughing. "It's pronounced Genshler-belligi." We started doing the show and the presenter says to me, "New leaders at the top of the Turkish league Gerry, which is a bit of a shock. Who are they?" I just rolled this name out, like it was always on the tip of my tongue!

Football has become more and more the world game over the last 25 years because it has taken a bigger and bigger hold in Asia. As I said, I used to go to Singapore to cover the World Cup or the Euros for ESPN, working for Andy Tate. I had a lot of people who followed me because of La Liga on Sky. Then I would be on ESPN doing the Premier League, so sometimes I'd be on for four or five hours on the Premier League, have an hour and a half break and come back on that night doing Spanish football. They would see my face for seven or eight hours over a Saturday and then Sunday was the same, so I had a big following in Asia. I watched football develop in Asia over 20 years and that really was fascinating, especially as it became so important to the game from a financial point of view. There was big money to be made on the television deals. I had a chat with Richard Scudamore from the Premier League about it, probably 10 or 12 years ago. I was doing ESPN, covering seven countries in Asia. He wanted to know how many people were watching. "Over 100million and growing every month." He couldn't believe it. By the end of that season, it was 200million and more who were watching. It was just crazy, crazy figures, and constantly going up and up. I put Scudamore in touch with Andy Tate and from there they started negotiating deals for the Premier League. That's where the big money started coming in. The snowball, once you start rolling it down the hill, it just gets bigger and bigger and bigger as it's moving along. That Asian TV money is what has really fuelled the Premier League juggernaut over the last decade or so.

That business side of the game has been really interesting and I've been able to help a few people out with my connections. Sky were always interested in the Northern Ireland scene, especially when the TV rights were coming up for grabs. When that was coming due, I got a phone call from Sky to keep a particular date free, on a Friday, to make sure I was around. They didn't tell me any more than that. A couple of days before that Friday, I got a call, "You're going to have to meet somebody in Belfast around eight o'clock in the morning."

"Who am I meeting?"

"Vic Wakeling's coming to Belfast."

Vic was the managing director at Sky. I met him at a coffee shop on the Lisburn Road - he got picked up by a limo at the airport, and he told me he was meeting the head of the Irish FA, Howard Wells. I gave him a bit of background on the committee and all of that, and then Vic asked what he was up against, the competition. He said he thought he'd been stitched up the last time the rights had been dished out. He said he'd made a good offer, but then he was told three days later that the BBC had offered £100,000 more. He felt that he'd been used to get more out of the BBC. But I knew Howard and I knew he wasn't like that. I said, "If you make an offer, and he likes it, he'll take it. It doesn't matter what anybody offers." Then I told him Sky had a presence in Northern Ireland. "We've covered all the schoolboy football. I've been covering that for Sky, all the schoolboy internationals, we've had cameras at Coleraine, Glentoran and Windsor Park."

There were none of the league games being shown live at that time, there was just a highlights package on a Saturday. Vic started writing up a deal to show so many live Irish league games as well as the international games and it was a really good deal. It was going to put the clubs and the players on the map. I thought it was really good for the development of Irish league football. He was still a bit unsure and he said, "If I knew what the BBC had really paid them, I'd feel happier." It so happened that I knew, so I told him and he worked around the figures from there. Anyway, they got the rights and he asked me to go to the press conference afterwards. There was a lot of opposition from the likes of the BBC and the papers, because they thought Sky was using their muscle to push the BBC out, which wasn't the case. They just wanted to get a deal where they could develop football. Vic got up and told them all about the presence we already had across the country at all these different grounds. "The reason I know that is because Gerry Armstrong told me, because he's been covering it." He got me to start talking about what Sky did. That won a lot of people round, the fact that at least five or six live games would be shown on Sky Sports of various league teams, and I was covering the games. I enjoyed that because it was an opportunity to bring something back to the grassroots of the game in Northern Ireland.

When we went back to live in Belfast, it did mean a huge amount of travelling because I used to have to fly over to do all the games. I remember covering a tournament at the end of the season, and there was an Italian club, there was Barcelona, there was Ajax and somebody else, four big clubs, all played in Amsterdam, and I went out to cover the games. It finished on the Sunday night then I flew from Amsterdam to Singapore to cover a dinner on the Monday night, a 16 hour flight and I was only there for like 24, maybe 30 hours - I actually managed to get a game of golf in, but your body clock's all over the place. But every week, it was flights. If Sky wanted me to cover a game in Germany, I had to go to Germany. And if they wanted me to cover a game in Finland, I had to go there. It was great fun, but it was hard because I had to leave the family behind. That was difficult.

Initially it wasn't so bad, because Deborah could come with me but obviously as Caitlin and Marianna got older, you couldn't keep taking them out of school. Before Marianna came along, I remember saying to Deborah one week, "I've got to go away this weekend to work on a game in Spain, it's the Classico, why don't you come with me?" So we went over to Madrid, we had a lovely hotel room, about 500 yards from the stadium. I'd got her a ticket and a pass to come in and watch the game, but she turned her nose up at it, "I don't really want to watch the game." Real Madrid against Barcelona, the biggest game in the world, can you believe it?! But the thing was, I was going to be in there for six or seven hours, so in the end, she decided to come in with me. We got there about an hour and a half before kick-off so I could start work, and we went into the Bernabéu Stadium. I love that place, it's vast, but at that time, it was pretty empty.

I took her down onto the pitch because I had to do a link for Sky Sports News, a couple of bits of information about who's fit and who's not fit. I went to do the interview and she wasn't really too bothered about being there. Deborah was standing out of shot and then she comes running over to me. "Look who's coming out of the tunnel!" The players had started to come out, Zinedine Zidane, Ronaldo and David Beckham, all the stars from Real Madrid.

"That's David Beckham!" I just shrugged. "Oh my God!"

"Did you not know that David Beckham played for Real Madrid?!"

I was introducing her to what I was doing as a career and gradually she was becoming more interested in sport and football and we had loads of trips after that. Everywhere I went, she went.

As Marianna was getting a bit older and coming towards school age, we decided it would be good for her and Caitlin to move to Spain to bring them up there so they could learn a new language, the way Ciaran and Brendan had. I thought that was a big asset. We moved out there and I was commuting into Sky. I'd fly out the Saturday morning, wouldn't be back till probably the Monday. But then if they wanted me to do the Champions League, I'd fly out again on Tuesday and fly back Thursday. It's not that glamorous, it's really hard work and you're on your own a lot. There was a lot of flights, lot of hotels, and I didn't particularly like the fact that I was away a lot. At least at the weekends, it was easy to bring Deborah and the kids with me to London, we had a season ticket at the Marriott in Kensington, I used to stay 100 nights a year there, but at least I would be able to spend a lot more time with them.

We did manage to work in a few other trips. We were going to Gatwick one weekend, and Deborah was flying back home with Marianna and I was off to Athens, to commentate on a game between Greece and Northern Ireland. On the spur of the moment, I said, "Why don't you just come with me to Athens. Marianna hasn't been there before. It's another place for her to go." I started taking them to a lot of the games that I was commentating on, and the experience she got and the places she saw was fantastic for a young girl. I think all of that's great for kids. I wanted her to understand and see the places that I've been to. From an education point of view, if you go to these places and find out about the cultures, that certainly helps broaden your mind. Obviously, that couldn't happen when it was the school term and I just hated being apart from her and the kids and not watching them grow up. On top of that, Deborah was really busy too because she had a couple of restaurants that she ran and she worked her fingers to the bone because it's hard work in Spain. You've got six or seven months that you really work around the clock while the season is on and you can make your money, so that was tough.

All of that travelling was the downside of being a sports commentator and sports analyst and being in demand. But the other side of it was that the work was fantastic. Doing live TV is all about doing your homework, that makes all the difference for me. I had a good memory, a lot of the time I didn't write that many notes down, but I knew the players, I knew the information. I used to amaze a few people who were sitting and watching by not having an awful lot of notes but having a memory that told me everything I needed to know. I liked the analysis too. I was lucky that I was able to do both, but covering the games live, co-commentating, is something different. It's like you're actually playing there yourself!

We had five or six years in Spain, but then we had to come back to England, basically because I had that much work going on in London and I was under a lot more pressure. As the girls got older, we couldn't take them out of school, they couldn't travel with me the same way any longer, so we moved to a place just outside London, Sindelsham, a lovely part of the world. We spent two and a half years there. I was home every night, I didn't have to stay in hotels, I was able to drive to work and drive home again, that was great. Deborah started doing a course in make-up in Oxford Street that was probably the best course for make-up artists in Europe at the time, people were coming from America, from Australia, from everywhere to get on this course, and she excelled at that sort of thing. She's very artistic and she got the highest mark of any of the students. She had done lots of stuff in fashion, she was a model herself, and she wanted to stay in that industry.

It was okay for the first year or so, but then Deborah started feeling restless, she wasn't really well, she was suffering. She didn't feel that she was going anywhere and I think at that stage, she was suffering really badly from depression, which I was not totally aware of. I sort of dismissed it all to be honest, I was one of those who thought, "There's nothing wrong, just get on with it." I was one of those type of people. But she had had it from when she was a child. I've learned more in the last five or six years, especially during the lockdown where my wife actually came out and spoke about her own depression, how she's struggled with bulimia and anorexia, how it all made her feel, her suicidal thoughts. She was really brave to come out and talk about that, I take my hat off to her. I gradually learned more as every year passed. I think she missed her dad growing up, and then she lost her mum when she was only 17, and her mom had brought her up virtually on her own, so she had difficult times growing up. Deborah is a real trooper. When she was 18 or 19 she bought her own home, she had a mortgage, she was working three jobs, which all shows her character and determination.

But she wasn't settled in England so we moved back to Northern Ireland for a wee while, but the draw of Mallorca was there and we went back there again until three years ago. When Sky lost the contract to show La Liga, it didn't make any sense living there and having to go to London or Ireland to commentate, so we moved back to Belfast three years ago. But again, one door closes another door opens. I've been doing commentary work in Dublin with Virgin Media which has been a lot of fun, with Niall Quinn, Brian Kerr, Keith Andrews, Damien Delaney and they're all great professionals. It's great when you're able to work with those guys. Everybody has their own opinion on football - 90% of the time we'll see it exactly the same but there's 10% where you see things differently and it's great that you can hear other people's opinions and how they envisage football should be played. Even at 67 now, I'm still learning, I find it interesting and I'm enjoying it. There are plenty more commentaries left in the tank yet!

CHAPTER TWENTY-TWO

....

GERRY & FRIENDS

Back in 2018, we moved back to Belfast which brought my journey full circle I suppose, back to the place it all started. I'm not the same person I was back when I left to go to Tottenham more than 40 years before, but Belfast isn't the same place either. It's a city that has changed for the better and one where I am very hopeful for the future that lies ahead of it.

As a teenager, I remember the barricades going up when the Troubles started. The milkman couldn't get in, you couldn't get bread. Maybe a day or two later, they organised things where they let the milk floats come in and the bread vans come in because otherwise, we wouldn't have had anything to eat. Living through that, it does have a huge effect on you from a mental point of view. I think in my case, it made me stronger and more resilient. I never really worried too much about anything in my life, but it depends on the individual, your attitude. I didn't mind getting in a scrap or having to fight with somebody on the way to school and on my way back home from school. That was how it was. All we saw on TV was movies, where the Indians were always the bad guys and the cavalry were always killing them. And if you go back to history to see who owned the land, and who took it from who, that's crazy! But that's the way history portrays it. As you get older and wiser you start to see things from every perspective which is so important. I think everybody should say, "If I was in his or her shoes, how would I look at that situation?"

You look at the situation with me and Deborah. Go back to those times when the Troubles were happening and the idea of a Catholic and a Protestant getting married would have caused all kinds of problems and almost certainly wouldn't have happened. But by the time we got together, those attitudes were becoming far less important. Northern Ireland has become a much more open and inclusive culture in that sense, which is so important for the future. We're all human beings, it's who we are that matters, not the labels that people put on us.

I think the world is changing. I don't know what it's going to mean to Britain, being out of the EU, out of Europe. Northern Ireland, because it's part of the island of Ireland and the border situation with Brexit, it might cause problems but I think the people here are dead set against that, whatever their political persuasions. People will demand that we keep the peace. A lot of change has happened here and I'm thrilled by it. I remember about 12 or 13 years ago, it was coming up to our wedding anniversary, the 12th of July, which is also the big celebration for the Orange Order. We were thinking of something nice to do but in Northern Ireland, it's difficult because everything closes down because of the parades. I said, "I'd love to go to the parade!" Deborah said, "Are you crazy, everybody will know who you are." I didn't care, so we went and stood there. They were waving all the Union Jacks, the guys are marching up with the bowler hats on and their sashes - and I knew most of them! They were coming over and talking and shaking my hand, it was funny. I don't see anything wrong with that. I enjoyed listening to the music, watching people enjoy themselves, what's the problem? That I could do that, when everybody knows my background, that I'm from the Falls, what's that if it isn't a sign of our progress?

We don't have any politics in our house. Deborah is from a unionist background, I'm coming from a republican background, but it's not important as an issue for us. It's all about being happy, looking after each other, showing a little bit of respect. I think that can be a lesson that everybody can learn. There's a lot of things still to be resolved in this country, but I have to say people have moved forward in the years that I've been away. I've come back and found a people that just wants to live in peace and have happiness. They don't need all the divisive rubbish that went on for so long. I think politicians have taken too much away from the people and the people are now starting to voice their opinions, which is a good thing.

I go back to that photo of my mum with Norman Whiteside's mum, meeting up and having a cup of tea together because of the World Cup in 1982. I just think of the impact of that team and how that helped start a ripple effect that ran through the country for many years. Billy Hamilton was brought up in a Protestant unionist background. I was coming from the Falls Road. Norman Whiteside was from the Shankill. By playing football together, we actually started to integrate as people. I love the fact that in Northern Ireland, the big push now is for integrated education. If you go back to when I grew up in the '50s and '60s, it was all segregated. Now they're integrating and I think that is a positive step forward, I think you can do an awful lot with that. Integrated schools would be such a big thing for the future in Northern Ireland because the working class people who came from the Shankill Road are no different to the working class people on the Falls Road. We showed that in 1982. We are led to believe different things by politicians and leaders, but as you get older, you see things through a different set of eyes. That integration is the route to a positive future.

I've really enjoyed coming back to Belfast and getting to see a lot of the family again. I've still got brothers and sisters here, as well as my dad over in Omagh. I've got a brother Eugene, who's also living there and we spend a lot of time with him and his wife Maggie. We are very close and we are always in stitches when we get together, there's never a dull moment.

My sister Rosaleen lives in Belfast, she's retired now, she worked in the housing executive. I have another brother Sean, who is a plasterer, he's still working, he's living in Belfast. But then I've got a sister down in Dublin, Mary, she's been there for 45 years now. She's widowed now, with three daughters, so I see her from time to time. But the rest of my family are in England still. My younger sister Gráinne, she still lives in St. Albans, where I used to live. Kevin was an electrician, he went to London to live and work and bought his own house and his family's all there, then my sisters Sinead and Joanne, they're still living in England as well.

We were at a family reunion in the late summer of 2021, the first we'd had in nearly three years because of the lockdown. I hadn't seen some of them for so long. We all got together along with my first wife Ann who still comes to all the family gatherings. She and Deborah get on so well, they spend time chatting away to each other. I'm very happy about that because Ann had to put up with an awful lot, especially during the time I was with Caron.

Deborah is a shining light, my right hand, the person that I trust absolutely. We've been together 18 years now and it keeps on getting better each day. Sky losing La Liga and us coming back to Belfast, it's been a blessing in its way. I'm here 24/7 more or less and as a result, we've probably got to know each other better in the last three years than in the previous 15 years and we get on even better now. I call her the White Witch, because her instincts are good, I trust her 100%. I just love the fact that we get on so well. I try and do my bit around the house now I'm home more. I'll go in the kitchen and clean up and as soon as I've finished, Deborah will go in there and do it properly! I always ask her, "Is that a bit more properly Protestant clean in there now?" We have a fabulous time together, we're always laughing and joking. After all the things I've done over the years, to have found Deborah, I can't tell you how lucky I am.

But maybe it was meant to be. We just clicked and it fell into place very naturally. When I asked her about why she would want to be with me rather than all the other guys who were a lot younger than me, she always said it just felt right. Deborah was big into fortune tellers and psychics, she watched them on TV and she loved going to see them. She went to different ones in Northern Ireland and when we were out in Mallorca, she went to see a girl called Sabrina, who was recommended to her. She came back and said, "Oh my God, this girl is unbelievable." She told her that she had met the person that she had known years and years ago from a different life and that she was happy now because we were reunited. I must admit, I don't really go in for that sort of thing but about six months later she said to me, "Why don't you go and see Sabrina?"

I decided I'd go, not say who I was or who had recommended me, nothing. I spoke to her in Spanish, we chatted away, I didn't give her any information at all. And she went through everything. A lot of it was straightforward, but then she started getting to the points where she seemed to know stuff that I didn't think she could know. She said, "I can see you in chains and handcuffs." I said, "I've been arrested a few times and had the cuffs put on me!" She said, "No, no, no, in a boat, a boat." She was going back hundreds of years ago, she said, "You were separated from the person who you were in love with. You were chained on a ship and taken away to the colonies." There were a lot of similarities with what she had told my wife. Who knows? But I think too many things have happened in our life together for them to be just coincidences and there are a lot of things that happen that are beyond our understanding.

I think what I have found over the years is that basically, we are all the same, whatever our race, religion, nationality. Covid did get people together and help people to understand everybody else's problems. It wasn't just one city or country dealing with it, it was everywhere. There was no distinction between us. I could see people bonding and starting to work together to try and help each other. I hope that continues as we come out of it, because I think it was a lesson for us all in that way.

I was very fortunate that I was able to play at the top level of football and do well from the game, but you have to put something back. I've been trying to do more in the last six or seven years. I just think it makes you feel good when you do that. I've been involved with the children's hospice for the last couple of years, but before that I took on the ambassador's role of the Northern Irish homeless football team. I'm involved with the Lighthouse charity in Belfast, because there's so many friends and family that I know who have committed suicide in the last three or four years. I felt that I could help and I became an ambassador for them. If you can help, if you can do something, you have to. I think just as a human being, it's the right thing to do. Deborah is exactly the same. She wasn't embarrassed to say, "I've suffered from depression for a long, long time," and I know that helped a lot of people because we had so many messages from people saying that knowing that had helped them with their own problems. Lockdown had a huge impact on people and we're going to continue to see that for years to come. Everybody's different. Some people can cope with pressure, some can't. Circumstances are totally different.

During lockdown, we spent our time putting our "Gerry & Friends" show online to try and entertain people and keep them mentally focused. Nobody wanted to go out. Nobody wanted to go into the shops. Nobody wanted to mix. Everyone was on their own and it did feel very lonely in that sense early on. Deborah said to me one night, "Nobody's working. Nobody's able to see their friends or go out, people are really depressed, they're stuck inside. Why don't you do a show and talk to the fans? You love talking about football and you love talking about life." It sounded a good idea, but I had no clue how to go about it. Sophie, my niece, is very good on social media, she sorted it out with Deborah and with Marianna. They set it all up for me. We put out a message that we were doing a show on a Thursday night, five past eight, just after the applause for the NHS and it started off like that, just a questions and answers thing. I thought it'd only be maybe 20 minutes but we were on for over an hour, it was great. The questions were really good, so I said we'd do it again the next week, and suddenly we were getting thousands of people tuning into it.

It kept building and after four or five weeks, it made sense to get other people on board. I got Billy Hamilton on, we had Luther Blissett, Graeme Souness, John Barnes, then we branched out a bit and we had Carl Frampton on, Jimmy Nesbit. On the anniversary of the game against Spain, I got 10 or 11 of the lads from that team on. Bronagh Gallagher did a show, she was hilarious. The shows were lasting two hours or more. We tried to keep it a mixture, Dame Mary Peters was a great person to talk to, she was brilliant, she's a fantastic lady. I did an interview with her at the running track. It was all done on a shoestring, no budget at all, we were spending hours and hours on it, but people started responding and helping with a bit of sponsorship.

We had access to people in the music industry too. Deborah has a brother and sister and two cousins, that's the only close family she's got. The oldest cousin, Johnny, he was in a band, they were doing okay. We went to watch them, 15, 16 years ago, playing really small venues where there were maybe 100, 150 people. They were really good. Then they got a big breakthrough where they were asked if they'd go on tour with U2, across America. The band was Snow Patrol and the rest is history! But it shows you the importance of getting a break and then making the most of it. We've had so much fun with them over the years, watching their career evolve and develop. Their parents, Deborah's aunt and uncle, the effort they put in to help Johnny was massive. Bradley, the other cousin, he's a really good photographer, he did weddings and stuff like that, a professional photographer. The band asked him to go and take professional shots at the gigs for them and from that, all of a sudden, he was taking professional shots for U2 and became the photographer for both bands! It just shows you how doors can open and things happen in life. I think it's all about sliding doors. And so that's how we got Jonny Quinn on "Gerry & Friends"!

Putting something back into my community has always been important to me and going all the way back, I've always done charity events. When I was at Watford, when I was at Tottenham, come Christmas time you would go to the children's hospital, give out presents and things. There's a lot of players who were very keen to do it. At Watford, the whole team went round the Watford General Hospital, just near the ground at Vicarage Road. I saw how powerful that was, an early example of how you can harness the power of football for the good, an early version of that spirit of '82 if you like, but I'll give you a recent example of how it still works. I got a message from a guy who wanted to show me a photograph. His dad died of Covid in November 2020, he'd been a big fan of the national team, he was at the World Cup in '82 and '86. He showed me these photos of his dad. In the first he was with Eusebio, then with Pat Jennings, then me, then George Best and his girlfriend Mary Stavin. It was just a wee conversation we had, but the guy went away happy that I took a few minutes to talk to him. It took me 10 or 15 minutes, but that made his day in a difficult time. That's the power of football, of sport, that it connects people in that way.

Your health is your wealth and that is true for all of us. There's a lot of people who have ended up with serious illnesses, and they've got all the money in the world but it means nothing then. That's what I found out at the hospice, seeing the kids there, maybe five or six years old, and you knew that within a couple of weeks, they're not going to be there. How do they cope with that as a parent, a brother or sister? You have to put yourself in that position and think, how do you think they feel? Anything I can do, I will. People should help each other, that's my mantra.

On a personal level, I'm happier now probably than I've ever been. The fact that I'm spending more time with the family, with Deborah and Marianna, that I'm getting to speak to my father a lot more, that's fantastic. I couldn't ask for more.

Marianna is still at school, she's got aspirations to become a singer or an actress. She's really set her heart on that, so we'll see how far she can go. She's had leading roles in productions of "Annie" and "Matilda" and just the other day she made her debut singing with Brian Kennedy. She has her life in front of her but I want her to make her own decisions. She's got her own mind, she's very determined, very focused and single minded. She takes after her dad! She's a very bright girl, never given us any trouble and she has an old soul, beyond her years.

Caitlin is over at university in Glasgow, she's in her third year now, studying international fashion branding, so the finals aren't so far away. It hasn't been easy being a student during the pandemic, but she's doing great and we're proud of what she is achieving. Aishleen has recently moved back to London after being a senior nurse at St George's Hospital in London. She's got a new job down there and she's settling into life with Theo, my first grandson, who is 10 now. Where does the time go? Ciaran still lives and works in the Brighton area too. His little boy Keir is four now. Brendan is up in London where he's a train driver, and he's got my third grandson Elliott, who is three, to keep him busy as well. I'm proud of them all. They're good kids, I've never had too many problems with them. They've maybe had more with me!

Doing this book has obviously been mostly about reflecting on the past, but I still have plenty of goals left for the future. I've got my own whiskey coming out this year called "Spirit of '82", and that's going to commemorate the 40th anniversary of the 1982 World Cup. Writing this book is something that's been talked about many times, but it felt like now was the right time to do it and I've really got the writing bug now! I'm still working, there are charities I'm involved in, I've still got loads of challenges ahead of me.

So, coming to the last page of this book, what else can I tell you?

I can tell you one thing for sure – this isn't the end!

ACKNOWLEDGEMENTS

I have many people to thank for their help and support throughout my life, too many to name in these acknowledgements. Many of them appear over the pages that follow and I hope I've done justice to the support that they've given me on my journey.

As far as the book goes, it started with William Adamson who first got in touch with me about the idea a couple of years ago, and we've taken it on from there. Stuart Curtis and all his staff at Curtis Sport have played a big part in putting it all together and getting the finished book into your hands.

Thanks to the wonders of modern Zoom technology, I've talked to Dave Bowler every Friday afternoon for most of 2021, going through all the stories and the ups and downs of my life and career, and he has pieced all of that together into this story. It's been a lot of fun going back through it all. But don't think we've finished yet, there's more to get stuck into next year!

Thanks to Paul Ferguson and the Belfast Telegraph for their help with some of the photographs in the book. From my club football days, thanks to Richard Walker and Alan Cozzi for providing pictures from the Watford FC Archive and to Paul Camillin at Brighton & Hove Albion for sorting out pictures from my time there. Those pictures are used courtesy of BHAFC and The Argus.

I think I've been very fortunate in my life, especially with those sliding doors moments. One door closes and another one opens. It happens for a reason, I do believe in fate but at the same time, you have to grab your opportunities when they come. My attitude has probably been the biggest part of that, my determination. None of my coaches would ever say I didn't have the right attitude. They all know how hard I worked on it, and if you put in the effort you get the rewards. But equally, you need good people around you to teach you, to help you and to support you and I've been very fortunate on that front throughout my life.

You'll read all about the players, coaches and clubs that have had an impact on my life and if I started listing them all now, that would need another book! I've been lucky to play for my country, to represent some great clubs, work for good coaches, have some fabulous mentors and play with some wonderful players, players better than myself who have passed their experience on and made me strive even harder to improve. I'd like to thank everybody I played with, whatever team – and whatever sport!

It was the same when I worked as a coach, both in terms of the people I worked for and with, as well as the players. Then when I went to work in television, a lot of people helped show me the ropes and have continued to be great colleagues and friends over many, many years. We'll be coming back to those days again.

Obviously, the biggest thank you I owe is to my family. I'm especially sad that my mum isn't around to see this book come out because as I found out recently, she was always busy keeping notes on my career, pasting things into scrapbooks and keeping the photos! Sadly, she died 10 years ago and that was a great loss to us all. She was at the heart of the family. You can never replace your mum, you only get one. My dad is still with us at 91, bright as a button and keeping himself busy all the time – he puts us all to shame with his energy, he's amazing! My grandmother Hannah was a big influence on me too, she helped bring me up and she kept all the Gallaghers in check!

My brothers and sisters, grandparents, uncles and aunts, cousins, nephews, nieces and all, they've been part of my journey too. We're a big family but we all look out for each other and we all know that we've got good people that we can turn to when we need them.

To Ciaran, Brendan, Aishleen, Caitlin and Marianna, I have to thank the kids for putting up with their dad over all the years, through the bad as well as the good! It hasn't always been plain sailing, but I'm so proud of all of them and the lives they've made and are making for themselves.

Finally, without Deborah, I could never have done any of this. Since we met, she's been a very special part of my life, she has been my rock. Behind every great man there's an even greater woman, as they say! We've been through a hell of a lot in the last 18 years, but she's a soulmate for me. Without her, I would be lost. She has my love and my thanks always.

GERRY ARMSTRONG INTERNATIONAL STATS

INTERNATIONAL	APPEARANCES	STARTS	SUB	GOALS
Northern Ireland (1977-1986)	63	56	7	12

TEAM SCORED AGAINST	NUMBER OF GOALS	TEAM SCORED AGAINST	NUMBER OF GOALS
Belgium	2	Israel	1
Bulgaria	2	Portugal	1
Finland	1	Republic of Ireland	1
France	1	Spain	1
Honduras	1	Wales	1

World Cup	APPEARANCES	GOALS
1982	5	3
1986	1	0

INTERNATIONAL CAREER BY TOURNAMENT

COMPETITION	GOALS
World Cup Qualifiers	5
World Cup Finals	3
European Championship Qualifiers	3
British Home International Championship	1
TOTAL	12

INTERNATIONAL CAREER BY GAME

DATE	FIXTURE	RESULT	COMPETITION	GOALS
		YEAR: 1977		
27th April	West Germany v Northern Ireland	L 5-0	International Friendly	-
28th May	Northern Ireland v England	L 1-2	British Home Championship	-
3rd June	Northern Ireland v Wales	D 1-1	British Home Championship	-
11th June	Iceland v Northern Ireland	L 1-0	FIFA World Cup Qualifier	-
16th November	Northern Ireland v Belgium	W 3-0	FIFA World Cup Qualifier	2 GOALS

240

YEAR: 1978

13th May	Scotland v Northern Ireland	D 1-1	British Home Championship	-
16th May	England v Northern Ireland	L 1-0	British Home Championship	-
19th May	Wales v Northern Ireland	L 1-0	British Home Championship	-
20th September	Republic of Ireland v Northern Ireland	D 0-0	UEFA European Championship Qualifier	-
25th October	Northern Ireland v Denmark	W 2-1	UEFA European Championship Qualifier	-
29th November	Bulgaria v Northern Ireland	W 0-2	UEFA European Championship Qualifier	1 GOAL

YEAR: 1979

7th February	England v Northern Ireland	L 4-0	UEFA European Championship Qualifier	-
2nd May	Northern Ireland v Bulgaria	W 2-0	UEFA European Championship Qualifier	1 GOAL
19th May	Northern Ireland v England	L 0-2	British Home Championship	-
22nd May	Scotland v Northern Ireland	L 1-0	British Home Championship	-
25th May	Northern Ireland v Wales	D 1-1	British Home Championship	-
6th June	Denmark v Northern Ireland	L 4-0	UEFA European Championship Qualifier	-
17th October	Northern Ireland v England	L 1-5	UEFA European Championship Qualifier	-
21st November	Northern Ireland v Republic of Ireland	W 1-0	UEFA European Championship Qualifier	1 GOAL

YEAR: 1980

26th March	Israel v Northern Ireland	D 0-0	FIFA World Cup Qualifier	-
16th May	Northern Ireland v Scotland	W 1-0	British Home Championship	-
20th May	England v Northern Ireland	D 1-1	British Home Championship	-

241

23rd May	Wales v Northern Ireland	W 0-1	British Home Championship	-
11th June	Australia v Northern Ireland	W 1-2	International Friendly	-
15th June	Australia v Northern Ireland	D 1-1	International Friendly	-
18th June	Australia v Northern Ireland	W 1-2	International Friendly	-
15th October	Northern Ireland v Sweden	W 3-0	FIFA World Cup Qualifier	-
19th November	Portugal v Northern Ireland	L 1-0	FIFA World Cup Qualifier	-

YEAR: 1981

25th March	Scotland v Northern Ireland	D 1-1	FIFA World Cup Qualifier	-
29th April	Northern Ireland v Portugal	W 1-0	FIFA World Cup Qualifier	1 GOAL
19th May	Scotland v Northern Ireland	L 2-0	British Home Championship	-
3rd June	Sweden v Northern Ireland	L 1-0	FIFA World Cup Qualifier	-
14th October	Northern Ireland v Scotland	D 0-0	FIFA World Cup Qualifier	-
18th November	Northern Ireland v Israel	W 1-0	FIFA World Cup Qualifier	1 GOAL

YEAR: 1982

23rd February	England v Northern Ireland	L 4-0	British Home Championship	-
24th March	France v Northern Ireland	L 4-0	International Friendly	-
27th May	Wales v Northern Ireland	L 3-0	British Home Championship	-
17th June	Northern Ireland v Yugoslavia	D 0-0	FIFA World Cup	-
21st June	Honduras v Northern Ireland	D 1-1	FIFA World Cup	1 GOAL
25th June	Spain v Northern Ireland	W 0-1	FIFA World Cup	1 GOAL

1st July	Austria v Northern Ireland	D 2-2	FIFA World Cup	-
4th July	France v Northern Ireland	L 4-1	FIFA World Cup	1 GOAL
13th October	Austria v Northern Ireland	L 2-0	UEFA European Championship Qualifier	-

YEAR: 1983

30th March	Northern Ireland v Turkey	W 2-1	UEFA European Championship Qualifier	-
27th April	Northern Ireland v Albania	W 1-0	UEFA European Championship	-
24th May	Scotland v Northern Ireland	D 0-0	British Home Championship	-
28th May	Northern Ireland v England	D 0-0	British Home Championship	-
31st May	Northern Ireland v Wales	L 0-1	British Home Championship	-
21st September	Northern Ireland v Austria	W 3-1	UEFA European Championship Qualifier	-
16th November	Germany v Northern Ireland	W 0-1	UEFA European Championship Qualifier	-

YEAR: 1984

4th April	England v Northern Ireland	L 1-0	British Home Championship	-
22nd May	Wales v Northern Ireland	D 1-1	British Home Championship	1 GOAL
27th May	Finland v Northern Ireland	L 1-0	FIFA World Cup Qualifier	-
12th September	Northern Ireland v Romania	W 3-2	FIFA World Cup Qualifier	-
14th November	Northern Ireland v Finland	W 2-1	FIFA World Cup Qualifier	1 GOAL

YEAR: 1985

27th February	Northern Ireland v England	L 0-1	FIFA World Cup Qualifier	-
27th March	Spain v Northern Ireland	D 0-0	International Friendly	-

Date	Match	Result	Competition	
11th September	Turkey v Northern Ireland	D 0-0	FIFA World Cup Qualifier	-
16th October	Romania v Northern Ireland	W 0-1	FIFA World Cup Qualifier	-
13th November	England v Northern Ireland	D 0-0	FIFA World Cup Qualifier	-

YEAR: 1986

Date	Match	Result	Competition	
26th February	France v Northern Ireland	D 0-0	International Friendly	-
26th March	Northern Ireland v Denmark	D 1-1	International Friendly	-
12th June	Brazil v Northern Ireland	L 3-0	FIFA World Cup	-

CLUB CAREER STATISTICS

CLUB	YEARS	APPEARANCES	GOALS	INTERNATIONAL CAPS
Tottenham Hotspur	1975-1980	84	10	27
Watford	1980-1983	76	12	21
Real Mallorca	1983-1985	55	13	9
West Bromwich Albion	1985-1986	8	0	3
Chesterfield	1986	12	1	3
Brighton & Hove Albion	1986-1989	47	6	0
Milwall (LOAN)	1987	7	0	0
Crawley Town	1989-1990	25	6	0
Glenavon	1990	7	2	0
TOTAL		321	50	63

TOTTENHAM CAREER

SEASON	APPEARANCES	GOALS
1976-1977	21	3
1977-1978	19	2
1978-1979	10	1
1979-1980	30	4
1980-1981	4	0
TOTAL	84	10

WATFORD CAREER

SEASON	APPEARANCES	GOALS
1980-1981	24	3
1981-1982	33	7
1982-1983	19	2
TOTAL	76	12

REAL MALLORCA CAREER

SEASON	APPEARANCES	GOALS
1983-1984	31	8
1984-1985	24	5
TOTAL	55	13

WEST BROMWICH ALBION CAREER

SEASON	APPEARANCES	GOALS
1985-1986	8	0
TOTAL	8	0

CHESTERFIELD CAREER

SEASON	APPEARANCES	GOALS
1986	12	1
TOTAL	12	1

BRIGHTON & HOVE ALBION CAREER

SEASON	APPEARANCES	GOALS
1986-1987	31	4
1987-1988	11	1
1988-1989	5	1
TOTAL	47	6

MILLWALL CAREER (LOAN)

SEASON	APPEARANCES	GOALS
1987	7	0
TOTAL	7	0

CRAWLEY CAREER

SEASON	APPEARANCES	GOALS
1989-1990	25	6
TOTAL	25	6

GLENAVON CAREER

SEASON	APPEARANCES	GOALS
1990	7	2
TOTAL	7	2